24 World Championships

Left to right:
Lou Gehrig,
Earle Combs,
Tony Lazzeri,
and Babe Ruth
prior to the
1932 World Series.
(UPI/Bettmann)

Mickey Mantle, in the twilight of his illustrious career, bats against the Baltimore Orioles, August 4, 1968. (UPI/Bettmann)

Dave Righetti acknowledges the praise of fans and teammates alike following his July 4, 1983 no-hitter against the Boston Red Sox. It was the first Yankee no-hitter since Don Larsen's perfect game in the 1956 World Series. (New York Yankees Archives)

Paul O'Neill,
1994 American League Batting Champion
(Yankees Magazine)

Willie Randolph (Robert Adamenko)

Tommy John (Yankees Magazine)

Rickey Henderson (Yankees Magazine)

(National Baseball Library)

(Yankees Magazine)

(New York Yankees Archives)

The Yankees

An Authorized History of The New York Yankees

Phil Pepe

Published by Taylor Publishing Company
1550 West Mockingbird Lane
Dallas, Texas 75235

Library of Congress Cataloging-in-Publication Data
Pepe, Phil.
The Yankees : an authorized history of the New York Yankees / Phile Pepe.—Updated and rev. paperback ed.
p. cm.
ISBN 0-87833-142-5
ISBN 0-87833-234-0 (3rd rev. ed.)
1. New York Yankees (Baseball team)—History. I. Title.
[GV875.N4P53 1997]
796.357'64'097471—dc21 97-30428
CIP

Dedication

For David Philip Pepe, Jr.,
Rachel Marie Peckman,
and Nicole Siena Pepe,
the next generation,
with all my love.

BACKGROUND: *The Grandstand at the original Yankee Stadium as seen from the bleachers.*

INSET: *The 1908 New York Highlanders. In 1913 they became The New York Yankees.*
(New York Yankees Archives)

Table of Contents

Yankee Stadium, 1927 (New York Yankees Archives)

Introduction

It must have been some diabolical ploy that conspired for me to end up covering the Yankees for almost three decades as "beat" writer for two newspapers, the New York World Telegram & Sun and the New York Daily News.

As a kid growing up in Brooklyn, I rooted fiercely for the Dodgers—doesn't it sometimes seem that the world grew up in Brooklyn, rooting for the Dodgers—and I despised the Yankees for what they did to my Dodgers every October.

How unkind the fates were to me, snatching my Dodgers away from Brooklyn and depositing them some 3,000 miles away (I covered only one game in my beloved Ebbets Field), then forcing me to cover the hated Yankees.

The year was 1959, my Dodgers were gone, and I was assigned to fill in for the regular Yankees writer on a trip to Cleveland, Detroit and Chicago.

The first Yankee I spent any time with was Yogi Berra, the same Y. Berra who had made my young life so miserable through so many Octobers. I was in the lobby of the hotel in Cleveland when Yogi asked me what I was doing.

"Nothing," I glibly replied.

"Wanna take a walk?" he asked.

"Sure," I wittily responded.

Carmen Berra's birthday was coming up and Yogi said he was going to a department store to buy her a present. I tagged along. I was impressed when he went to the women's wear department and picked out a beautiful negligee, more impressed with his warmth and friendliness. Yankees weren't supposed to be warm and friendly. Not to Dodgers fans.

But how are you going to hold a grudge against Yogi Berra?

As I matured, I came to realize that my hatred of the Yankees as a youngster was nothing more than a grudging respect for their excellence and their professionalism.

The manager of the Yankees when I became the team's beat writer in 1962 was Ralph Houk. In those formative years, I learned more baseball from Houk than from any other single person. He would sit patiently and answer my questions, which probably were inane. He would carefully explain his strategy, the reasons for moves that I questioned.

Houk never lost his temper with me. Not once. And I never thanked him for educating me. I do now.

Of the more than 1,100 players who have worn the Yankees uniform since 1903, I had the good fortune of covering, meeting or knowing more than 400 of them, as well as every Yankees manager from Casey Stengel to the present.

Through no effort on my part, and largely because the Yankees have been a dominant team in my tenure as a baseball writer, I have witnessed some of the most memorable events in baseball history. Such as:

- Roger Maris' 61st home run in 1961.
- Mickey Mantle's blast off Bill Fisher that almost made it out of the stadium.
- Mantle's final game as a Yankee.
- Whitey Ford's record scoreless innings streak in the 1961 World Series.
- Mantle's game-winning home run off Barney Schultz in the 1964 World Series.

- Chris Chambliss' pennant-winning home run in 1976.
- Reggie Jackson's three home runs in Game 6 of the 1977 World Series.
- Ron Guidry's 18-strikeout game in 1978.
- Bucky Dent's home run in Boston in 1978.

In one way or another, I have been associated with the Yankees for more than three decades, more than half my life. For that reason, and for hundreds of others, it's an honor being associated with this, an authorized history of the sport's most famous team, The Yankees.

Phil Pepe
Englewood, N.J.
November, 1994

31 Years of Confident Service
THE BRONX SAVINGS BANK
Branch Office 12 WESTCHESTER SQUARE
SAFE DEPOSIT VAULTS
HALF A POUND! HALF A DOLLAR!
Burma-Shave
NO BRUSH
NO LATHER
CLEAR HEADS CALL FOR
Calvert
WHISKIES
THE YANKEES USE
LIFEBUOY
PROTECTS HEALTH
—STOPS B.O

UPI

Yankees owner George Steinbrenner doesn't mind being doused with champagne by Andy Pettitte after his team won its second world championship in three years—the fourth for Steinbrenner in his 26 years as "Boss" of the Yankees. (AP/Wide World)

Bombers Again

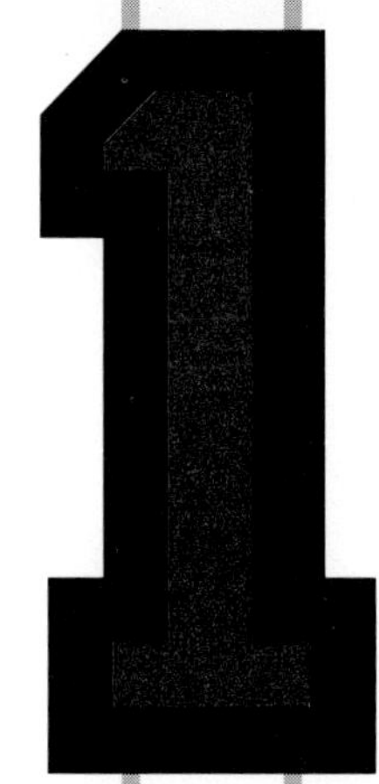

At the precise moment Yankees third baseman Scott Brosius gathered in Matt Sweeney's soft ground ball and threw it across the diamond to Tino Martinez for the final out of the 1998 World Series, the debate was afoot.

Was this Yankees team the greatest in baseball history? Or merely one of the greatest?

Let future baseball historians decide. Suffice it to say that the 1998 New York Yankees had finished off the greatest season any baseball team ever enjoyed.

The 1998 Yankees won 114 games in the regular season, more than any American League team ever. They won their last seven postseason games, including a four-game World Series sweep of the San Diego Padres that was the 16th sweep of a seven-game World Series in history, the first sweep since 1990 and the first Yankees sweep since 1950.

The New York Yankees, the most famous and most successful of all sports teams, had won their 35th pennant and 24th world championship, more than twice as many as any other team.

The 1998 season was one in which individual performances grabbed the headlines. Mark McGwire of the St. Louis Cardinals, with 70 home runs, and Sammy Sosa of the Chicago Cubs, with 66, surpassed the records of Babe Ruth and Roger Maris. And Cal Ripken, Jr., of the Baltimore Orioles ended his incredible consecutive-games streak at 2,632. But in terms of team accomplishments, the Yankees ruled over baseball.

Including the regular season and the postseason, the Yankees won 125 games and lost 50, a winning percentage of .714, the number of home runs the mighty Babe Ruth hit in his career.

"I'd have to say right now they are as great as any team there has ever been," said Yankees owner George Steinbrenner, his emotions spilling over into tears of joy as he clutched the World Series trophy. "You couldn't say that until they won the Series, but now that they've done it in four straight, they've got to be."

The world championship climaxed a five-year Yankees renaissance during which they reached the postseason four times and won two world championships.

In 1994, the Yankees were a runaway train charging headlong toward another championship, but that train was derailed by circumstances beyond their control. The season was stopped abruptly on August 12, when the Players Association voted to strike. There would be no more baseball in 1994—no playoffs, no World Series.

In 1995, the Yankees put on a late rush and slid into the playoffs through the back door, as the American League's first "wild card" entry in baseball's newly expanded playoff format. Their captain and spiritual leader, Don Mattingly—who had played so elegantly for 12 seasons, who had taken his place in Yankees lore alongside Babe Ruth, Lou Gehrig, Joe DiMaggio, Mickey Mantle and Reggie Jackson—was finally going to get a chance to play in the postseason.

But Mattingly, the Yankees and their fans were forced to suffer one more disappointment—a defeat by the Seattle Mariners in five heart-pounding, pulse-quickening games.

In 1996, the Yankees started all over again with a new manager. Joe Torre was brought in to replace Buck Showalter, the young manager who had begun the upswing in the Yankees' fortunes. In 35 years, covering more than 4,200 games as a player and manager, Torre had never even been involved in a World Series.

The Yankees erased the painful memories of recent disappointments by beating the Atlanta Braves in six games to win the World Series, returning to baseball's pinnacle after an 18-year drought.

Thurman Munson

For Joe Torre and hundreds of thousands of Yankees fans, it was worth the wait.

THE ROAD BACK TO GLORY

Where does one begin to chronicle the Yankees' demise after their singular success in the three-year period from 1976 through 1978?

Perhaps, it is appropriate to begin with the afternoon of Thursday, August 2, 1979, on the landing strip of Canton-Akron Airport. A twin-engine Cessna Citation, practicing takeoffs and landings, missed the strip attempting a landing and crashed. The pilot, Thurman Lee Munson, was killed instantly.

Steven L. Twardzik

Thurman Munson, captain of the Yankees, their heart and their soul, was only 32 at the time.

He had taken up flying so he could commute on off days between the Bronx and his home in Canton, Ohio, where he could spend more time with his growing family. Now, he was gone.

In 1977, Munson became the first American Leaguer in 22 years to hit over .300 and drive in 100 runs for three consecutive seasons. Because of knees deteriorating from the constant squatting and standing demanded by his position as a catcher, he no longer would be the player he once was. But Munson still had a lot of good baseball remaining in him when he died.

His absence left a void that would be impossible to fill. His leadership, his competitiveness, his ability to perform in the clutch were immeasurable, and irreplaceable. On the day Munson died, the Yankees were in fourth place, 14 games out of first. The following night, a tearful Yankee Stadium crowd came to pay homage to the fallen leader.

The Yankees' starting team took the field. The catcher's position was vacant. On the huge scoreboard in right centerfield was this message:

"Our captain and leader has not left us–
Today, tomorrow, this year, next...
Our endeavors will reflect our
love and admiration for him."

For the remainder of the season, the Yankees merely went through the motions, finishing fourth, 13 $^{1}/_{2}$ games out of first.

But they rebounded in 1980 with a new manager,

Dick Howser, and with Rick Cerone, obtained from Toronto in a trade for Chris Chambliss, filling Munson's catching position. The Yankees won 103 games, set an American League attendance record of 2,627,417, and finished three games ahead of the Baltimore Orioles in the American League East and, once again, faced the Kansas City Royals in the American League Championship Series.

This time, it was all Kansas City. With George Brett hitting home runs in the first game and the third, a decisive three-run shot off Goose Gossage in the seventh inning, the Royals swept the series in three games.

In his first season as a Yankee in 1981, free-agent signee Dave Winfield helped the team win its 33rd pennant and throughout the decade of the '80s he was a major all-around talent. (Bob Adamenko/Yankees Magazine)

The following season heralded the arrival of free agent Dave Winfield, signed to a 10-year contract for a record $20 million. It also brought the second longest strike in baseball history.

Because a two months players strike interrupted the season in June, it was decided to play the season in two halves. Winners of the first half in each division would play the winners in the second half to determine the division champion, who would then go on to play in the League Championship Series. When the strike came, the Yankees led the AL East by two games over Baltimore and so were first half AL East champions.

When play resumed in August, the Yankees, a largely veteran team, suffered from the layoff. And because they had already earned a berth in the division playoff, they lacked incentive and finished sixth. The Milwaukee Brewers won the second half and were the Yankees opponents for the division title in a best-of-five series.

The Yankees won the first two games in Milwaukee, lost the next two in New York, then pounded out 13 hits in Game 5, including home runs by Reggie Jackson, Oscar Gamble and Rick Cerone, to advance to the American League Championship Series. Waiting for them was a young, spirited, hell-for-leather group of Oakland Athletics managed by none other than Billy Martin.

But Yankees experience was too much for Oakland, which fell in a three-game sweep for the Yankees' 33rd American League pennant. Who could have predicted it would be their last for more than a dozen years?

Perhaps the beginning of the decline came with the 1981 World Series. For the third time in five years, it was the Yankees against the Dodgers and after the Yankees won the first two games at home, it looked like the same script as the previous two meetings. But the Dodgers swept the next four games and were world champions.

The 1981 season also was Reggie Jackson's last in pinstripes. A free agent, his five-year contract

On the final day of the 1984 season Mattingly topped teammate Dave Winfield .343 to .340 in a neck-and-neck race for the AL batting title. Here the two contestants congratulate each other after Winfield's final at-bat. (Bob Adamenko/Yankees Magazine)

If 1984 was Mattingly's breakout year then 1985 made him a superstar. That season he became the first Yankee since Thurman Munson in 1976 to be named the American League's Most Valuable Player. Don hit .324 with 35 home runs, 211 hits and his 145 RBI and 48 doubles led the league. (John McKeon/Yankees Magazine)

INSET: *In 1983, a 22-year-old first baseman-outfielder from Indiana joined the Yankees for good. That year he wore number 46 and batted a respectable .283 in 91 games. (Yankees Magazine)*

In his second year as a Yankee, Jimmy Key led all American League pitchers with 17 victories. (Steve Crandall/Yankees Magazine)

LEFT INSET: *Dave Righetti's July 4, 1983 no-hitter against the Red Sox was one of the club's biggest highlights of the 1980s. "Rags" went on to become the Yankees' all-time saves leader with 224. (Yankees Magazine)*

RIGHT INSET: *On September 4, 1993 first-year Yankee Jim Abbott electrified Yankee Stadium fans with his first career no-hitter, a 4-0 victory over Cleveland. (Steve Crandall/Yankees Magazine)*

expired, Jackson decided to take his home run bat elsewhere. Without Jackson, the Yankees finished fifth in 1982, but enjoyed a resurgence in 1983, with a third place finish. On July 4, Dave Righetti pitched the eighth no-hitter in Yankees history.

Joining the Yankees to stay in 1983 was a young lefthanded-hitting first baseman named Don Mattingly, who would later add his name to the list of Yankees captains that included Lou Gehrig, Thurman Munson, Willie Randolph and Graig Nettles, and who would take his place among the team's roster of all-time greats.

In 1984, Mattingly and teammate Dave Winfield battled for the league batting championship right down to the final day of the season, Mattingly winning the title at .343 with a hit in his final at bat, thereby joining Babe Ruth, Lou Gehrig, Joe DiMaggio (twice), George (Snuffy) Stirnweiss and Mickey Mantle as the only Yankees to win a batting championship. A year later, he became the AL's Most Valuable Player, the 20th time a Yankee won the award, the first since Thurman Munson in 1976.

Mattingly singles up the middle against the Angels in Anaheim on July 23,1994 to record his 2,000th major league hit. Only five other players have tallied 2,000 or more hits as a Yankee, and all are in the Hall of Fame. (Focus On Sports)

In 1987, Mattingly would tie a major league record by hitting a home run in eight consecutive games, and set a major league record by clouting six grand slams in one season.

Paul O'Neill, being congratulated by Don Mattingly and Danny Tartabull, led the AL in batting in 1994 with a .359 average. (Steve Crandall/Yankees Magazine)

17

Luis Polonia, (opposite page) back in his second stint in Pinstripes, hit .311 and was a catalyst on the basepaths. (Lou Rocco/Yankees Magazine)

Although in the 1980s no team won as many games as the Yankees, from 1987 through 1992, they failed to finish higher than fourth.

On October 29, 1991, the Yankees named as their manager, William Nathaniel (Buck) Showalter III. He was 35 years old at the time, the youngest manager in baseball. He had spent seven years as a player in the Yankees farm system. He had played 793 minor league games, but not one in the major leagues.

Buck Showalter was young, he was bright, he was enthusiastic, and he brought with him a work ethic, a single-mindedness and a fierce intensity that soon would infect his players around him.

A Hall of Famer in waiting, Wade Boggs was his typical prolific self in the Yankees' climb back atop the AL East. Boggs' .342 BA in 1994 was fourth best in the league and he was named to All-Star team for the 10th consecutive time, his ninth straight as a starter. (Lou Rocco/Yankees Magazine)

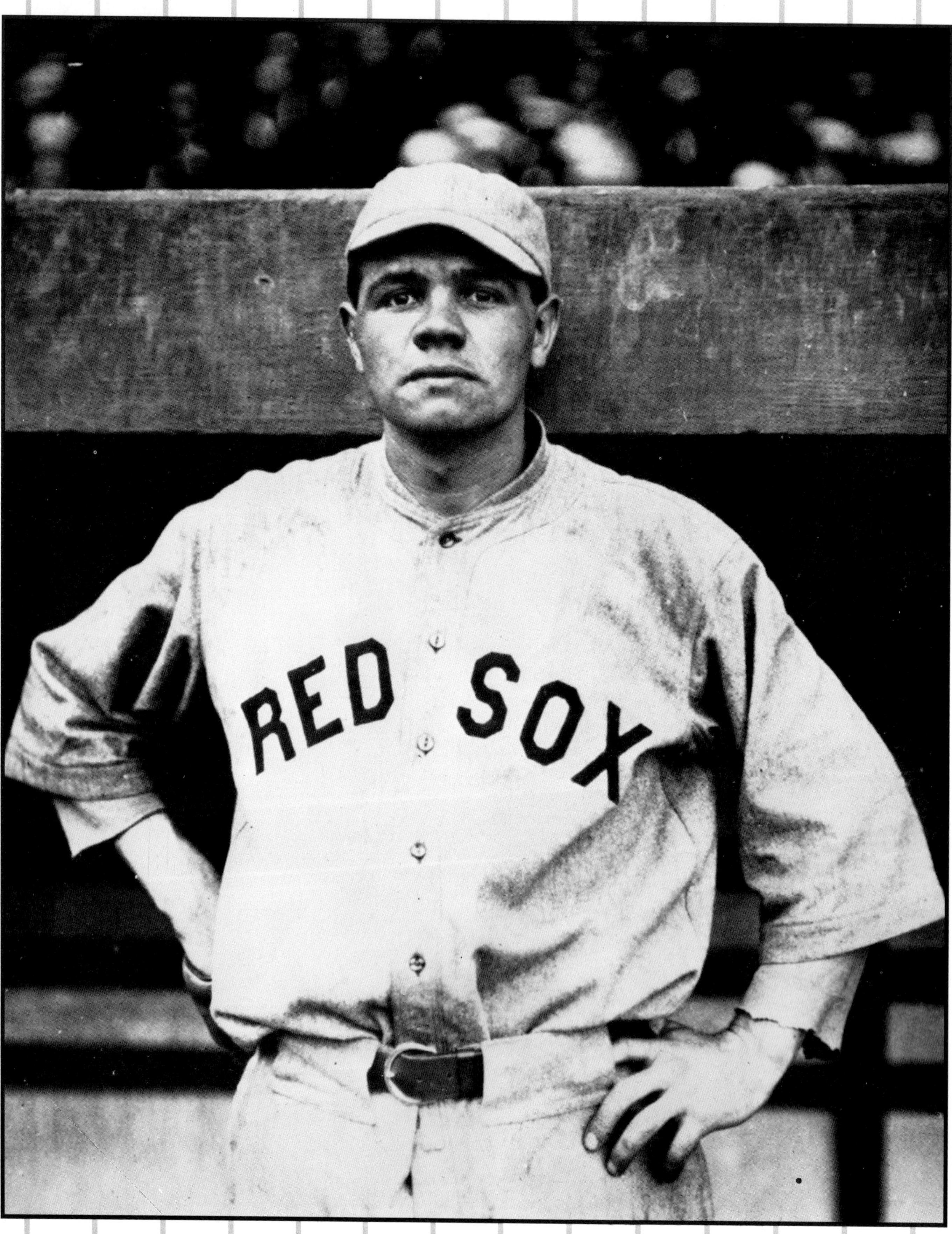

George Herman "Babe" Ruth was the shining light of Harry Frazee's Boston Red Sox. His sale to the Yankees would change the course of baseball history. (UPI/Bettmann)

In The Beginning

For the want of a nail the shoe was lost. For the want of a shoe the horse was lost. For the want of a horse the rider was lost. For the want of a rider the battle was lost. For the want of a battle the kingdom was lost.

And because H. Harrison (Harry) Frazee was more interested in Broadway theater than he was in baseball, the game's balance of power shifted from Boston to New York and the course of baseball history was changed for all time.

Harry Frazee was born in Peoria, Illinois, but he was a New Yorker by adoption and by inclination, a Ruynonesque character who walked with a swagger; an opportunist who could wheel and deal with the best of them. In Peoria, he worked as a bellhop. Later he moved to Chicago and in time became the owner of the Cort Theater.

But Broadway was Frazee's goal, his dream and his passion. He moved to his Shangri-la, New York City, and purchased the Longacre Theater, where he produced his own shows, a string of box office smashes such as "Nothing But the Truth," "Leave It To Jane," and his biggest success, "No, No, Nanette."

Harry was an operator, a dabbler. He was involved in the promotion of the Jack Johnson-Jess Willard heavyweight championship fight in Havana in 1915. But he was not a sportsman by any means. He was interested only in making a fast buck, which led him and two others to purchase the Boston Red Sox on November 1, 1916.

At a 1919 American League owners meeting, four men who figured prominently in Yankees history got together for this picture. From left: Yankees co-owner Colonel Tillinghast L'Hommedieu Huston, Red Sox owner Harry Frazee, Yankees co-owner Jacob Ruppert and Washington's Clark Griffith. The latter was the first Yankees manager in 1903 when they were known as the Highlanders. (UPI/Bettmann)

Frazee had little interest in baseball and less in the city of Boston. He would not leave his beloved New York, operating the team as an absentee owner, excoriated by Red Sox players and the Boston press. He will live in infamy as the man who ruined the Red Sox and made the Yankees the greatest name in sports, but that was a bum rap. From the beginning, it was apparent his intention was to build the Red Sox into a powerhouse, then sell the team for a hefty profit.

Between December 1917 and April 1918, Frazee traded for catcher Wally Schang, outfielder Amos Strunk, pitcher Bullet Joe Bush, first baseman Stuffy McInniss, and second baseman Dave Shean.

Frazee heard a rumor that the Washington Senators were planning to sell the great Walter Johnson, and already had an offer of $50,000. Broadway Harry bid the princely sum of $60,000 and was accused of trying to buy the American League pennant. His offer for Johnson was refused, but the Red Sox won the American League pennant anyway, by 2½ games over the Cleveland Indians, then defeated the Chicago Cubs in the World Series in six games. It was an historical occasion. The Red Sox have not won a world championship since.

The shining light of

Harry Frazee was an operator and a dabbler. In addition to owning the Boston Red Sox, he was a theatrical producer and was involved in the promotion of the Jess Willard-Jack Johnson heavyweight championship fight in Havana in 1915. (UPI/Bettmann)

Harry Frazee's 1918 Red Sox was a 23-year-old man-child out of Baltimore named George Herman Ruth, affectionately known as "Babe."

Ruth had been purchased by the Red Sox midway in the 1914 season from the Baltimore Orioles, then of the International League. At the time, Ruth was three months past his 19th birthday. He was a huge barrel-chested, spindly-legged young man, crude and often obscene and given to excesses, on and off the field. He drank too much, ate too much and spent too much time and energy pursuing women.

He could hit a baseball—when he hit it—to faraway places, reaching distances no other man reached. But it was as a pitcher that the Red Sox were most interested in Ruth. He appeared in only five games in 1914, winning 2 and losing 1, but the fire-balling left-hander showed enough promise for the Red Sox to place him prominently in their plans for the 1915 season.

Harry Frazee. (National Baseball Library, Cooperstown, NY)

Young Ruth took his place alongside a formidable pitching staff that included Rube Foster, Ernie Shore, Dutch Leonard, Smoky Joe Wood and Carl Mays. Ruth, the rookie, won 18 games and a star was born. Only Foster and Shore, with 19, won more. The Red Sox won 101 games and took the

American League pennant by one game over Detroit.

In 1916, Ruth won 23 games, led the league in ERA with 1.75, in starts with 41 and in shutouts with 9.

"He was already the best lefty in the league," said Ruth's teammate, Harry Hooper. The Babe was all of 21.

The following season, Ruth won 24 games, had a 2.01 ERA, completed 35 of 38 starts and pitched six shutouts. But there was a growing controversy over the young Ruth, who not only was the best left-handed pitcher in the American League, he was its best home run hitter, too.

New York's first American League franchise moved from Baltimore in 1903 and was called the Highlanders. Their first owners were Frank Farrell, a prominent New York racing figure, and Bill Devery (above with his family), a former New York City chief of police. (UPI/Bettmann)

In 1915, in a mere 92 at-bats, young Ruth belted four home runs. The Red Sox, as a team, hit 14. The league leader, Braggo Roth, hit 7.

The controversy over how best to use Ruth raged between the traditionalists, who subscribed to the theory that a pitcher who could win 23 or 24 games, was infinitely more valuable than a home run hitter, and the new breed, who saw Ruth's home run potential as the wave of the game's future. Slowly, the new breed was winning out. In 1918, Ruth pitched in 20 games and played leftfield or first base in 72 others. He hit 11 home runs, tying Philadelphia's Tilly Walker for the league lead.

By 1919, Ruth became a full-time outfielder and part-time pitcher. He started 15 games and won 9, but launched the staggering total of 29 home runs, two more than the all-time baseball record that had existed since 1884. Ruth's 29 homers were a remarkable 17 more than any other player in the game, in either league; they were more than were hit by 10 entire major league teams; and they were all but four of the total hit by Ruth's Red Sox teammates.

As the popularity of the mighty Babe Ruth escalated, he was becoming a dilemma for Harry Frazee. He had grudgingly paid the Babe $5,000 for the 1917 season, raised him to $7,000 in 1918, but when Ruth asked for a hike to $12,000 for the 1919 season, Frazee went ballistic. Not even his top actors, his biggest stars, were paid that much money.

A rare centerfield view of Hilltop Park. (National Baseball Library, Cooperstown, NY)

Eventually, Frazee agreed to sign Ruth to a three-year contract for $10,000 per year.

But 1919 was not a very good year for Harry

To manage the New York Highlanders in 1903, owners Frank Farrell and Bill Devery hired Clark Griffith (right) away from the Chicago White Sox and gave him carte blanche to spend what it took to bring in the best players available. In their first year the Highlanders finished fourth in an eight-team league. Griffith, the player-manager, won 14 games as a pitcher.

Pitcher Jack Chesbro (below right) came to the Highlanders from Pittsburgh of the National League. In 1904, he started 51 games, completed 48, pitched 454.2 innings, posted a 1.84 ERA and won an all-time record 41 games.

Griffith raided the National League for such stars as Wee Willie Keeler (below left) who came over from Brooklyn and batted .318 for the Highlanders in 1903, the fourth best BA in the American League. (TOP PHOTO: *New York Yankees Archives;* BOTTOM PHOTOS: *National Baseball Library, Cooperstown, NY)*

Before he was dubbed "the Babe," Ruth (below right) was a teenage sensation at St. Mary's School for Boys in Baltimore, MD. He first signed as a professional with the Baltimore Orioles (left) of the International League and was their star pitcher. Ruth was purchased by the Red Sox from the Orioles midway in the 1914 season, (below left) three months past his 19th birthday. He was not only a great pitching prospect but the team's best hitter . (all photos: Babe Ruth Museum)

The Highlanders' home was Hilltop Park, a 10,000-seat wooden stadium on Broadway and 168th Street, in Upper Manhattan overlooking the Hudson River. They battled Washington on Memorial Day 1910 in front of a swollen crowd of 21,000, many of whom were left standing. The Highlanders won the contest 3-0 in one hour and twenty minutes. (New York Yankees Archives)

Frazee. He suffered a series of flops in the theater and found himself so short of cash, he had trouble paying the mortgage on Fenway Park and was in danger of losing his show business empire. Given a choice between baseball or Broadway, Frazee opted for Broadway. His only solution was to put his most valuable piece of baseball property on the market. George Herman Ruth, the Babe, was for sale.

And Frazee knew exactly where to go to get his price–to a couple of his New York cronies, Col. Jacob Ruppert and Col. Tillinghast L'Hommedieu Huston, owners of the New York Yankees.

The Yankees had been in existence for 17 years, the last five under the ownership of Ruppert and Huston, and never had won a championship. Just four times in their 17 seasons had they finished higher than fourth in the American League, which came into existence in 1901 to rival the established National League.

There was no New York representative among the eight charter members of the American League, but league president, Ban Johnson, recognized the importance of a New York team to his fledgling league. In 1903, the league's third year in existence, Johnson arranged for two prominent, if somewhat shady, New Yorkers, to purchase the Baltimore team for $18,000 and move it to New York.

The co-owners were Frank Farrell, who owned gambling establishments and a stable of race horses, and Bill Devery, former New York City Chief of Police, who had been under investigation for corruption, but never charged.

The New York team was called the Highlanders and they played their home games at 10,000-seat Hilltop Park on Broadway and 168th St. in Upper Manhattan. To lead their team, Farrell and Devery hired Clark Griffith away from the Chicago White Sox as manager and gave him carte blanche to spend what it took to bring in the best players available in an effort to compete with the successful New York Giants of the National League.

Griffith, still an effective pitcher himself (he

In 1913, the Highlanders became the Yankees and the team left Hilltop Park to become co-tenants with the Giants of the National League at the nearby Polo Grounds. The above photo, taken on April 4, 1913, is believed to be the first team photo of the New York Yankees. (UPI/Bettmann)

would win 14 games in 1903), raided the National League for such stars as infielder Wid Conroy, catcher Jack O'Connor, outfielder Wee Willie Keeler and pitchers Jack Chesbro and Jesse Tannehill, who won 36 games between them. The Highlanders, however, still finished fourth.

The following season, Chesbro started 51 games, completed 48 of them, pitched 454.2 innings and won an all-time record 41 games. The Highlanders finished second, three games behind Boston.

In 1913, the team changed its name from Highlanders to Yankees and, having outgrown Hilltop Park, moved into the Polo Grounds as tenants of the powerful, far more popular, New York Giants.

The grandiose plans and high hopes for New York's American League franchise never materialized and Farrell and Devery could no longer afford the losses they were amassing. Their search for new ownership led them to a pair of Colonels, who had been tipped off by Giants' manager John McGraw

In 1915, the Yankees were purchased for $460,000 by Colonels Tillinghast L'Hommedieu Huston (above) and Jacob Ruppert (right). Huston was a self-made millionaire who made his fortune in the harbor improvement business in Cuba. Ruppert was a member of the New York National Guard Silk Stocking Regiment, a four-term congressman, and heir to the Ruppert Brewery. (both photos:UPI/Bettmann)

ABOVE: *Jacob Ruppert (at left) during summer maneuvers with the New York National Guard Seventh Regiment, also called the Silk Stocking Regiment, in the late 1880s.*

RIGHT: *Jacob Ruppert just after he was made a colonel in the National Guard by New York Governor Hill in 1889. Ruppert was 22 at the time. (all photos: UPI/Bettmann)*

The Ruppert Brewery on Third Ave. and 91st St. in Manhattan in 1932, its heyday.

that the Yankees were for sale and suggested to his friends that they buy the team.

Col. Jacob Ruppert was the multi-millionaire scion of the Ruppert Breweries, a short, chunky, lifelong bachelor. He was a patron of the arts, a meticulous dresser, a member of the New York National Guard "silk stocking" regiment and somewhat aloof. He was a shrewd businessman and well-connected politically, having served four terms in Congress.

Col. Tillinghast L'Hommedieu Huston, despite an aristocratic name, was one of the boys, a gruff, hard drinking, card-playing, self-made multi-millionaire. An Army engineer during the Spanish-American war, he made his fortune in the harbor-improvement business in Cuba.

Cols. Ruppert and Huston paid $460,000 for New York's American League baseball team, which had finished sixth, seventh, eighth and tied for sixth in the previous four years as their hired-gun players began to age.

Ruppert's entry into baseball was not motivated by a great love for the game or to further his image as a sportsman. It was purely a business decision. His master plan was to change the name of the team to the "Knickerbockers," as a promotional and advertising tool for his brewery's best-selling beer. But an avalanche of editorial objections to the plan in the New York newspapers caused Ruppert to abandon his plan and keep the name "Yankees."

Ruppert and Huston were willing to spend what was necessary to put a winning team on the field. In 1915, they purchased first baseman Wally Pipp from Detroit and pitcher Bob Shawkey from Philadelphia. The most significant change for the Yankees, however, was the appearance of pinstripes on their uniforms for the first time on April 22 of that year.

In the first three years under the ownership of Huston and Ruppert, the Yankees finished fifth, fourth and sixth under manager Wild Bill Donovan. Ruppert decided it was time to hire a new manager and asked American League President Ban Johnson for a suggestion. "Get Miller Huggins," Johnson said. Huggins (above) had managed the St. Louis Cardinals for the previous five seasons. (New York Yankees Archives)

In the first three years under new ownership, the Yankees finished fifth, fourth and sixth under manager Wild Bill Donovan. Huston liked Donovan, but Ruppert was growing increasingly impatient with the team's lack of progress. He decided it was time to hire a new manager and while Huston was away in Europe, Ruppert asked AL president Ban Johnson if he could suggest a replacement.

"Get Miller Huggins," Johnson said.

Huggins was a tiny firebrand, five feet, six inches tall, and barely 140 pounds. He had played 13 years in the National League with Cincinnati and St. Louis, carving out a workmanlike, if unspectacular career, as a second baseman. For the past five years, he had managed the Cardinals without great success, but Ban Johnson was known to have an eye for talent.

"He's a fine manager," the league president said, "and we'll take a good man away from the National League."

Huggins became manager of the Yankees in 1918. In his first season, he improved the team to fourth place. In his second, they finished third. But the best, and the biggest, was still to come.

(UPI/Bettmann)

A Babe In The Bronx

It was, by all accounts and from all perspectives, a match made in heaven—George Herman Ruth and New York. The brash, bold, boisterous, braggadocios Babe, known for his booming bat and his nocturnal forays, in the world's greatest metropolis, the center of commerce, industry, communication and bright lights; the insatiable insomniac in the city that never sleeps.

The deal was consummated with a contract of sale signed on the day after Christmas, 1919, and the transfer from the New York Yankees to Harry Frazee of a check in the amount of $25,000, but the announcement would not come until January 5, 1920.

Under terms of the agreement, the Yankees would send Frazee three additional payments of $25,000, establishing the sale price at $100,000, twice as much as ever was paid for any other player. In addition, Col. Jacob Ruppert agreed to a loan of $300,000 to Frazee, guaranteeing his mortgage on Fenway Park.

While the city of New York in general, and Yankees fans in particular, were ecstatic with the news of the acquisition of the mighty Babe, Ruth, himself, was less than enthusiastic.

When the deal was announced, Ruth was spending the off-season in California, playing a series of exhibition games, golfing and partying. Informed of the sale, Ruth was hardly warm to the idea of pulling up stakes. He proclaimed his love for the Boston area, for the great Red Sox fans, for his farm in Sudbury, and for his new business enterprise—part ownership of a cigar factory.

Ruth enjoyed playing the role of the rural life on his farm in Sudbury, MA. (UPI/Bettmann)

Perhaps, as has been speculated, Ruth was merely campaigning for a new contract. He still had two years remaining on his three-year, $10,000-per deal with the Red Sox. If he was to go to New York, Ruth insisted, he would have to have a new contract with a substantial raise. He even asked for a percentage of the sale price. The Yankees agreed to pay Ruth the munificent sum of $20,000 for 1920. Ruth dropped his demand for a percentage of the sale price and the Babe's attitude toward coming to New York changed abruptly. He professed his approval of the deal, said he was excited about coming to New York and vowed his dedication to his new team.

Ruth met up with his new teammates in Penn Station on February 28 for the train trip to Jacksonville for spring training, where the newcomer was the center of attention. An expanded press corps of 13 reporters was in camp to chronicle the Babe's every move, and he gave them ample copy for the stories they sent back to their newspapers.

The newest Yankee was less than a smashing success in spring training. He wasn't hitting and fans rode him unmercifully. One in particular was so vociferous, Ruth went up into the stands after him.

Ruth continued to maintain that "spring

With the acquisition of Babe Ruth (at right), manager Miller Huggins and owner Jacob Ruppert had the Yankees franchise pointed in the right direction. (UPI/Bettmann)

training don't mean nothing," and when reporters asked him if he thought he could match his 1919 total of 29 home runs, the Babe boldly bellowed, "I'll hit 50 this year."

It was an outrageous boast since no team in either league hit 50 home runs the previous season. The Yankees led the majors with 45 homers. It was not a tailend team that Ruth was joining. In their second season under Miller Huggins, the Yankees won 80 games, 20 more than the previous year, and finished third, up a notch from 1918. Frank "Home Run" Baker led the team with 10 home runs. First baseman Wally Pipp, shortstop Roger Peckinpaugh and leftfielder Duffy Lewis each belted seven, and centerfielder Ping Bodie slugged six home runs, inspiring a cartoon by Robert Ripley in a New York newspaper depicting the Yankees' sluggers with the accompanying caption, "Murderers Row." Babe Ruth had not yet joined the team and Lou Gehrig was still a student at Columbia.

Babe Ruth, already immensely popular in Boston, became an idol to America's youth after joining the Yankees in 1919. Five thousand boys came out to see the growing legend in Syracuse in the summer of 1922. (UPI/Bettmann)

Ruth's Yankees debut came on April 16 in

Like Ruth, Carl Mays (left) also came from the Red Sox and won 26 games in 1920 and a league-leading 27 in 1921. However, he never lived down the tragedy of throwing the pitch that hit Cleveland infielder Ray Chapman in the head, killing him. (New York Yankees Archives)

First baseman Wally Pipp (right) gave American League pitchers headaches by hitting seven home runs in 1918. (New York Yankees Archives)

ABOVE: *The original Murderers Row of Wally Pipp (far left), Roger Peckinpaugh (center), and Frank "Home Run" Baker (far right) was augmented in 1919 by Babe Ruth (second from left) and in 1920 by Bob Meusel (second from right). (UPI/Bettmann)*

Frank Baker (left) led the 1918 Yankees with 10 homers and acquired the nickname "Home Run." (New York Yankees Archives)

Roger Peckinpaugh (right), the Yankees shortstop from 1913–1921, also is the youngest manager in Yankees history. At 23 and only in his second year of major league baseball, he managed the team for 20 games in 1914. (New York Yankees Archives)

In the "Golden Age of Sport" Ruth was the greatest hero of them all and he rubbed elbows with celebrities like former heavyweight champion James J. Corbett (above left). Ruth and Corbett hosted a Thanksgiving dinner for an orphanage in Spokane, WA. (UPI/Bettmann)

Shibe Park, Philadelphia. He had asked Huggins to allow him to play centerfield because he was concerned about running into walls in left or right and injuring himself. Huggins complied. But Ruth dropped a fly ball that allowed the Athletics to score two unearned runs that beat the Yankees. At bat, Babe stroked a pair of singles.

In the home opener a week later, Ruth pulled a rib cage muscle after batting once and left the game. It was not an auspicious debut for the big man, who did not hit his first home run until May 1. After that first one, they came in bunches. He hit 12 home runs in the month of May, 12 more in June. On July 15, he hit his 29th homer, matching his major league record set the previous season. On August 4, Ruth had 37 homers and a 26-game hitting streak that hiked his batting average to a season-high .391.

His home run production slowed in August. He hit only seven in five weeks, but Ruth finished strong, with 10 homers in his final 24 games.

His 54 home runs were astounding. George Sisler, second in the American League, had 19. The National League champion, Cy Williams of Philadelphia, hit 15. Babe's 54 homers in 1920 were more than any

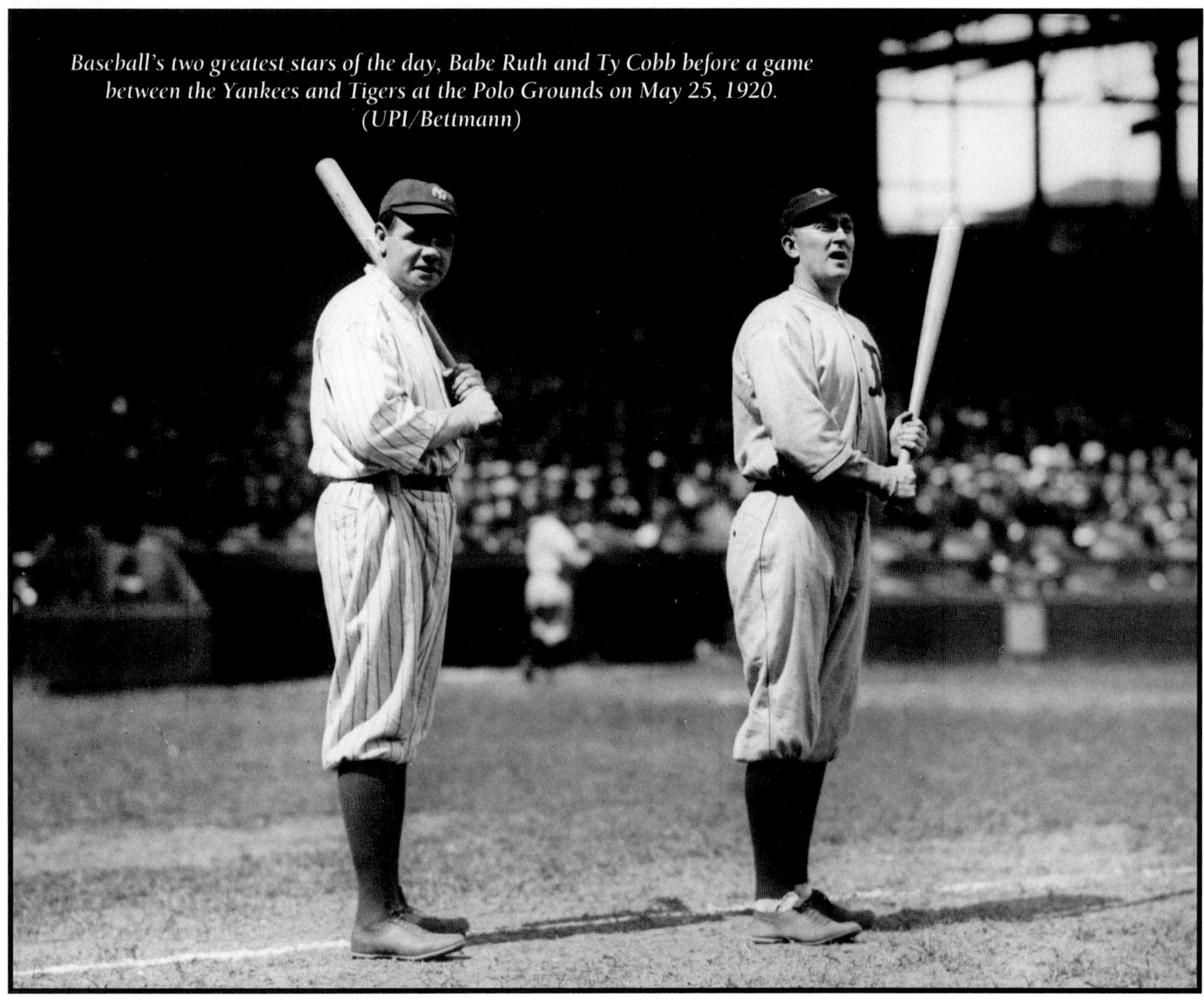
Baseball's two greatest stars of the day, Babe Ruth and Ty Cobb before a game between the Yankees and Tigers at the Polo Grounds on May 25, 1920. (UPI/Bettmann)

team except the Phillies, who hit 64, and, of course, his Yankees, who belted the astonishing total of 115 homers.

Ruth finished fourth in the league in batting at .376, had 36 doubles, 9 triples, scored 158 runs, drove in 137, stole 14 bases and produced an all-time record slugging percentage of .847. Still, for the second straight year, the Yankees finished third.

The mighty Ruth's contribution to baseball was more than just home runs and increased attendance. The game was reeling from the 1919 "Black Sox Scandal," in which eight members of the Chicago White Sox were brought to trial for conspiring to throw the World Series to the Cincinnati Reds. The eight never were convicted, but newly-appointed commissioner, Judge Kenesaw Mountain Landis, meted out his own arbitrary justice and banned all eight from the game for life.

Public confidence in the integrity of the game was at an all-time low. Suspicion and skepticism abounded. The game needed a savior and Babe Ruth was the perfect angel of mercy. His booming home runs, and his bombastic behavior gave the game a larger-than-life hero that fans could embrace.

Attendance soared. In 1920, the Yankees surpassed the one million mark for the first time in the club's history, drawing 1,289,422, doubling the previous year's total. All because of Babe Ruth and the interest engendered by his booming home runs.

He was part of a majestic era, a golden era of sports, at a time when the names were magic. Jack Dempsey. Red Grange. Johnny Longden. Bobby Jones. Bill Tilden. But he was the greatest hero of them all. He hit the most and the longest home runs, ate the most hot dogs, drank the most beer, had the flashiest cars, was seen with the most dazzling women, wore the most fashionable clothes, had the most prodigious appetite, the heartiest laugh and the most booming voice, the biggest belly and the skinniest legs. And he saved baseball.

The 1921 World Series between the Yankees and Giants was played entirely at the Polo Grounds in Manhattan. (UPI/Bettmann)

Ed Barrow left the Red Sox and was appointed Yankees General Manager on October 29, 1920. In 1921, the Yankees won their first American League pennant. (New York Yankees Archives)

1921 New York Yankees, the club's first American League Champions.

TOP ROW: *Jack Quinn, Tom Rogers, Alex Ferguson, Elmer Miller, Mike McNally, Rip Collins, William Piercy, Frank Baker, Harry Harper, Al De Vormer, Fred Hofmann, Bob Meusel, Bob Roth, Roger Peckinpaugh.* MIDDLE ROW: *Aaron Ward, Bill Fewster, Wally Pipp, Bob Shawkey, Wally Schang, Babe Ruth, Carl Mays, Waite Hoyt, N.L. Hawke* FRONT ROW: *John Mitchell, Eddie Bennett (mascot), Miller Huggins (manager), Charles O'Leary (coach), Frank Roth (coach). (New York Yankees Archives)*

When the game needed a hero, a savior, George Herman Ruth, The Babe, stepped in to accept the role, capturing the imagination of a public that had become suspicious, that had grown disillusioned, that felt betrayed. Babe Ruth was the right man at the right time. He may have been the only man who could save baseball, who could capture the fancy of a skeptical American public. Who is to say for certain that we would still have baseball as we know it now were it not for him?

His name blared from newspaper headlines almost daily. Italian-Americans in New York loved baseball and they loved Babe Ruth. "The Bambino," they called him, using the Italian word for "baby," and the nickname took hold.

Stories about Ruth soon became legendary. He was assigned to room with veteran outfielder Ping Bodie and when reporters, constantly in search of new stories about the Babe, inquired how it was rooming with a hero, Bodie replied, "I don't know. I never see him. I room with his suitcase."

Despite their improvement on the field and their success at the gate, Jake Ruppert, now taking a greater interest in the operation of his baseball team, remained unfulfilled. He wanted a championship and he would stop at nothing to get one. Toward that end, he hired Ed Barrow away from the Red Sox as general manager, a move that raised eyebrows in baseball circles. Was this the trailer to the sale of Ruth by the Red Sox to the Yankees?

In truth, Barrow had nothing to do with Ruth's sale to New York. He was, in fact, vehemently opposed to it. He did, however, engineer the deal that brought catcher Wally Schang and pitcher Waite Hoyt from the Red Sox to the Yankees.

Schang became the team's regular catcher in 1921 and batted .316 with six homers and 55 RBIs. Hoyt won 19 games and the two newcomers helped push the Yankees over the top. They won 98 games, finished four and a half games ahead of Cleveland, and were American League champions for the first time in the history of the franchise. Ruth improved on his 1920 statistics. He batted .378, belted 59 home runs and drove in 171 runs.

The 1921 World Series was played in one ballpark, the Polo Grounds, shared by the Giants and Yankees. The Yankees won the first two games of the best-of-nine Series on back-to-back shutouts by Carl Mays and Waite Hoyt. The Giants evened the series by winning games three and four, despite Ruth's first Series home run. The Yankees won game five,

Although Giants general manager John McGraw (at left) extended a friendly hand to Yankees manager Miller Huggins, the two organizations were not always on good terms. The Yankees' increasing popularity and success on the field led the Giants to boot them out of the Polo Grounds and force them to build their own stadium. (New York Yankees Archives)

but when Ruth had to sit out the remainder of the Series with an infected arm, the Giants swept the last three games to win the Series, five games to three. The Giants of John McGraw had put the upstart Yankees in their place.

The same two teams met in the 1922 World Series. The Giants easily won the National League pennant, but the Yankees barely took the American League pennant by one game in a dogfight with the St. Louis Browns. Ruth and slugger Bob Meusel missed the first month of the season. The two had been suspended by Commissioner Landis for participating in an unauthorized barnstorming tour.

Ruth would hit only 35 home runs and drive in 99 runs during the regular season. In the World Series, he was held to just two hits, a single and a double, and one RBI as the Giants swept the Series in four games, the first year under a new format of a best-of-seven World Series.

Because of their back-to-back world championships and their dominance over their tenants, hostilities between the Giants and Yankees escalat-

The original site of Yankee Stadium, February 1921, looking northeast from 157th Street. Construction began on May 5.

The bleachers and main grandstands take shape in late summer of 1922.

By July, 1922, (above) construction was well on its way.

A centerfield perspective (left) on November 1, 1922.

An aerial view (right) of the construction and surrounding area in September, 1922.

(All construction photos courtesy of Ballpark Classics Inc./Osborn Archives)

Underwood & Underwood

Fans file into new Yankee Stadium.
(New York Yankees Archives)

Opening Day—April 18, 1923

LEFT: *Raising Old Glory at Yankee Stadium for the first time. (UPI/Bettmann)*

RIGHT TOP: *Opening Day of Yankee Stadium. Pictured from left are Colonel Ruppert, Commissioner of Baseball Judge Kenesaw Mountain Landis, Colonel Huston and Red Sox owner Harry Frazee. (UPI/Bettmann)*

RIGHT BOTTOM: *Yankees owner Colonel Ruppert with manager Miller Huggins and Boston manager Frank Chance before the first game ever played at Yankee Stadium. (UPI/Bettmann)*

Yankees manager Miller Huggins (left) and owner Jacob Ruppert confer during spring training in the early 1920s. (New York Yankees Archives)

ed. John McGraw was envious of the Yankees' success at the gate. Because of the enormous popularity of Babe Ruth, the Yankees outdrew the Giants in their own ballpark, a humiliating situation for the landlord. Fans were switching their allegiance from the established Giants to the new team in town. Something had to be done, decreed McGraw, the Napoleonic leader of the Giants. The Giants had to be saved. He informed the Yankees their lease would not be renewed following the 1922 season.

With his team in danger of being homeless in the 1923 season, Ruppert moved swiftly. He purchased a 10-acre parcel of swampland in the Bronx for $1.5 million and construction began on a magnificent new structure on May 5, 1922. It took 45,000 cubic yards of earth as fill, 20,000 cubic yards of concrete, eight tons of reinforced steel, one million board feet of Pacific Coast fir for bleachers and 284 days to build the edifice that would quickly become the most famous sports stadium in the world.

The state-of-the-art structure would be called Yankee Stadium and it would sit just across the Harlem River from the Polo Grounds.

Wednesday, April 23, 1923, came up raw and windy in New York City. The midday temperatures struggled vainly to climb into the 50s. But the temperature be damned. Hearts and hides were warmed because spring had come to New York, heralded by the opening of the baseball season.

On that day, Bloomingdale's announced a sale of men's two trouser suits for $24.75. Loft's advertised chocolate covered coconut candy for 24 cents a pound, and the A&P had Brer Rabbit molasses for 7 cents, Grandmother's bread for 5 cents and Pacific toilet paper for 5 cents a roll.

Pola Negri was starring in "Bella Donna" at the Rivoli; Vera Sheppard completed a record 69 consecutive hours of dancing; and a raid on Oscar Carr's Garage in North Hampton uncovered a 250-gallon still and a large quantity of liquor and mash.

The big news on Wednesday, April 18, 1923, however, was in the Bronx, where Gov. Al Smith and Mayor John Hyland, Baseball Commissioner Kenesaw Mountain Landis, police commissioner Richard Enright and bandmaster John Philip Sousa helped dedicate the newest, largest, most modern stadium in baseball.

There was no ballpark to be compared with the magnificent new edifice. Yankee Stadium was the last word in athletic facilities.

They came to the South Bronx by street car, by bus, by subway and by automobile on that cold and windy April day, hordes of fans attracted by a sense of history, a feeling of pride, a spirit of togetherness. The official attendance was announced as 74,217, with an additional 15,000 milling around outside, having been denied admittance to the stadium.

Those fortunate to make it inside had reason to be uplifted—by the beautiful surroundings, by watching Yankees shortstop Everett Scott play in his 986th consecutive game, by Bob Shawkey's three-hitter against the Boston Red Sox. But the climax came early. It came in the third inning when, quite fittingly, the mighty Babe Ruth hit the first home run in the new stadium, a "four base drive into the right field bleachers with two mates on that drove the fans into a frenzy," according to James Cruisenberry, writing in the *New York Daily News* the following day.

The mighty Babe "showed it could be done," wrote Cruisenberry, "and above all, it probably returned the old time confidence of the Babe. He hadn't been going so good on the spring training trips. He was in great condition, but he wasn't smacking them. The season opened and on the first day—in his second time at bat—he smacked one as he never smacked before. It was great!"

Before he became "Papa Bear," George Halas wore the Pinstripes. In 1919, he appeared in 12 games as an outfielder. (New York Yankees Archives)

In time, Yankee Stadium became the best known sports palace in the world.

It was there that Knute Rockne of Notre Dame made his famous "win one for the Gipper" speech in 1928, and Army battled heavily favored Notre Dame to a 0-0 tie in 1946.

It was there that Joe Louis made the world free for democracy by knocking out the pride of Nazi Germany, Max Schmeling in the first round in 1938, and Sugar Ray Robinson melted under June heat and humidity against light heavyweight champion Joey Maxim in 1952.

It was there that in 1961 Roger Maris hit his 61st home run and Don Larsen pitched the only Perfect Game in World Series history in 1956, and Al Gionfriddo made "the catch" against Joe DiMaggio in 1947.

It was there that thousands bade weepy farewells to Lou Gehrig and Babe Ruth.

There have been 31 World Series played in Yankee Stadium, three All-Star games, three NFL championship games, 30 title fights, 19 Fordham-NYU football games, 21 Army-Notre Dame games.

Pope Paul VI and John Paul II celebrated mass there, Billy Graham and Billy Sunday preached there, Nelson Mandela was greeted there, Billy Joel and U2 and Pink Floyd performed there.

The Bronx became baseball's capital, Yankee Stadium its castle, and Babe Ruth its king.

If Yankee Stadium was not "the House That Ruth Built," it certainly was, by his popularity and because of his prodigious home runs, the house that Ruth made legendary.

A Home Of Their Own

In their new home, the Yankees enjoyed their fourth consecutive year of attracting more than one million paying customers and won their third straight American League pennant, by 16 games over the Detroit Tigers.

Babe Ruth bounced back with another spectacular season. He led the American League in home runs with 41, tied for first with Tris Speaker in RBIs with 130, led in runs with 151, in walks with 170 and in slugging percentage with .764. Although his batting average of .393 was the highest in his major league career, he finished second in the league batting race, 10 points behind Detroit's Harry Heilmann.

The Giants also won their third straight pennant and the two intra-city rivals who had shared the same field for the previous 10 seasons, met again in the World Series. This time the Yankees had a home of their own and hosted the Series opener.

The Giants won Game 1, 5-4, on a ninth inning, inside-the-park home run by one Charles Dillon "Casey" Stengel, who drove a Joe Bush change-up into deepest left centerfield. Rounding second, Stengel lost his shoe, but he hobbled around the bases and slid home with what would be the winning run.

After three games, the Giants led, two games to one, but the Yankees would sweep the next three to win the first world championship in their history. Ruth hit three home runs and batted .368 for the Series.

In the first World Series game ever played in Yankee Stadium in 1923, the New York Giants won on a ninth inning inside-the-park home run by, of all people, Casey Stengel. (UPI/Bettmann)

With Ruth at the top of his game, not yet at his physical peak at age 28, and dominating baseball with his barrage of home runs, the Yankees appeared invincible, likely to monopolize the world championship throughout the decade of the 20s. The only things that could stop Ruth were his ego, his contentiousness and his lifestyle. They did.

The Yankees slipped a notch in 1924, finishing second to Washington, but not through any fault of Ruth. He again led the league in home runs with 46 and won his only batting title with a .378 average. But age was beginning to creep up on several of Ruth's teammates and the Yankees slipped just enough to prevent them from catching the Senators, a formidable opponent with such stars as Goose Goslin, Sam Rice, Bucky Harris, former Yankee Roger Peckinpaugh and the legendary "Big Train," Walter Johnson, who won 23 games.

Late in the season, the Yankees acquired a player who was to have a profound impact on future Yankees teams when they purchased the contract of Earle Combs, a 23-year old speedy centerfielder.

To ease his disappointment at not making it to the World Series for the first time in four years, Ruth went off to Cuba for a vacation of revelry. Ruth partied, drank, ate and reportedly blew his entire 1924 salary at the gaming tables. When he reported for spring training in 1925 in St. Petersburg, where the Yankees had moved

ABOVE: *At the end of the 1924 season, the Yankees added an important piece to their future championship puzzle when they purchased the contract of 23-year-old speedy centerfielder Earle Combs.*

The Yankees' talented doubleplay combination, which would be intact through the glorious late 1920s, arrived three months apart in 1925. First came shortstop Mark Koenig (right top), then second baseman Tony Lazzeri, (right bottom) who had hit 66 home runs in one minor league season. (All photos: New York Yankees Archives)

their spring headquarters, Ruth was 30 pounds overweight. His complexion was sallow. He looked haggard and drawn and run-down despite the added weight. His face was puffy, his eyes sunken and bloodshot.

"Everybody figured he was washed up," said Earle Combs. "He was just a wreck."

Ruth started spring training by catching the flu. Then he broke a finger in a clubhouse prank. He recovered from his infirmities and worked hard to lose the excess weight, but he also continued to party hard. On the trip north, the Yankees stopped off to play a game in Asheville, N.C. As Babe climbed off the pullman, his face turned gray, he started breathing heavily, his eyes closed and he tottered for a moment, then pitched face first onto the cement platform.

Ruth was rushed to the hospital and the New York newspapers blared big, bold headlines that suggested the mighty Babe was at death's door. He was taken to New York for more tests and the word was that he was suffering from influenza and indigestion. Although there was suspicion that the press was not disclosing the true nature of his ailment. W.O. (Bill) McGeehan called Ruth's ailment, "The stomach ache heard round the world."

Ruth remained hospitalized while the Yankees lost 16 of their first 24 games. Not only were they without their great slugger, the rest of the team was beginning to show signs of age. By the last week of May, Ruth checked out of the hospital and began working out. Against the objections of his doctors, he returned to

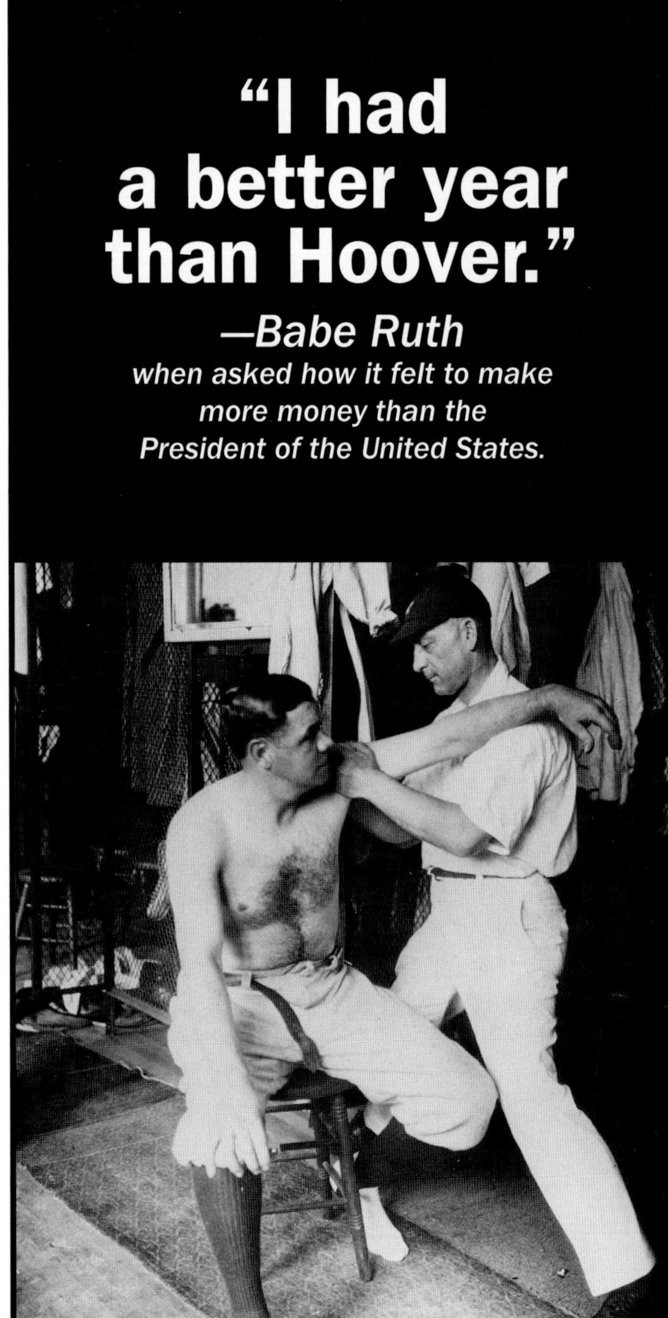

Ruth's off-the-field activities frequently landed him in the trainer's room. Here Ron "Doc" Woods prepares Ruth's throwing arm prior to a game. (UPI/Bettmann)

the lineup on June 1, but he was obviously weakened. That didn't stop the Babe from continuing his reckless lifestyle.

On a trip to St. Louis in August, Babe vanished once the team hit town and did not show up until five minutes before game time the following day. Manager Miller Huggins was livid. He fined Ruth $5,000 and suspended him indefinitely, which made Ruth even more livid than his manager.

"I ought to choke you to death," he threatened the diminutive manager. To members of the press, Ruth said, "I will not play for him. Either he quits or I quit."

General manager Ed Barrow interceded to bring about an uneasy truce between the Yankees star and their manager. Ruth's suspension was lifted on September 9, after nine days. Babe played in only 98 games, but still managed to swat 25 homers to go along with 66 RBIs and a .290 average. Bob Meusel, who had told his ailing running mate, "Don't worry, Babe, I'll show them how you hit them," made good on his boast by leading the American League with 33 homers. But the Yankees won only a pathetic 69 games and finished seventh.

Even while the Yankees were hitting bottom, steps were being taken to return the team to contention. In June, they purchased the contract of a sensational minor league shortstop named Mark Koenig. In August, they bought another minor league phenom, second baseman Tony Lazzeri. And on June 3, manager Huggins made a daring, if desperate, move. He

replaced the veteran, but aging, Wally Pipp with a 22-year-old out of Columbia University named Henry Louis Gehrig.

Lou Gehrig, the son of German immigrants who grew up in the Yorkville section of New York, and whose mother worked as a cook and housekeeper at a Columbia fraternity house, received a signing bonus of $1,500 and a salary of $2,000 to play the remainder of that season in Hartford. He joined the Yankees six weeks into the start of the 1925 season only to find Pipp solidly entrenched at first base, a position he had held down for the Yankees for 10 seasons.

"I was so discouraged at my slim prospect for getting regular work at first," Gehrig said, "that I asked Hug to try me in the outfield," which already had Ruth, Combs and Meusel. Gehrig made his Yankees debut on June 1 as a pinch-hitter for shortstop PeeWee Wanninger. Gehrig was retired, but the date of that plate appearance would be etched into the baseball records forever.

The following day, fate was to intervene in Gehrig's behalf and alter the course of baseball history. Pipp was struck on the head in batting practice.

He was a son of German immigrants, he grew up in the Yorkville section of Manhattan and he attended the High School of Commerce and Columbia University. Lou Gehrig replaced Wally Pipp at first base on June 3, 1925 and played a record 2,130 consecutive games. (National Baseball Library, Cooperstown, NY)

"I just couldn't duck," Pipp later recalled. "The ball hit me in the temple. Down I went. I was too far gone to bother reaching for any aspirin tablets, as the popular story goes."

Pipp was knocked into semi-consciousness and taken to a nearby hospital, where he remained for two weeks. In his absence, Gehrig got his chance to start at first base, and a career, a record and a legend was launched.

Gehrig was sitting in the dugout when Huggins approached him. "You're my first baseman today," the manager said, "and from now on."

Opportunity was knocking for Gehrig, and Lou was quick to answer its call. In his first game as a regular, batting sixth behind Ruth and Meusel, Gehrig singled twice and doubled in his first three at bats. Now that he had become the regular first baseman for the Yankees, he was determined not to be dislodged. In his first season, Gehrig batted .295 with 20 home runs and 68 RBIs in what amounted to little more than half a season.

During the 1926 World Series, Babe Ruth heard about a New Jersey boy who was gravely ill. He visited the boy in the hospital and promised to hit a home run for him in Game 3 of the Series. He hit three home runs. Two years later the boy, Johnny Sylvester, was the Babe's guest at a game at Yankee Stadium. (UPI/Bettmann)

Reports of Ruth's demise as a ballplayer, like reports of his death, were grossly exaggerated and Ruth was determined to prove he had some good years left. He reported to spring training for the 1926 season in his best shape in years. He had moved from Boston to New York's Ansonia Hotel on Broadway and 73rd St., and he spent the winter working out regularly in a New York gym. His weight was down to 222 and his stomach was flat.

The Yankees opened the 1926 season by winning 13 of their first 18, then ripped off 17 out of their next 21 for a 30-9 record on May 29. They slumped in August, but managed to win the pennant by three games. Ruth regained his batting form to hit .372, second in the league, and to lead the league by wide margins in home runs with 47 and RBIs with 145, proving there was life in the old boy yet. Gehrig had 16 homers and 107 RBIs.

The Yankees met the St. Louis Cardinals in the 1926 World Series, one of the most memorable ever. The Yankees won Game 1 and the Cardinals came back to even the Series in Game 2. After that game, a fan from Essex Fells, N.J., managed to get word to Ruth that a young boy named Johnny Sylvester, an avid fan of Babe's, lay near death in a hospital. He had undergone a serious operation and apparently had lost the will to live.

The next day, a telegram from the Babe arrived at the boy's bedside. In it, Ruth promised to hit a home run for little Johnny in the game that day. He hit three.

Not even the Babe's heroics could save the Yankees in the World Series. It came down to a decisive seventh game in Yankee Stadium and to one at-bat in the seventh inning. With the bases loaded, two outs and the Cardinals leading, 3-2, old Grover Cleveland Alexander struck out young Tony Lazzeri to kill off the Yankees last threat.

With two outs in the ninth, Ruth drew a walk, but with slugger Bob Meusel at bat, the Babe, thinking he could catch the Cardinals unaware, attempted to steal second. He was thrown out to end the World Series.

The Yankees were back, but not all the way back, and to a man, they dedicated themselves to winning the world championship the following year and they broke from the starting gate like a runaway train. On July 5, the Washington Senators came to Yankee Stadium for a doubleheader. The Yankees swept both games, winning the first, 12-1, and taking the second, 21-1.

It was days like this that Col. Ruppert had in mind when he said, in answer to what he considered a perfect day at the stadium: "When the Yankees score

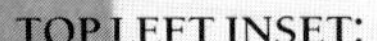

TOP LEFT INSET:
The crowd gathered to wait for the gates to open including 75-year-old Jack Taylor (top right inset) who arrived from Texas with his tricycle and dog and pitched a tent outside the main ticket window.

BOTTOM LEFT INSET:
Yankee fever was rampant during the 1926 World Series.

BOTTOM RIGHT INSET:
On October 2, part of the record-breaking Game One crowd descends the elevated subway line outside Yankee Stadium.

BACKGROUND:
Inside, the crowd of 61,658 watched the Yankees beat the Cardinals 2-1 on a three-hitter by Herb Pennock. Lou Gehrig singled home Babe Ruth with the winning run in the sixth inning. (UPI/Bettmann)

Hit a home run and get a box of
Holeproof Ex
3 to 4 times more wear
HELMAR
THE QUEEN OF CIGARETTES
ORANGE DRINK
CANDY
ICE CREAM CONES
MURAD

Overshadowed by his more famous teammates Ruth and Gehrig, was slugger Bob Meusel. The 6-3, 190-pound outfielder had a lifetime BA of .309 and led the American League in home runs (33) and RBI (138) in 1925. (New York Yankees Archives)

eight runs in the first inning and slowly pull away."

With the sweep, the Yankees opened a 12-game lead. They would finish with a record of 110-44, $19^1/_2$ games in front of the Philadelphia Athletics. The 1927 Yankees, forever identified as "Murderers Row," are considered by most baseball observers as the greatest team ever assembled. They batted .307 as a team. The eight regulars batted .320. Ruth, of course, was the leader, belting the astounding total of 60 home runs. He batted .356 and led the league in runs. Gehrig batted .373, led the league in doubles and RBIs (175). Pulled along in friendly rivalry with Ruth, Gehrig slugged 47 homers (the combined total 147 homers by Ruth and Gehrig accounted for 25 percent of the home runs in the league). Earle Combs batted .356 and led the league in hits and triples. Bob Meusel batted .337. Tony Lazzeri batted .309 and was third in the league with 18 homers. Waite Hoyt led the league with 22 wins, in winning percentage and earned run average. The Yankees completed their perfect season with a four-game sweep of

"When the Yankees score eight runs in the first inning and slowly pull away."

—Col. Jacob Ruppert,
when asked what he considered a perfect day at the ballpark.

A rare photo of the 1927 Yankees on the eve of the World Series against the Pirates as they gather in Babe Ruth's room at the Roosevelt Hotel in Pittsburgh. (Left to right) Bob Meusel (standing), Dutch Reuther, the Babe, Mark Koenig, Pat Collins, Benny Bengough, and Joe Giard (standing). (UPI/Bettmann)

the Pirates in the World Series.

In 1984, Hoyt was asked to write the foreword for a book on the 1927 Yankees. As a broadcaster for the Cincinnati Reds into the 1980s, Hoyt was uniquely qualified to compare Murderers Row with other great teams, including Cincinnati's Big Red Machine of the 70s. He argued that no team came close to the '27 Yankees.

"Instead of delving into facts and figures," Hoyt

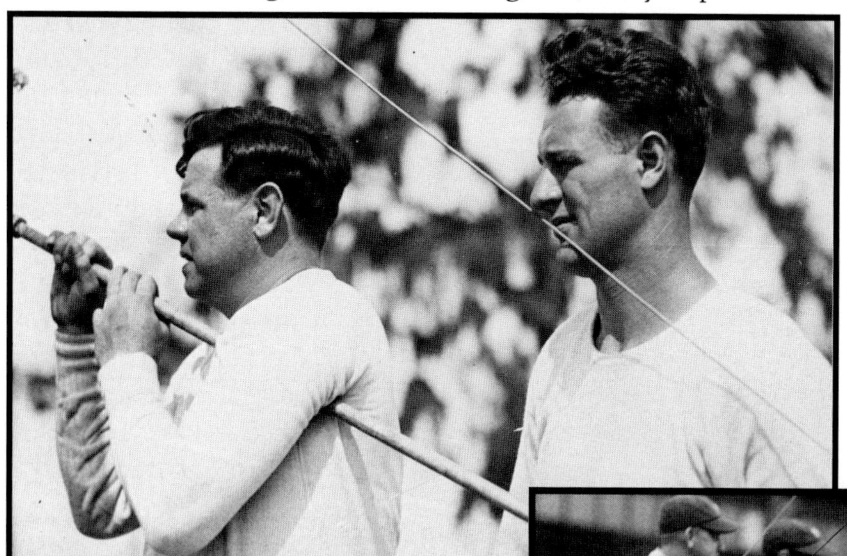

The Babe and Lou at the batting cage (left) in spring training in 1928 and later that same season (below) in New York. (UPI/Bettmann)

wrote, "I should like to deal with the even more collective state of mind of our team. Huggins termed it well. He preached 'attitude.' Sometimes he used a similar word, 'disposition.' There could not have been a group with a better attitude and disposition than that ball club. There was no flamboyant display, no back slapping, no cheering, for this was before the days when professional athletes reacted to teammates' accomplishments with congratulatory enthusiasm. Our only concession to high-spirited behavior occurred after a victory in Yankee Stadium. On the way from the players' bench to the clubhouse, we chanted 'Roll Out the Barrel,' which became our theme song.

"We were a contingent of 25 divergent personalities, yet each of us was totally dedicated to a peak effort and result...and in our performance each of us maintained a sophisticated dignity. We were never rough or rowdy, just purposeful.

"Huggins instituted a rigid program of behavior for those men who were not in the starting lineup. If you were an extra for the day, you were expected to pay attention to the game. There was to be no talk about anything but baseball, no sitting slouched with feet up and chin resting on cupped hands. We sat like third-grade kids in front of a hard-shelled teacher.

"I recall one incident vividly. Our bullpen was out in leftfield, atop a slightly graded embankment in the open space between the main grandstand and the bleachers, and it was provided with a wooden bench. A telephone was installed so that Huggins could phone down to 'get so and so ready.' There also was a connecting telephone in the mezzanine box of Ed Barrow (general manager), who from that vantage point, could oversee the whole stadium. One day, Barrow cast a critical eye toward the bullpen. It was a hot day, and one player was stretched out on the bench, apparently taking a snooze. The bull-pen phone rang. Barrow snorted, 'Tell that lazy (bleep) to sit up straight. Get his feet on the ground. What the hell does he think we're paying him for?'"

The Yankees made it three straight pennants and two straight world championships in 1928 and while Ruth's average slipped to .323, the lowest of his career for a full season, his power numbers held firm with 54 homers and 142 RBIs, both tops in the league. There were, however, telltale signs that season that forewarned of troubled times ahead. After taking an $11\ ^1/_2$ game lead on July 1, the Yankees

A new cast of Yankees thrived in the McCarthy era. Hall of Fame catcher Bill Dickey (top left) had arrived in 1928. Vernon "Lefty" Gomez (above right) arrived in 1930. Later that year the Yankees purchased the contract of Charlie "Red" Ruffing (bottom left) from the Boston Red Sox. Gomez led the league with 26 wins in 1934. Ruffing led the league with 21 wins in 1938. In 1932, the Yankees added a rookie shortstop named Frank Crosetti (below right) from San Francisco to team with second baseman Tony Lazzeri, also from San Francisco. Crosetti was a Yankee for 37 consecutive seasons as a player and a coach. (New York Yankees Archives and National Baseball Library, Cooperstown, NY)

went into an August slump that saw them slip into second place. They regrouped to sweep a three-game series from the first place Athletics in September and won the pennant by 2 1/2 games.

In the spring that followed, manager Huggins warned of imminent danger. He told the press that he was concerned that his team was aging, and exhorted his players to intensify their efforts for the 1929 season.

It was the season in which numbers appeared on major league uniforms for the first time and the Yankees were the innovators. Better to identify the players, they reasoned. Not that the cast of Murderers Row needed to be identified.

In assigning uniform numbers, the Yankees simply gave each player the position he occupied in Huggins' batting order, therefore Earle Combs was No. 1, Mark Koenig No. 2, Babe Ruth No. 3, Lou Gehrig No. 4, Bob Meusel No. 5, etc.

Huggins proved to be a prophet of doom as the Yankees finished second, 18 games behind Connie Mack's Athletics, interrupting their string of three pennants. But Huggins didn't live to see his unhappy prediction come true. He contracted a rare skin infection, which he dismissed as merely a boil on his neck, and died on September 25 at the age of 50.

Always the prankster, Ruth takes it upon himself to get a good photograph of his teammate Gehrig at Philadelphia's Shibe Park. (UPI/Bettmann)

At Huggins' funeral, Ruth wept uncontrollably, telling the press, "I loved that little guy." Standing nearby, a relative of the fallen manager sneered sardonically, "What a phony. He took five years off Miller's life."

In Huggins' absence, coach Art Fletcher was chosen to manage the team for the remainder of the season. Fletcher was asked to take the job full time in 1930, but declined, preferring to remain as a coach. The job was offered to Eddie Collins and Donie Bush. When both star players refused, Ruth dropped hints among his friends in the press that he would welcome the opportunity to be the team's player-manager.

Instead, the job was given to former pitching star Bob Shawkey, who had managed successfully at the Yankees' top farm team in Newark.

Ruth's three-year, $70,000-per contract had run out and negotiations opened for a new deal. The Babe asked Ruppert for $100,000, at which the owner balked and submitted his counter-offer. Two years at $80,000 per year. Ruth agreed, giving rise to a story, probably apocryphal, that Ruth was asked how it felt earning more money than the President of the United States (Herbert Hoover's salary was $75,000).

Ruth is reported to have replied, "I had a better year than Hoover."

Bob Meusel had been sold to Cincinnati following the 1929 season as the dismantling of Murderers Row escalated, and right-hander Red Ruffing was acquired from Boston. Ruth earned his money with a league-leading 49 homers, 154 RBIs and a .359 average. Gehrig batted .379, second in the league to Al Simmons' .381, led the league with 174 RBIs and belted 41 homers. But the Yankees finished third, 16 games out.

Shawkey was deemed a bust as a manager, too openly critical of his players, and the search was on for his replacement. Ruth intensified his quest for the job and campaigned openly that he had earned the chance to manage the team. Ruppert said he would give the Babe every consideration, while others scoffed: "He can't manage himself, how's he going to manage 25 other guys?"

Ruppert already had his man picked out. He was friendly with Joe McCarthy, who had just completed the final year of his contract as manager of the Chicago Cubs, and who was not getting along with Cubs' owner, Bill Veeck.

Ruppert brought McCarthy to New York in 1931, a

After Ruth left the Yankees following the '34 season, Gehrig stood alone as the Yankees' leader until his health failed in early 1939. (National Baseball Library, Cooperstown, NY)

move that dismayed Ruth and didn't sit well with his teammates. McCarthy was a humorless disciplinarian (he banned pre-game card-playing in the clubhouse), and he never played in the major leagues.

Despite a sharp increase in his weight and his disappointment at not getting the job, Ruth was second in the league in batting with a .373 average, his highest in eight seasons, tied Gehrig in home runs with 46 and was second to Gehrig in RBIs, 184-163. Still, the Yankees finished second, 13 1/2 games behind Philadelphia.

Ruth was in his 19th major league season in 1932. He had passed his 37th birthday and he had slowed perceptibly. He played in only 133 games, his fewest since 1925, the year of the "Belly Ache." His average skidded to .341, his home runs to 41, his RBIs to 137. The new king of clout in the American League was Jimmie Foxx of the Athletics, who led the league with 58 homers and 169 RBIs. Nevertheless, the Yankees, assembling a new cast of heroes such as Ruffing, shortstop Frankie Crosetti, catcher Bill Dickey, outfielder Ben Chapman, and pitchers Lefty Gomez and Johnny Allen, won 107 games and beat out Foxx's A's by 13 games.

Representing the National League against the Yankees in the 1932 World Series were the Chicago Cubs, a team with which the Yankees shared bad blood. For one thing, there was the bitterness of McCarthy at having been fired by the Cubs after the 1930 season. For another, there was the saga of Mark Koenig, the beloved shortstop of the '27 Yankees.

Koenig, who had been traded along with Waite Hoyt to Detroit during the 1930 season, was picked up by the Cubs for their pennant run in August of the 1932 season. His experience, excellent defense and .353 average may have been the difference in

In 1931, less than two years after the death of Miller Huggins, the Yankees hired Joe McCarthy (at right) away from the Chicago Cubs to be their 12th manager. A stern disciplinarian who never played in the major leagues, McCarthy was not a popular choice among the Yankees, especially Ruth, (inset) who campaigned for the job himself. (New York Yankees Archives and UPI/Bettmann)

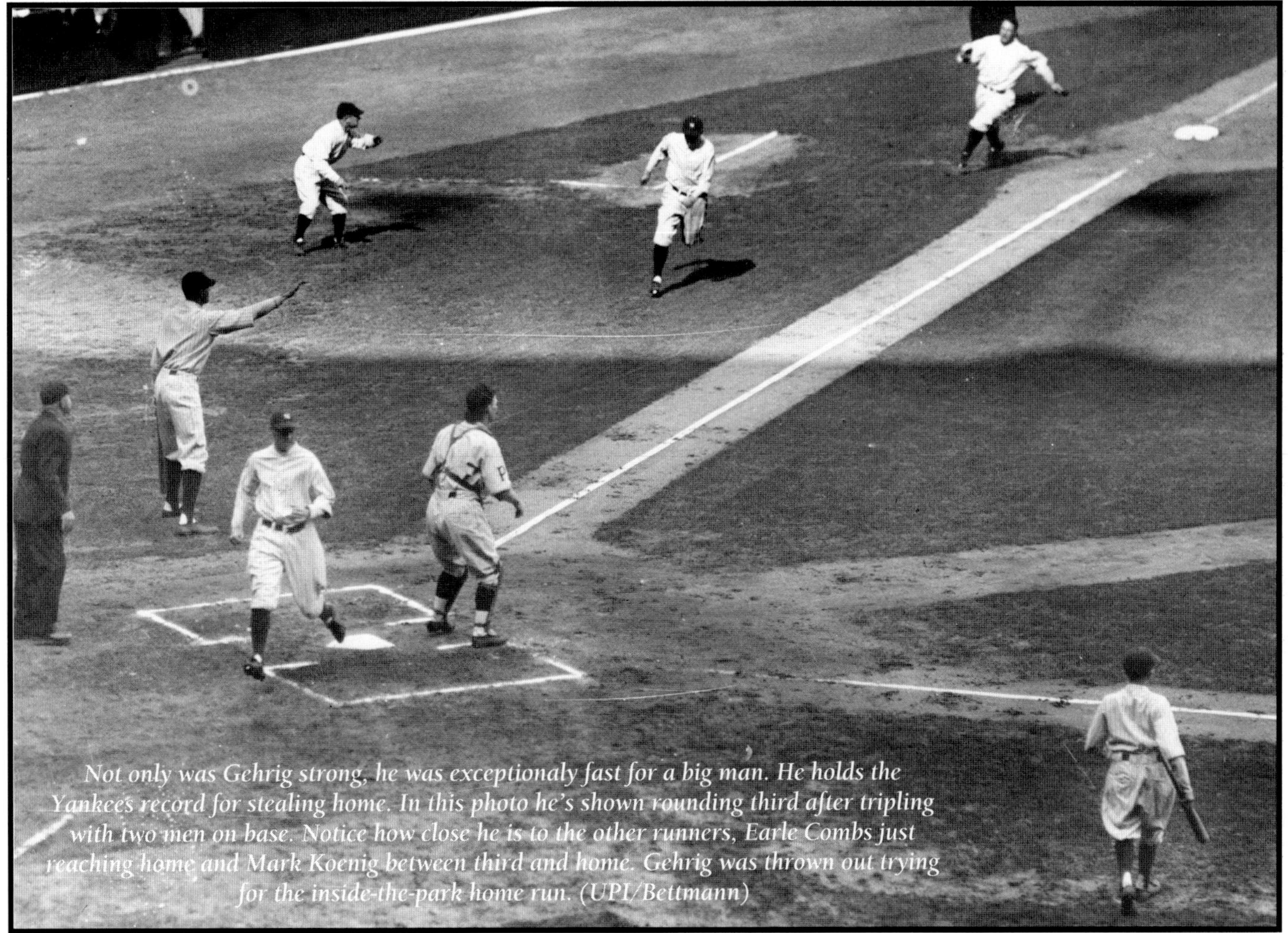

Not only was Gehrig strong, he was exceptionaly fast for a big man. He holds the Yankees record for stealing home. In this photo he's shown rounding third after tripling with two men on base. Notice how close he is to the other runners, Earle Combs just reaching home and Mark Koenig between third and home. Gehrig was thrown out trying for the inside-the-park home run. (UPI/Bettmann)

Chicago's four-game margin over Pittsburgh. But Koenig was voted only a half share of the pennant and World Series money, which outraged his old Yankees teammates, Babe Ruth in particular. He called the Cubs cheapskates and they responded with a savage and blistering verbal attack against Ruth throughout the Series, which was one of the most hostile in memory.

The Yankees won the first two games at Yankee Stadium, then traveled to Chicago for Game 3, where the ugliness continued as the Chicago fans joined their Cubs in the verbal assault.

The score was tied, 4-4, in Game 3 when the Yankees came to bat in the fifth. After Joe Sewell grounded out, Ruth came to bat. What happened then has been the subject of much debate, conjecture and interpretation. What is fact is that Ruth took a strike and pointed out to the field, took another strike, pointed again, then hit Charlie Root's next pitch, a changeup, into the centerfield seats.

By pointing, was Ruth saying he was going to hit a home run? Did he call his shot?

Cubs manager Charlie Grimm's version of what happened is that Cubs' pitcher Guy Bush was needling Ruth from the bench, and the Babe's response was to point to the mound as if to tell Bush, "You'll be out there tomorrow."

Ruth further obfuscated the legend by, at different times, confirming and denying that he had called his home run. During spring training of the following year, Ruth was attending a dinner party when one of the guests asked him about the "called shot." This was his response, as detailed by sportswriter Grantland Rice in his book, "The Tumult and the Shouting."

"The Cubs had bleeped my old teammate Mark Koenig by cutting him in for only a measly, bleeping half share of the Series money. Well, I'm riding the bleep out of the Cubs, telling 'em they're the cheapest pack of bleeping crumbums in the world. We've won the first two and now we're in Chicago for the third game. Root is the Cubs' pitcher. I park one into the stands in the first inning off him, but in the fifth it's tied four to four when I'm up. The Chicago fans are giving me hell.

"Root's still in there. He breezes the first two pitches by—both strikes. The mob's tearing down Wrigley Field. I shake my fist after that first strike. After the second, I point my bat at these bellerin' bleachers—right where I aim to park the ball. Root throws it and I hit that bleeping ball on the nose, right over the bleeping fence.

"'How do you like those apples you bleep, bleep, bleep,' I yell at Root as I head towards first. By the time I reach home, I'm almost fallin' down I'm laughin' so hard. And that's how it happened."

The Yankees went on to sweep the '32 World Series, which would be the last in which the mighty Babe Ruth ever played.

As his time was rapidly running out, the Babe would have a few more moments. In 1933, he hit the first home run in the first All-Star game ever played, in Chicago's Comiskey Park, but his batting average for the 1933 season slipped to .301, his home runs to 34, his RBIs to 103.

Before the 1934 season, Col. Ruppert offered Ruth the chance to go to Newark to manage the Yankees' top farm team. If he was sincere about managing, this would be a good learning experience for him and an opportunity to prove to the baseball world that he had managerial ability. Ruth refused. He would play one more year. On July 14, he hit the 700th home run of his career. He would end up with 714 homers, but for the 1934 season, at age 39, his numbers declined to a .288 average, 22 home runs, 84 RBIs.

Babe Ruth's career with the Yankees officially came to an end on February 26, 1935, when Col. Ruppert summoned the press to his brewery office. The Babe was there and Ruppert revealed to the press the contents of a terse note he had written to the aging slugger. It said:

Brooklyn-born Waite Hoyt came to the Yankees from the Red Sox in 1921. He led the league with 22 victories in 1927 and won a career-high 23 in 1928. He went on to become the longtime radio voice of the Cincinnati Reds. (New York Yankees Archives)

Mr. George H. Ruth:

You are hereby notified as follows:
1. That you are unconditionally released.

(Signed) Jacob Ruppert

Only three months and five days earlier, the Yankees had another announcement for the press. They had purchased the contract of an outfielder, one Joseph Paul DiMaggio, the son of a Martinez, Calif., fisherman, from San Francisco of the Pacific Coast League.

With the mighty Babe Ruth gone, Lou Gehrig became the field leader of the Yankees, and their captain, but it should not be dismissed as mere coincidence that, after finishing second for three straight seasons, with the arrival of Joe DiMaggio in 1936, the Yankees won the first of an unprecedented four consecutive world championships.

By 1938, Gehrig began to slide noticeably, his batting average dipping below .300 for the first time since 1925. His home runs declined from 37 to 29, his RBIs from 138 to 115. In the World Series against the Cubs, won by the Yankees in a four-game sweep, Lou made only four hits, all singles, in 14 at-bats.

Most were not alarmed. Gehrig was just past his 35th birthday, a time when production figured to decline. But those who knew him best suspected there was some problem other than age.

Gehrig never complained about anything physical, but his frustration at a sudden loss of power manifested itself in an uncharacteristic number of thrown bats.

"To see that big guy coming back to the dugout

On July 4, 1939, Lou Gehrig Day was held at Yankee Stadium and Babe Ruth, now retired, came to embrace his old teammate. (UPI/Bettmann)

after striking out with the bases loaded would make your heart bleed," Lefty Gomez said.

Convinced he had several years of good baseball left, Gehrig accepted a $3,000 pay cut to $36,000 without complaint and reported for spring training in 1939, determined to work harder than ever and restore the big numbers to his record. But by mid March, Gehrig had played in only 10 exhibition games, his average was barely over .100 and he had failed to get an extra base hit. His reflexes had slowed, his power was almost non-existent and he labored doing even the simple things on the field that once he had performed so instinctively.

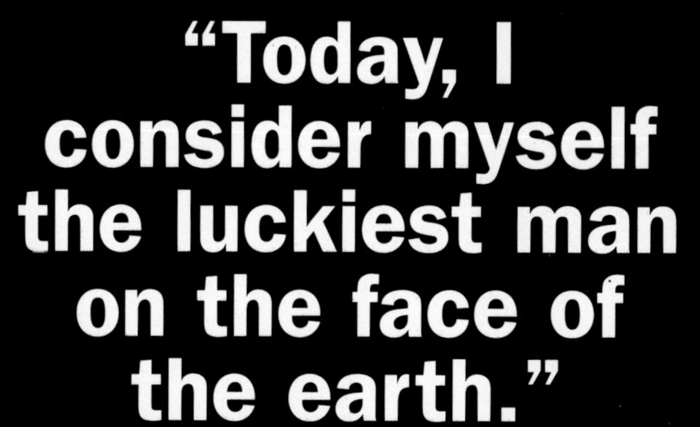

On May 2, the Yankees opened a series in Detroit. Gehrig had played in eight games, extending his incredible iron-man consecutive game streak to 2,130, but he was batting a mere .143. In 28 at bats, he had only four hits, all singles, and one RBI. It destroyed him that he was so helpless.

On the team's arrival in Detroit, Gehrig waited for McCarthy in the hotel lobby. The two went to the manager's room and Lou got right to the point.

"I'm benching myself, Joe," he said.

"Why?" the manager asked.

"For the good of the team, Joe," Gehrig said. "Nobody has to tell me how bad I've been and how much of a drawback I've been to the club. I've been thinking ever since the season opened, when I couldn't start as I hoped I would, that the time has come for me to quit."

That afternoon, Gehrig sat on the bench and watched as Babe Dahlgren went out to play first base for the Yankees. The Iron Man streak was over. Lou Gehrig would not play another game for the Yankees.

Gehrig was rapidly declining physically. His hair was graying swiftly, his body falling apart perceptibly, the weight loss unable to be reversed.

In June, Gehrig, growing weaker by the day, went to the Mayo Clinic in Rochester, Minn., for a series of tests. The diagnosis was made by Dr. Harold C. Habein.

"This is to certify that Mr. Lou Gehrig has been under examination at the Mayo Clinic from June 13 to June 19, 1939, inclusive.

"After a careful and complete examination, it was found that he is suffering from amyotrophic lateral sclerosis. This type of illness involves the motor pathways and cells of the central nervous system and in lay terms is known as a form of chronic poliomyelitis (infantile paralysis).

"The nature of this trouble makes it such that Mr. Gehrig will be unable to continue his active participation as a baseball player."

The letter was dated June 19, 1939, Gehrig's 36th birthday.

The condition was irreversible. There was no known treatment for ALS, now called "Lou Gehrig's Disease."

Soon after his return from the Mayo Clinic, the Yankees planned a "Lou Gehrig Appreciation Day." It was held at Yankee Stadium on July 4.

More than 62,000 showed up at the big ballpark. All Gehrig's old teammates of the famed Murderers Row were there, including the mighty Babe himself, now in retirement.

As baseball writer Sid Mercer, serving as master of ceremonies, presented gifts to Gehrig, and announced that Gehrig's uniform number 4 would be retired, never to be worn by any other Yankee, the huge crowd began to chant:

"We Want Gehrig... We Want Gehrig..."

Gehrig slowly pulled a handkerchief from his pocket, blew his nose, wiped his eyes, and walked laboriously to the microphone.

"Fans, for the past two weeks you have been reading about a bad break I got. Yet, today, I consider myself the luckiest man on the face of the earth..."

The speech went on for several minutes. When it was over, there was a thunderous roar from the crowd. Ruth, never the best of friends with Gehrig, walked over to his former teammate and threw a burly arm around Lou's neck, squeezing him in tender embrace.

Less than two years later, on June 6, 1941, 13 days short of his 38th birthday, Lou Gehrig, baseball's legendary Iron Horse, was dead.

LOU GEHRIG'S FAREWELL ADDRESS

Yankee Stadium
"Lou Gehrig Appreciation Day"
July 4, 1939

New York Yankees Archives

"Fans, for the past two weeks you have been reading about the bad break I got. Yet today I consider myself the luckiest man on the face of the earth. I have been in ballparks for seventeen years, and have never received anything but kindness and encouragement from you fans. Look at these grand men. Which of you wouldn't consider it the highlight of his career just to associate with them for even one day? Sure I'm lucky. Who wouldn't consider it an honor to have known Jacob Ruppert? Also, the builder of baseball's greatest empire, Ed Barrow? To have spent six years with that wonderful little fellow, Miller Huggins? Then to have spent the next nine years with that outstanding leader, that smart student of psychology, the best manager in baseball today, Joe McCarthy? Sure I'm lucky. When the New York Giants, a team you would give your right arm to beat, and vice versa, sends you a gift—that's something. When everybody down to the groundskeepers and those boys in white coats remember you with trophies—that's something. When you have a wonderful mother-in-law who takes sides with you in squabbles with her own daughter—that's something. When you have a father and a mother who work all their lives so you can have an education and build your body—it's a blessing. When you have a wife who has been a tower of strength and shown more courage than you dreamed existed—that's the finest I know. So I close in saying I may have had a tough break, but I have an awful lot to live for."

National Baseball Library, Cooperstown, N.Y.

5

Joltin' Joe

There should have been a ceremony, a blare of trumpets, a drum roll to signal the changing of the guard.

Babe Ruth played his last game as a Yankee on Monday, September 30, 1934. One year, eight months and three days later, Joe DiMaggio played in his first game as a Yankee. It was the dawning of a new era.

Young DiMaggio had signed as a 17-year old shortstop to play with his home town minor league team, the San Francisco Seals, following in the footsteps of his older brother, Vince. He appeared in only three games in his first season and was converted to the outfield for the following year.

The 1933 season was a huge one for the young outfielder. He batted .340, hit 28 home runs, drove in 169 runs and set a Pacific Coast League record by hitting safely in 61 consecutive games. DiMaggio was the toast of San Francisco, the home town boy starring for the home town team, and he attracted interest from every major league club. But a knee injury suffered during the 1934 season, caused most teams to lose interest.

The Yankees, however, through scout Bill Essick, did not back off, although DiMaggio's injury saved them a good deal of money. Where DiMaggio's value had been estimated as upwards of $100,000, the Yankees were able to purchase his contract from the Seals for $25,000 and five players.

DiMaggio extended his consecutive hit streak to 56 games with three hits in Cleveland on July 16, 1941 including this seventh inning triple. Indians third baseman Ken Keltner takes a late throw from the outfield. The following night Keltner made two spectacular plays to help put an end to the streak. (UPI/Bettmann)

The Yankees elected to have DiMaggio remain with the Seals for the 1935 season in order to be certain his knee healed fully before he came to New York. It proved to be a wise decision as DiMaggio tore the Pacific Coast League apart, batting .398 with 270 hits, 48 doubles, 18 triples, 34 home runs and 154 runs batted in.

While DiMag was tearing up the PCL, the Yankees, Ruth-less for the first time since 1919, finished second for the third consecutive season.

The following spring, DiMaggio and fellow northern Californians Frank Crosetti and Tony Lazzeri set out from their home by auto, across the country to St. Petersburg, Florida, for spring training.

"Five days it took us," DiMag would say years later. "One of my biggest thrills was reporting to my first spring training. I'll never forget walking into that dingy clubhouse with nails to hang our clothes on, and seeing Bill Dickey, Charlie Ruffing and Lou Gehrig. I always followed the Yankees and to meet those fellows, those great stars, was a big thrill."

From Day One, DiMaggio was the talk of training camp. His matchless grace in centerfield, his power at the plate, made him an immediate sensation. And he had a spectacular spring, so much so that sportswriters were saying that the great Gehrig, second fiddle to Ruth for so many years, was destined to

(UPI/Bettmann)

He came out of San Francisco, a son of a fisherman, and after batting .398 for the Seals in 1935, Joe DiMaggio arrived in New York the following year and continued the line of succession of Yankee superstars.

National Baseball Library, Cooperstown, NY.

(UPI/Bettmann)

By the time he was 21, Joe DiMaggio had become a household name throughout America. It wasn't always that way. Even in his home town of San Francisco, his name was often misspelled in his early years as a member of the Seals.

His name appeared in print as "DeMaggio," as "deMaggio" and as "diMaggio." It wasn't until the Seals were making arrangements for an engraved gold watch to be presented to the young slugger to commemorate his 61-game hitting streak in 1933 that the issue was resolved.

Joe had signed his Seals' contract "DeMaggio," but his older brother, Tom, witnessing the signature, signed his name "DiMaggio."

"How do you really spell your name, Joe?" inquired Seals vice president, Charley Graham.

"Spell it any old way," the outfielder replied.

But Graham persisted, Tom DiMaggio insisted, and it has been "DiMaggio" ever since.

"Ol' Reliable" Tommy Henrich. (New York Yankees Archives)

play the same role to the newcomer.

The anticipation of DiMaggio's arrival in New York was at fever pitch as the season drew near, but late in spring training, Joe burned his foot severely with a heating lamp and had to be hospitalized. His long-awaited debut as a Yankee came on May 3, 1936, at Yankee Stadium in a game against the St. Louis Browns. Joe played left field and batted third, behind Crosetti and Red Rolfe, and ahead of Gehrig. He slammed out two singles and a triple in six at bats, scored three runs and knocked in another as the Yankees demolished the Browns, 14-5.

DiMaggio had a rookie season that more than lived up to his advance billing, one that few rookies ever have had. He batted .323 with 29 home runs and 125 RBIs and led the league with 22 outfield assists. Largely through the efforts of Joe D, the Yankees returned to the pinnacle of baseball, winning their first American League pennant in four years, then beating the Giants in six games in the World Series. It was the first of four consecutive world championships for the Yankees, during which time DiMaggio vaulted to the top of the game, a superstar of monumental proportions.

The "Yankee Clipper" batted .346 and drove in 167 runs in 1937, and led the league in homers with 46 and slugging percentage with .673. In 1938, he batted .324 with 32 homers and 140 RBIs. In 1939, he led the league with a .381 average and had 30 homers and 126 RBIs, winning his first of three Most Valuable Player awards.

The Yankees slipped to third in 1940, but through no fault of DiMaggio, who had another marvelous season, a league-leading .352, 31 homers and 133 RBIs. And he was to reach the crowning achievement of his glorious career in 1941.

Ominous clouds hovered over Yankee Stadium on the morning of Thursday, May 15, 1941. The winds of war wafted from across the ocean. Closer to home, in the Bronx, New York, Joe DiMaggio was in a slump.

The Great DiMaggio had come through preseason adversity with his customary style. He had reported two weeks late for spring training because of a contract dispute. Having won his second consecutive American League batting championship in 1940, DiMaggio anticipated a hefty raise from his salary of $32,000.

When his 1941 contract arrived at his San

Francisco home and it called for a $2,500 cut, DiMaggio was outraged. And adamant. He held firm, refusing to budge from home until the Yankees upped the ante to $35,000.

Determined not to let his late start curtail his production, Joe worked hard in training, and batted safely in all 19 exhibition games in which he played. He missed not a beat when the season opened, hitting safely in each of the Yankees first eight games for an average of .528 that gave every indication this would be the greatest season of his six with the Yankees.

But on the morning of May 15, DiMaggio found himself in an horrendous three-week slump during which his average plummeted more than 200 points and dragged the Yankees down with him. As they prepared to face the Chicago White Sox, the Yankees had lost four straight, seven of their last nine, and tumbled 5 1/2 games out of first place. A frightening trend was being established.

One of the greatest catches in World Series history was made by the Dodgers' leftfielder Al Gionfriddo. It robbed Joe DiMaggio of a game-tying home run in the sixth game of the '47 Fall Classic. It occurred with two outs in the sixth inning with two Yankees on base and the Dodgers leading 8-5. The Yankees lost the contest, but won Game Seven 5-2. (New York Yankees Archives)

Now, on this hazy afternoon in Yankee Stadium, DiMaggio, hitless in his previous game, stroked a solid single to center off lefthander Edgar Smith to drive in rookie Phil Rizzuto, the five-foot, six inch, native New Yorker who had replaced Frank Crosetti at shortstop. It was not the end of DiMaggio's slump, his only hit of the day.

DiMaggio's single drove in the Yankees' only run in a 13-1 rout by the White Sox. Despite his single, DiMaggio's average dipped another two points to .304, but like a drop of rain in Johnstown, a crack in the sidewalk on a street in San Francisco and a misstep by Mrs. O'Leary's cow in Chicago, this single in the Bronx was the start of something.

AP/Wide World Photos

"'I would like to take the great DiMaggio fishing,' the old man said. 'They say his father was a fisherman. Maybe he was as poor as we are and would understand.'"

—From "The Old Man and the Sea," by Ernest Hemingway.

If the great streak had a modest beginning, it followed that pattern in its early days, hardly causing a ripple in the baseball waters. Although he hit safely in each of the next 12 games, only four times did Joe have a multiple hit game. It wasn't until Game 14 of the streak, in Washington on May 29, that the newspapers began to pay attention to what DiMaggio was doing. And then only in light of other events.

DiMaggio has often said, and others have parroted him, that a hitter has to be lucky to sustain a streak of any appreciable length. The truism of that theory was driven home on May 29.

It was a hot, humid day, the barometer rising steadily and the threat of rain hanging in the heavy air. Rain was imminent when Tommy Henrich homered in the top of the fifth to put the Yankees ahead, 2-1. The Senators tied the score in the bottom of the inning, sending the game into the sixth, when the Yankees batted around, breaking the game wide open, but the heavens finally burst with a thunder-

On June 29, 1941, in Washington, DiMaggio tied and broke George Sisler's American League record by hitting in his 41st and 42nd consecutive games in a doubleheader against the Senators. (UPI/ Bettmann)

storm that rendered the field unplayable. The game was halted, everything that happened in the sixth inning was eradicated with the official records reverting to the fifth.

All batting records were official although the score was recorded as a 2-2 tie.

DiMaggio had singled in the aborted sixth, but that was washed away. Fortunately, Joe D had stroked a single in the fourth off Steve Sundra to extend his streak to 14 games. DiMaggio scored on a single by Frank Crosetti, who stretched his hitting streak to 11 games. But first baseman Johnny Sturm was not so fortunate.

Sturm entered the game having hit in 11 consecutive games. He went hitless in the first five innings, but singled in the ill-fated sixth. That hit was disallowed and Sturm's streak was at an end. In calling attention to that unfortunate development, the writers parenthetically made mention of the good fortune of DiMaggio and Crosetti, whose batting streaks were still intact. It was the first mention in print that DiMag was on a hitting streak.

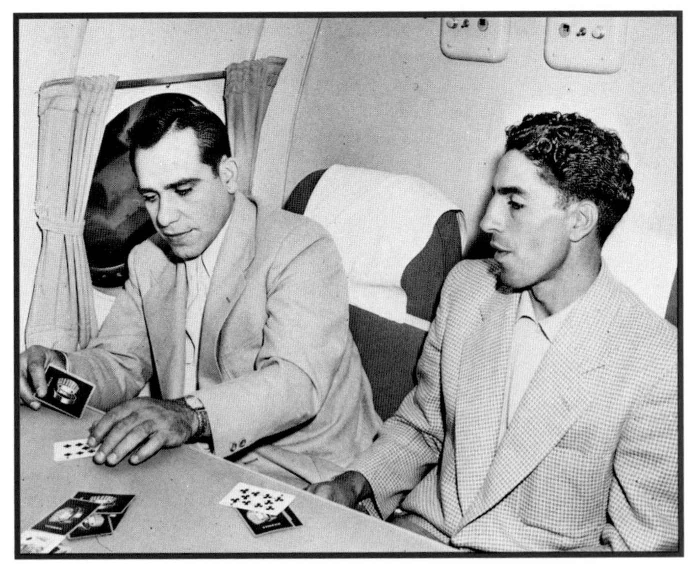

Pals Yogi Berra and Phil Rizzuto passing the time on a chartered flight . (UPI/Bettmann)

Vic Raschi won 21 games for three consecutive seasons from 1949-51. (New York Yankees Archives)

Adolph Hitler continued his march on Europe, storming into Poland and Czechoslovakia, and Joe DiMaggio continued his assault on American League pitchers; although, to be accurate, it had not yet become an assault. After the close call in Washington, DiMaggio extended his streak to 21 with one hit each in five of the next six games.

On June 7 in St. Louis, DiMaggio lashed out three singles to extend his hitting streak to 22 games. Not only was he only halfway to the all-time record, his wasn't even the longest hitting streak alive in the American League at the time. Starting on May 15, the same day as DiMaggio, Ted Williams of the Boston Red Sox, having played one extra game, had hit in 23 straight.

On Sunday, June 8, both the Yankees and Red Sox played doubleheaders, New York in St. Louis, Boston in Chicago. While Williams was horse-collared (0-for-5, with four walks), DiMaggio homered twice and drove in four runs in the first game of his doubleheader, doubled and knocked in three runs in the second. He had increased his streak to 24 games and shook off the mighty Williams.

"I certainly was conscious of my streak," Williams said in later years. "And DiMaggio's was just starting to get into the papers then. I went to Chicago with 23 games and did a big and glorious zero, and Joe carried on."

Carry on he did. A single in Game 25, a single and homer in Game 26, another homer in Game 27, singles in each of the next three games. On Saturday, June 21, DiMaggio singled against Detroit to extend his streak to 34 games, passing Rogers Hornsby's National League record. It was then, DiMaggio later told sportswriter Dan Daniel, that he began to get serious about his own streak.

One week later, on June 28, the Yankees met the Philadelphia Athletics in Shibe Park. They pounded out 14 hits for a 7-4 victory that moved them into first place. Charlie Keller's home run in the seventh extended the Yankees record of having hit at least one homer in 23 consecutive games. They would eventually take the streak to 25 straight games with a homer before it was stopped.

But all the focus was on the individual hitting streak of DiMaggio. With a double in the fourth, he became the fourth player in major league history to hit safely in 40 straight games; tying Ty Cobb's 1911 streak, one behind George Sisler's 19-year old modern record, four behind Willie Keeler's all-time mark set in 1897.

Charlie "King Kong" Keller drove in 100 runs three times. In 1941 he tallied a career-high 122 RBI, only three behind league-leader Joe DiMaggio. (New York Yankees Archives)

Allie "The Chief" Reynolds is the only Yankee to pitch two no-hitters, both in the same season, 1951. (New York Yankees Archives)

As luck would have it, the Yankees were scheduled for a doubleheader in Washington on Sunday, June 29, and the prospect of seeing DiMaggio tie and break the modern record on the same day, crammed 31,000 into Griffith Stadium despite temperatures that reached 100. They were not disappointed.

Batting against the baffling knuckleball of Dutch Leonard, DiMaggio lined out to centerfield in his first at bat. In his second, Leonard's knuckler fluttered erratically, putting him behind in the count, 3-0. Joe looked at third base coach Art Fletcher for a sign, and got the go-ahead to hit.

"I owe a lot to (manager) Joe

The Yankees celebrate clinching the 1947 pennant. (Front row from left) Allie Reynolds, unindentified, Ralph Houk, Bobo Newsom, Aaron Robinson, Joe Page, manager Bucky Harris, part owners Del Webb and Larry MacPhail, coach Red Corriden, broadcaster Russ Hodges, coach Charlie Dressen, Mel Allen and baseball writer Joe Trimble. (Back row from Left) George McQuinn, Joe DiMaggio, Phil Rizzuto, Karl Drews, Tommy Henrich, Frank Shea, and George Stirnweiss. (New York Yankees Archives)

McCarthy for the streak," Joe would say in later years. "He never gave me the take sign. Always let me take my rips."

With the count 3-0, DiMaggio took his rip, but popped it feebly to third.

DiMaggio came to bat for the third time in the sixth inning. On a 1-1 count, Leonard tried to slip a fast ball by Joe. It was a mistake. DiMaggio tagged it on a line to left center, the ball splitting Washington outfielders George Case and Doc Cramer and rocketing to the fence 422 feet away. The partisan Washington crowd erupted as DiMaggio pulled into second base having tied Sisler's modern record of hitting safely in 41 consecutive games.

Baseball players are a notoriously superstitious lot, and the great DiMaggio was no exception. He would always make certain to touch second base on his way to his defensive position in centerfield. And on the day he started his hitting streak in the Pacific Coast League, he had placed a small bandage on his hand to protect a stone bruise. Thereafter, he instructed the trainer to bandage the hand in exactly the same manner every day of his 61-game streak and long after the bruise had healed.

Imagine DiMaggio's chagrin when he came to bat for the first time in the second game and discovered his favorite bat, the one he had used through much of the streak, was gone. It had been stolen from the bat rack by a souvenir-hunting fan. DiMaggio was disheartened, but his teammate, Tommy Henrich, had an idea. Earlier in the season, Henrich in a hitting slump, had borrowed a bat from DiMaggio. Henrich came alive with it at the plate. He offered to return DiMaggio's bat, "for luck," and Joe accepted.

The lucky bat failed to perform its magic in DiMaggio's first three at-bats. In the seventh inning, he faced Red Anderson, likely his final at-bat of the game. Anderson's first pitch whistled inches from DiMag's chin. Joe jumped back and wordlessly got back into the box, setting himself with his "lucky bat" held high off his right shoulder. On the next pitch, DiMaggio blistered a line drive into leftfield for a clean hit and the record. Once again, the crowd erupted with an ear-piercing roar.

After the game, DiMaggio told reporters: "Sure, I'm tickled. It's the most excitement I guess I've known since I came into the majors."

Sisler was quick to acknowledge the coronation of a new king of streaks and the end of his record. In a telegram to DiMaggio, Sisler said, "Congratulations. I'm glad a real hitter broke it. Keep going."

Having surpassed Sisler's modern major league record, DiMaggio's next goal was the all-time mark of 44 by Wee Willie Keeler, a record Joe admitted he knew and thought little about. His focus was Sisler, but with that gone, sportswriters pointed toward No. 44.

It came on July 1, in the second game of a doubleheader against the Red Sox at Yankee Stadium. Lured by DiMaggio's streak, 52,832 piled into the big ballpark on a hot and humid Tuesday afternoon. DiMaggio extended his streak to 43 games with his third at bat, on a questionable call by the official scorer of a ball that handcuffed Sox third baseman Jim Tabor. As if to take the onus off the scorer, Joe singled cleanly in his next at-bat.

In the second game, he left no suspense to the huge crowd, singling over the head of shortstop Joe Cronin in the first inning to arrive at No. 44, thus tying Keeler's unpublicized record.

To surpass Keeler, DiMaggio had to wait only until his third at-bat in game No. 45. He had been robbed by rightfielder Stan Spence's one-handed stab of a vicious liner to right in his first at-bat, and bounced to third baseman Tabor in his second. But in the fifth, he drilled a line drive over the leftfield fence, a ball hit so viciously it disappeared from view before Joe had time to admire his record-breaking hit.

"I don't believe anybody but a ballplayer is in a position to appreciate just what it means to hit safely in 45 straight games," Yankees manager Joe McCarthy said admiringly.

Said Ted Williams: "I really wish I could hit like that guy Joe DiMaggio. I'm being honest. Joe's big and strong and he can club the ball without any effort. These hot days I wear myself out laying into it, and I lose seven or eight pounds out there. When it's hot, I lose my snap or something."

At the time, Williams was batting .401.

DiMaggio continued a torrid pace through the early part of July with at least two hits in seven of eight games to arrive at 52 straight without the added pressure of chasing a record. Every game merely extended his own record.

Now, newspapers not only reported the extension of DiMaggio's streak, the daily question was when would DiMaggio be stopped, and who would be the one to stop him? Some thought he might extend the streak through the remainder of the season.

On July 17, the war heated up between Germany

Opening day 1948 in Washington. President Harry S. Truman, southpaw, throws out the first ball as managers Joe Kuhel of Washington and Bucky Harris of the Yankees look on. (New York Yankees Archives)

and Russia on the Russian front, and that night, lured by the great DiMaggio, 67,468 jammed Cleveland's Municipal Stadium. It would be the largest crowd in the major leagues in the 1941 season.

Left-hander Al Smith pitched for Cleveland against DiMaggio's closest friend, the irrepressible Lefty Gomez. But the hero—or villain—of the piece would be Indians third baseman Ken Keltner, acknowledged as the slickest fielding third baseman in the league.

On his first at-bat, Joe lashed a bullet down the line at third. Keltner speared it with a back-handed stab and threw DiMaggio out at first.

"I couldn't get out of the box quickly because of the rains the day before," DiMaggio remembered, "and Ken's long throw just nipped me."

There would have been no throw if Keltner had not been playing so deep.

"Deep?" DiMaggio said. "My God, he was standing in leftfield."

On his second at-bat, DiMaggio was walked and the crowd, pulling hard for the home team Indians in their struggle to catch the first place Yankees, nevertheless booed.

When he came to bat in the seventh, DiMaggio noticed that Keltner, still playing deep, had moved another step closer to the foul line. Joe knew he could easily have bunted for a base hit, but his pride would not permit him to take such a wimpish approach to extend the streak.

"He (Keltner) dared me to bunt on him," DiMaggio recalled, "but I didn't bunt during the entire streak."

Again, DiMaggio hit a wicked smash to third, just inside the line. Keltner hardly had to move to stab it on a short hop and throw DiMaggio out by a step.

When he came to bat in the eighth, Joe faced a new pitcher, reliever Jim Bagby. The Yankees had scored two runs to take a 4-1 lead and had the bases loaded with one out. On a 2-1 fastball, Joe smashed one hard and deep to short, but right at Lou Boudreau. The ball took a nasty hop as Boudreau was about to field it, but the Indians' shortstop recovered quickly, snared the ball at shoulder height and started a short-to-second-to-first double play.

The streak was over, ended at 56 games...but is it? More than a half century later, it still remained on the books, having survived dozens of challenges; a half century later, it was the oldest major record in baseball. The 56-game streak is special. A streak requires day-in, day-out consistency under the most gruelling pressure. Slumps are not permitted, bad days not allowed. One misstep and the streak is ended.

In 1948, the Yankees acquired left-hander "Steady Eddie" Lopat from the White Sox. Lopat teamed with Reynolds and Raschi to form one of the best trios of starting pitchers in the late '40s and early '50s. (New York Yankees Archives)

When it ended for DiMaggio, he was both relieved and glum.

"Nobody thought he would ever be stopped," said Phil Rizzuto. "We all thought it would just go on. When it ended, the way it ended, it was a shock. After the game, Joe asked me to stay behind. There were a lot of 'paisans' in Cleveland and they were mad that the streak ended. Keltner had to have a police escort to leave the stadium.

"We waited until the crowd was gone and Joe and I walked back to the Cleveland Hotel. We passed a bar and Joe turned to go in and I followed him.

"'No, Phil,' he said. 'You go back to the hotel. I want to be alone.'

"So I started walking back to the hotel alone and I hear him call me.

"'Hey, Phil,' he said. 'I forgot my wallet in the clubhouse. Give me all your money.'

"So I took out my money, all I had, and gave it to him. It came to $14.80. He never paid me back. He just forgot about it, that's how upset he was."

Many years later, Rizzuto reminded DiMaggio that he never paid back the loan and Joe offered to give him the $14.80.

"Are you kidding?" Rizzuto said. "Nothing doing. It's worth the $14.80 just to be able to tell that story."

Propelled by their centerfielder, the Yankees won the 1941 American League pennant by 17 games over the Red Sox. DiMaggio batted .357, but finished third in the batting race to Boston's Ted Williams, who hit an astounding .406, and

Vic Raschi's 21st victory, 11-3 over the Red Sox, clinches the 1951 pennant for the Yankees. (New York Yankes Archives)

Washington's Cecil Travis at .359. DiMaggio led the league with 125 RBIs, crashed 30 homers and won his second Most Valuable Player award.

The Yankees hooked up for the first time with the Brooklyn Dodgers in the '41 World Series. They split the first two games in Yankee Stadium and the Yankees took Game 3 in Brooklyn. Then came the turning point of the Series in Game 4.

Going into the top of the ninth, the Dodgers, led, 4-3. Relief pitcher Hugh Casey retired the first two Yankees in the ninth and faced Tommy Henrich. The count went to 3-2. Casey then threw what is believed to have been an illegal spit ball. Henrich swung and missed for strike three, but the ball darted down into the dirt and skipped past catcher Mickey Owen as Henrich reached first.

DiMaggio followed with a single and the Yankees rallied for four runs and a 7-4 victory. They won the next day to wrap up the Series in five games.

The United States was at war by the start of the 1942 season and it was only a matter of time before baseball's big stars would be called to join the war effort, DiMaggio among them. He managed to play the entire 1942 season before going off to serve in the Army. Before he left, DiMaggio led the Yankees to a second straight American League pennant, giving him six pennants in his seven seasons with the Yankees. But the St. Louis Cardinals beat the Yankees in a five-game World Series, after which DiMaggio went off to military service.

Despite DiMaggio's absence, the Yankees had enough talent remaining of draft exempt players to win the 1943 pennant and avenge their loss to the Cardinals with a 4-1 win in the World Series.

It wasn't until after 1943 that the full effects of the war took hold. The Yankees finished third and fourth with a team comprised of overage veterans and underage kids.

JOLTIN' JOE DIMAGGIO

"Who started baseball's famous streak
That's got us all aglow?
He's just a man and not a freak,
Joltin' Joe DiMaggio.
Joe, Joe DiMaggio, we want you on our side.
He tied the mark at 44, July the First, you know
Since then he's hit a good 12 more,
Joltin' Joe DiMaggio.
Joe, Joe DiMaggio, we want you on our side.

From coast to coast that's all you hear
Of Joe the one man show.
He's glorified the horsehide sphere,
Joltin' Joe DiMaggio.
Joe, Joe DiMaggio, we want you on our side.

He'll live in baseball's Hall of Fame,
He got there blow by blow.
Our kids will tell their kids his name,
Joltin' Joe DiMaggio.
Joe, Joe DiMaggio, we want you on our side.
We dream of Joey with the light brown bat.

And now they speak in whispers low
Of how they stopped our Joe.
One night in Cleveland, oh, oh, oh,
Goodbye streak DiMaggio.
Joe, Joe DiMaggio, we want you on our side."

The DiMaggio era ended after the 1951 season when Joe, bothered by a heel injury, slipped below .300 for the first time in his illustrious career and retired. (National Baseball Library, Cooperstown, NY)

By 1946, World War II was over and the great stars returned. The Yankees finished third, after Joe McCarthy resigned as manager–after sixteen brilliant seasons–over a dispute with the team's owners. The '46 season was distinguished by the first night game in Yankee Stadium on May 28, 1946, and by the arrival of two players who would make their marks as Yankees–Vic Raschi, a hard-throwing, fiercely competitive right-handed pitcher, and Larry Berra, a squat, oddly-shaped left-handed hitting catcher who was nicknamed "Yogi."

Baseball enjoyed the greatest boom period in its history, largely due to the euphoria and the economic upswing of the nation following the end of World War II. The Yankees drew more than two million fans to Yankee Stadium for the first time. They would top the two million mark in attendance in each of the next four seasons. A week after the end of the 1946 season, the Yankees sent veteran second baseman Joe Gordon to Cleveland for right-handed pitcher Allie Reynolds.

In 1947, DiMaggio won his third Most Valuable Player award, the Yankees returned to the top of the American League and polished off the Dodgers in a seven-game World Series, distinguished by the ninth inning of the fourth game. Bill Bevens, a journeyman pitcher for the Yankees, came one out away from pitching the first no-hitter in World Series history. But Cookie Lavagetto, an aging infielder, pinch hit a line drive off the rightfield screen in Ebbets Field for a two-run double that not only broke up the no-hitter, but gave the Dodgers a 3-2 victory. The hit would be Lavagetto's last as a major leaguer.

The Yankees slipped to third in 1948, when they

acquired Eddie Lopat, a crafty left-hander from the Chicago White Sox, but they came back in 1949 with a new manager to win one of the most exciting and most memorable pennant races in history.

After two seasons, Bucky Harris was let go as manager of the Yankees and replaced by "Casey" Stengel in a surprise move. Stengel was 59. After an excellent major league playing career with five National League teams, including the Dodgers and Giants, he had been a bust as a manager in the National League for Brooklyn and Boston, never finishing higher than fifth in nine seasons. He returned to the Pacific Coast League and managed Oakland with marked success. But that was still the minor leagues and his selection by the Yankees was a surprise.

Stengel proved to be an excellent choice, masterfully maneuvering an injury-riddled Yankees team by instituting a platoon system, right-handed hitters against left-handed pitchers, left-handed hitters against right-handed pitchers, to beat out the Red Sox for the 1949 American League pennant.

Stengel started the 1949 season, and his Yankees managerial career, without the team's super star and leader. Joe DiMaggio, suffering from a bone spur on his heel, missed the team's first 65 games, but Stengel's platooning had the Yankees in first place when DiMag returned on June 28 for a three-game series against the Red Sox in Boston.

For weeks, reporters kept asking Stengel when DiMaggio would be back.

"When Joe feels as though he wants to come back, I will put him in the lineup," was Stengel's standard reply.

"I knew when I was coming back," DiMaggio recalled. "But I wasn't talking. I was pointing for the series in Boston. We would play there only one more time and I wasn't going to give up that Boston ballpark. What better place to make my comeback?"

Secretly, DiMaggio began getting himself ready, taking batting practice in New York while the team was on the road.

"For four days I hit," he said. "Gus Niarhos caught and Al Schacht, 60 years old by then, pitched batting practice and we got some ball boys and bat boys to shag. I thought I got myself in fairly decent shape. I knew I was going to play in Boston, but nobody else did.

"I flew up to Boston the day of the game and went right from the airport to the ballpark. I put on my uniform and went out on the bench. The players were on the field and Stengel had his back to me, talking to the writers. He hadn't put up the starting lineup and they were asking him about it.

"'I can't give you the lineup yet,' he was saying, and he kept turning around to look at me. I didn't say a word. I just kept tying my shoelaces. He kept looking and finally I gave him a nod and he said, 'Now I can give you the lineup.'"

The comeback performance was nothing short of remarkable. DiMaggio hit a single and a two-run homer in the first game, won by the Yankees, 5-4. In the second game, the Red Sox jumped off to a 7-1 lead, but DiMaggio hit two homers to lead the Yanks to a 9-7 come-from-behind victory. In the third, he homered again, a two-run shot, in a 6-5 Yankees victory. Four home runs and nine RBIs in the three-game sweep.

The two teams jockeyed for position all season, taking turns in first place, until they came to the final two games in Yankee Stadium, with the Red Sox, now managed by Joe McCarthy, who came out of retirement in the 1947 season, leading by one game. They needed to win one out of two to clinch the pennant. The Yankees had to win both games.

In the first game, which was "Joe DiMaggio Day," attended by more than 69,000 fans, the Sox scored a run in the first and three more in the third against Allie Reynolds and reliever Joe Page. The Yankees came back with two in the fourth and two more in the fifth to tie, 4-4. It stayed that way until the eighth, when outfielder Johnny Lindell belted a home run to give the Yankees a 5-4 win.

They were tied going into the final game of the season, one game to decide the American League championship. Vic Raschi, a 20-game winner, started for New York against 23-game winner Ellis Kinder.

The Yanks pushed across a run in the first and that's how it stayed until the eighth as Raschi and Kinder hung zeroes on the scoreboard inning after inning. In the bottom of the eighth, the Yankees exploded for four runs. The Red Sox would answer with a rally of their own in the top of the ninth. They scored three runs before Raschi snuffed them out for a 5-3 win and the pennant.

The Yankees again met the Dodgers in the 1949 World Series and won it in five games.

The following year, the Yankees made it two straight pennants under Stengel, beating out the Tigers by three games thanks to a tow-headed, 21-year old lefthander from New York City named Edward "Whitey" Ford, who came up from the minor leagues in mid-season and won nine out of 10 decisions. Diminutive shortstop Phil Rizzuto, who

(UPI/Bettmann)

hit .324 and had 200 hits, was the American League MVP. The Yankees then polished off the Philadelphia Phillies "Whiz Kids" in a four-game sweep for their second straight world championship, with Ford winning the final game.

DiMaggio, still bothered by his bad heel, played in only 139 games, but batted .301 with 32 home runs and 122 RBIs, then added another homer in the Series. It was a fine season for the Yankee Clipper, but he was about to turn 36 and thoughts of retiring crept into his mind.

The Great DiMaggio knew he had stayed too long when he played in only 116 games in 1951, fell below .300 for the only time in his career at .263, hit only 12 homers and drove in 71 runs. He was aging and he was hurting. It was time to call it quits.

There was one last hurrah for DiMaggio, a home run and five RBIs in the 1951 World Series, won by the Yankees in six games over the New York Giants. In his 13 years as a Yankee, a career shortened by three years in the Army, he slammed out 2,214 hits, hit 361 homers, drove in 1,537 runs, had a lifetime batting average of .325 and played on 10 pennant winners and nine world championships. But now it was time to step aside for a younger man.

And the Yankees had been joined in 1951 by a younger man, one with the power and speed and gifts to be the worthy successor to Joe DiMaggio, to carry on the tradition of New York Yankees superstars. His name was Mickey Mantle.

In nine seasons as a manger with Brooklyn and Boston, Charles Dillon "Casey" Stengel had a winning record only once.
(UPI/Bettmann)

Casey: From Clown To Genius

In retrospect, it is hard to believe that Casey Stengel almost didn't become manager of the Yankees and that he did so only because General Manager George Weiss lobbied long and hard for his selection as a replacement for Bucky Harris. Co-owners Del Webb and Dan Topping were opposed to the idea, but they had agreed to let Weiss make all the baseball decisions for their team.

Still, Webb and Topping felt they should have some input on a decision of such import. Weiss began his campaign for Stengel by working on Webb first and convinced him that Stengel could do the job. Webb then took Weiss' arguments to Topping, who fell into line.

Viewed in the context of the time, Topping's and Webb's objections to Stengel were understandable. Stengel's entire major league career, 14 years as a player, nine years as a manager, had been spent in the National League. He was considered old for a manager; 59 when he was hired by the Yankees.

As manager of the Brooklyn Dodgers from 1934 through 1936, and the Boston Braves from 1938 through 1943, he had been a complete failure—two fifth place finishes, two sixths and five sevenths in his nine seasons, only once finishing better than .500.

In Boston, he was under constant vicious attack from acerbic *Boston Record* sports columnist Dave Egan, known as "The Colonel." Prior to the 1943 season, Stengel was struck by a car and incapacitated for two months with a broken leg. Summing up the season, Egan wrote, "The man who did most for baseball in Boston in 1943 was the motorist who ran Stengel down two days before the opening game and kept him away from the Braves for two months."

What's more, Topping and Webb considered Stengel a clown. While he had a productive 14-year major league career—a lifetime batting average of .284, two home runs and a .417 average for the Giants in the 1923 World Series—he was best remembered for such antics as arriving at the ballpark one day, doffing his cap and having a sparrow fly out.

That was hardly the sort of image Topping and Webb wanted for their dignified, reserved and business-like Yankees.

It was General Manager George Weiss who convinced Yankees co-owners Dan Topping and Del Webb to hire the 59-year-old Stengel to manage the Yankees in 1949. (New York Yankees Archives)

But Weiss knew another Casey Stengel. They had been friends for some 40 years and Weiss regarded Stengel as a knowledgeable baseball man, one who ate, slept and breathed the game and would talk baseball for endless hours. Weiss argued that in Brooklyn and Boston, Stengel had inferior talent. He pointed to the job Stengel did in winning the Pacific Coast League championship with Oakland in 1948 and he insisted his friend

The new manager of the Yankees with the four most important men in his baseball life: (from left) GM George Weiss, superstar Joe DiMaggio, and co-owners Del Webb and Dan Topping. (New York Yankees Archives)

would be a success with the Yankees.

Weiss had wanted to bring Stengel in as manager after Joe McCarthy resigned in 1946, but Larry MacPhail, then a one-third partner of Topping and Webb, opposed the idea. Bucky Harris was MacPhail's choice and he proved to be a favorite with Yankees players and fans, but not of Weiss. When MacPhail sold out his interest to Topping and Webb after the 1947 season, and the Yankees slipped to third in 1948, Weiss saw his chance to replace Harris and bring in Stengel.

Stengel was officially introduced as manager of the Yankees in New York's posh "21" Club on October 12, 1948, the day after the Cleveland Indians defeated the Boston Braves in the World Series. Dan Topping strode to a microphone, waited for the assembled press to hush and made the following announcement: "I'm happy to make the announcement that Casey Stengel has been appointed manager of the New York Yankees."

There was a smattering of applause from the writers in attendance, most of whom covered Casey as a player for the Giants and Dodgers and later as a rival manager. They knew him well and liked him. As John Drebinger of the *New York Times* said, "If you didn't like Casey, you didn't like anybody."

Stengel seemed somewhat nervous when he took the microphone, which may have been the last time he ever was nervous talking to anyone. He thanked "Bob" Topping, referring to the Yankees co-owner's playboy brother, a misidentification which would come to be known as a Stengel trait. He rarely remembered names, frequently misspelled or mispronounced them and often referred to acquaintances, and even close friends, as "Doctor."

Asked about his new team, Stengel candidly said, "I never had players like this."

The New York writers treated the selection of Stengel kindly and favorably, a view not shared as enthusiastically by all members of the press. In the *Boston Record*, under the column heading and picture of the Colonel, Dave Egan, were these words:

"Well, sirs and ladies, the Yankees have now been mathematically eliminated from the 1949 pennant race. They eliminated themselves when they engaged Perfesser Casey Stengel to mismanage them for the next two years, and you may be sure that the perfesser will oblige to the best of his unique ability."

In spring training, some writers noted that Stengel seemed in awe of the talent around him and overwhelmed by the enormity of his task. Joe DiMaggio, never a Stengel fan, took one writer aside one day and confided that the new manager seemed "bewildered."

If there was one thing on which Stengel had unanimous approval, it was his ability to handle, develop and bring along young players. He was regarded as an excellent teacher and one who was not afraid to entrust important assignments to rookies. Circumstances required Stengel to make immediate changes on the Yankees. Aging first baseman George McQuinn retired after the 1948 season, so Stengel moved right fielder Tommy "Old Reliable"

In 1949, his first season as manager of the Yankees, Stengel guided the team to his first American League pennant by beating the Red Sox and former Yankees manager Joe McCarthy (at left) on the final day of the season. (UPI/Bettmann)

Henrich to first base. He made Yogi Berra his every day catcher. And he gave important assignments to three rookies, outfielders Hank Bauer and Gene Woodling, and second baseman Jerry Coleman.

Stengel's biggest problem, however, was the absence for the first 65 games of the season of his team's biggest star, best player and leader, the great DiMaggio, because of his heel injury. This caused Stengel to reveal what would be his greatest managerial skill—the ability to maneuver his players by instituting a seldom used platoon system. Bobby Brown and Billy Johnson shared third base, Woodling and Bauer alternated in leftfield or right, and Cliff Mapes and Johnny Lindell platooned in center until DiMaggio returned.

His first season as manager of the Yankees was Stengel's most brilliant. He held his team together in DiMaggio's absence and a rash of injuries to other important players and directed his team to the pennant by sweeping the last two games against the Red Sox, with his greatest detractor, the Colonel, Dave Egan, looking on as a witness. Stengel's year was complete when the Yankees won the World Series from the Dodgers in five games.

In 1950, Johnny Lindell was sold to the St. Louis Cardinals and infielder George "Snuffy" Stirnweiss was traded to the St. Louis Browns. Three newcomers joined the Yankees, one of them a skinny second baseman whom Stengel had managed in Oakland and loved for his combativeness and his fierce desire to win. Casey suggested to Weiss that he purchase the contract of the tough guy and Billy Martin became a Yankee. Joe Collins took over as the regular first baseman with Henrich, now 37

World Series bunting became commonplace during Stengel's tenure as Yankees manager. From 1949 to 1953 the Yankees won an unprecedented five Fall Classics. (New York Yankees Archives)

LEFT: *Billy Martin, who played for Stengel in the Pacific Coast League, became teacher's pet in New York because of clutch plays like the one below: Martin came out of nowhere with the bases loaded in the seventh inning of the seventh game of the 1952 World Series to catch Jackie Robinson's wind blown pop-up. (UPI/Bettmann)*

BELOW: *Stengel with two of his star pupils, Yogi Berra (Casey called him "my assistant manager") and rookie Whitey Ford in this 1950 photo. (UPI/Bettmann)*

ABOVE: *Six Yankees plus manager Casey Stengel made the 1952 American League All-Star team. (From left) Mickey Mantle, Hank Bauer, Stengel, Allie Reynolds, Yogi Berra and Phil Rizzuto. Vic Raschi is not pictured. (UPI/Bettmann)*

Left-hand hitting Gene Woodling (right) and right-hand hitting Hank Bauer (above) could have played regularly with any other team yet they thrived in Casey Stengel's platoon system.

A former Marine, a combat pilot and a slick-fielding second baseman, the popular Jerry Coleman (below) later became a broadcaster for the Yankees and the San Diego Padres.

First baseman Joe Collins (lower right) played his entire 10-year career with the Yankees and was a mainstay on seven pennant winners and five world championships. (all photos: New York Yankees Archives)

years old, becoming a part-time player. In midseason, the Yankees called up from their Kansas City farm team a young lefthander named Whitey Ford, who would win nine of 10 decisions in the vital stretch run to Stengel's second straight American League pennant.

The Yankees finished three games ahead of the Detroit Tigers, then won the 1950 World Series from the Philadelphia Phillies in a four-game sweep.

Two seasons, two pennants for Stengel, and eight wins in nine World Series games. With that achievement, Stengel was solidly entrenched as manager of the Yankees and there were no more doubts about his ability to lead.

The 1951 season brought more changes. Henrich retired. Pitcher Tommy Byrne and outfielder Cliff Mapes were traded to the St. Louis Browns. Third baseman Billy Johnson was traded to the St. Louis Cardinals. Former star relief pitcher Joe Page was released. Newcomers to the Yankees were infielder Gil McDougald and a teenage adonis from Oklahoma with awesome power as a switch-hitter, blinding speed and a Lil' Abner build. His name was Mickey Charles Mantle.

The most versatile of the Stengel Yankees was Gil McDougald (inset) who was an All-Star at second, short and third. Here he's at third against the sliding Minnie Minoso. (New York Yankees Archives)

DiMaggio was hampered by injury and age and his heir apparent, Mantle, was having trouble connecting with American league pitching, but somehow the Yankees managed to win their third consecutive pennant. Yogi Berra led the team in home runs with 27 and RBI's with 88. Ford was serving a two-year hitch in the Army, but the pitching big three of Vic Raschi, Eddie Lopat and Allie Reynolds carried the team by winning 59 games and the Yankees finished five games in front of the Cleveland Indians.

A highlight of the season was two no-hitters by Reynolds, only the fifth and sixth in Yankees' history. On the night of July 12, in Cleveland, he no-hit the Indians. On September 28, in the first game of a doubleheader against the Boston Red Sox at Yankee Stadium, Reynolds was one out away from his second no-hitter when Ted Williams hit a foul pop between first and home. Catcher Yogi Berra settled under it, then dropped it.

It meant Reynolds had to get the game's greatest hitter out again to complete his second no-hitter of the season. On Reynolds' next pitch, Williams hit another foul pop, almost identical to the first. This

STENGELESE

On July 9, 1958, Casey Stengel appeared before the Senate Subcommittee on Antitrust and Monopoly. The committee, chaired by Senator Estes Kefauver of Tennessee, was looking into the legality of baseball's reserve clause and Stengel's testimony was thought to be important to their decision. The august body did not know what it had bargained for.

For 45 minutes, some 7,000 words recorded in the Congressional Record, the manager of the Yankees held the committee spellbound with his Stengelese. Safe to say, the hallowed walls would never be the same.

Following is a sampling of Stengel's testimony:

Sen. Kefauver: "Mr. Stengel, you are the manager of the New York Yankees. Will you give us very briefly your background and views about this legislation?"

Stengel: "Well, I started in professional baseball in 1910. I have been in professional ball, I would say, for 48 years. I have been employed by numerous ball clubs in the majors and in the minor leagues. I started in the minor leagues with Kansas City. I played as low as Class D ball, which was at Shelbyville, Kentucky, and also Class C ball and Class A ball and I have also advanced in baseball as a ballplayer. I had many years that I was not so successful as a ballplayer, as it is a game of skill. And then I was no doubt discharged by baseball, in which I had to go back to the minor leagues as a manager. I became a major league manager in several cities and was discharged. We call it discharged because there is no question that I had to leave."

UPI

Sen. Kefauver: "Mr. Stengel, are you prepared to answer particularly why baseball wants this bill passed?"

Stengel: "Well, I would have to say at the present time, I think that baseball has advanced in this respect for the player help. That is an amazing statement for me to make because you can retire with an annuity at 50 and what organization in America allows you to retire at 50 and receive money? I want to further state that I am not a ballplayer, that is, put into the pension-fund committee. At my age, and I have been in baseball, well, I will say I am possibly the oldest man who is working in baseball. I would say that when they start an annuity for the ballplayers to better their conditions, it should have been done, and I think it has been done. I think it should be the way they have done it, which is a very good thing. The reason why they possibly did not take the managers at that time was because radio and television or the income to ball clubs was not large enough that you could have put in a pension plan. Now I am not a member of the pension plan. You have young men here who are, who represent the ball clubs, they represent the players. And since I am not a member and don't receive pension from a fund which you think, my goodness, he ought to be declared in that, too, but I would say that is a great thing for the ballplayers. That is one thing I will say for the ballplayers, they have an advanced pension fund. I should think it was gained by radio and television or you could not have enough money to pay anything of that type.

"I have been up and down the ladder. I know there are some things in baseball 35 to 50 years ago that are better now than they were in those days. In those days, my goodness, you could not transfer a ball club in the minor leagues, Class D, Class C ball, Class A ball. How could you transfer a ball club when you did not have a highway? How could you transfer a ball club when the railroad then would take you to a town, you got off and then you had to wait and sit up five hours to go to another ball club?"

Sen. Kefauver: "Mr. Stengel, I am not sure that I made my question clear."

Stengel: "Yes, sir. Well, that's all right. I'm not sure I'm going to answer yours perfectly either."

Sen. Kefauver: "I am asking you, sir, why is it that baseball wants this bill passed?"

Stengel: "I would say I would not know, but I would say the reason they want it passed is to keep baseball going as the highest paid ball sport that has gone into baseball, and from the baseball angle—I am not going to speak of any other sport, I am not in here to argue about these other sports. I am in the baseball business. It has been run cleaner than any business that was ever put out in 100 years at the present time. I am not speaking about television or I am not speaking about income that comes into the ball parks. You have to take that off. I don't know too much about it. I say the ballplayers have a better advancement at the present time."

Sen. Langer: "I want to know whether you intend to keep monopolizing the world's championship in New York City?"

Stengel: "Well, I will tell you. I got a little concern yesterday (in the annual All-Star game, won by Stengel's American Leaguers, 4-3) in the first three innings when I saw the three players I had gotten rid of, and I said when I lost nine what am I going to do and when I had a couple of my players I thought so great of that did not do so good up to the sixth inning I was more confused but I finally had to go and call on a young man in Baltimore that we don't own and the Yankees don't own him, and he is doing pretty good, and I would actually have to tell you that we are more the Greta Garbo type now from success. We are being hated, I mean, from the ownership and all, we are being hated. Every sport that gets too great or one individual—but if we made 27 cents and it pays to have a winner at home, why would you have a good winner in your park if you were an owner? That is the result of baseball. An owner gets most of the money at home and it is up to him and his staff to do better or they ought to be discharged."

In 1950, the Yankees made a $100,000 investment in a new scoreboard. At the time it was the largest and most modern in the major leagues. (New York Yankees Archives)

time, Berra squeezed it for the final out of Reynolds' second no-hitter. A relieved Berra then raced to the mound and jumped into Reynolds' arms.

For the sixth time, the Yankees hooked up in the World Series with their neighbors from across the Harlem River, the New York Giants, who had won the National League pennant in dramatic fashion. Trailing the Brooklyn Dodgers by 13 1/2 games in August, the Giants came back to finish the regular season in a tie and force a three-game playoff. They split the first two games and the Dodgers took a 4-2 lead into the bottom of the ninth in the third game when Bobby Thomson exploded the "shot heard 'round the world," a three-run homer off Ralph Branca to win the league championship for the Giants.

The Yankees put an end to the Giants' magic, taking their third consecutive world championship in a six-game Series. With that championship came the end of another era. After 13 fabulous seasons, DiMaggio retired.

There was no mistaking Stengel's genius now, or the fact that he was solidly in command of the Yankees fortunes. With his success, Stengel's popularity skyrocketed. He was a character who became a favorite with photographers because of his distinctive, photogenic face and his willingness to mime and mug for the camera; and a favorite with the writers because of his riveting stories, his baseball acumen and his colorful language. Perhaps inadvertently, perhaps to avoid revealing his true thoughts, he engaged in a form of double-speak that became known as "Stengelese."

He would interrupt a conversation, or begin a monologue by poking a gnarled finger at his listener and say, "Now, wait a minute, doctor." In Stengelese, nothing ever started or began, it "commenced;" a player, or a manager, was never fired or released, he was "discharged;" a Baltimore chop, or a high bouncer to the infield, was a "butcher boy;" a rookie or an inexperienced person was "like Ned in the third reader;" and someone who had passed on was "dead at the present time."

Upon DiMaggio's retirement, Stengel was asked his evaluation of the famed Yankee Clipper.

"He's the best I've ever had," Stengel said succinctly and sincerely. Not satisfied to let it go at that, Stengel was off on one of his typical monologues.

"Now, wait a minute for crissakes," he said. "You're going into too big a man. Maybe he woulda been an astronaut if he wanted. He could hit some balls off the moon and see if they'd carry. There were a lot of great ones and Ruth could pitch, too, but this fella is the best I had. About DiMaggio, you don't have to falsify anything. He started in with a bang and never stopped. Of course when he played for me he was handicapped, but you wouldna knowed it if you didn't see him limping in the cabs and in the clubhouse. The best thing he had–and I'll give you a tip–was his head. He saw some of the faults of the pitcher and he would hit the ball and he didn't just hit on Sunday, neither."

Doubts that the Yankees could win without DiMaggio's leadership were soon dispelled. They finished three games ahead of the Indians in 1952 to win their fourth consecutive pennant, then beat the Dodgers in a seven-game World Series.

The highlight of the Series came in the bottom of the seventh inning of Game 7 with the Yankees ahead, 4-2. The Dodgers loaded the bases with one out and Stengel, always making the unorthodox move, summoned left-hander Bob Kuzava, to replace 16-game winner Vic Raschi. Kuzava had a record of 8-8 and only three saves during the regular season, but he was called in to face the left-handed hitting slugger, Duke Snider. When Snider popped out for the second out, it was assumed Stengel would bring in a right-hander to face the fearsome Jackie Robinson.

Again, Stengel went against the book by leaving Kuzava in. Robinson hit a high pop to the infield for what looked like the third out. But everybody froze momentarily as the ball, taken by a stiff wind, wafted back toward home plate. Finally, second baseman Billy Martin made his move, a mad dash toward the plate, catching the ball at his waist between the pitcher's mound and the third base foul line. Stengel looked on proudly as his boy from Oakland saved the day.

The Yankees held on to win the game and their fourth consecutive world championship, tying the major league record set by the Yankees of Joe McCarthy from 1936 through 1939.

In search of an unprecedented fifth straight world championship, the Yankees welcomed Whitey Ford back from military service in 1953 and he led the staff with 18 wins. For the third straight year, the Yankees beat out the Cleveland Indians, this time by seven games, and for the second straight year, they faced the Brooklyn Dodgers in the World Series.

This time, the Yankees took care of the Dodgers in six games for their fifth straight world championship. Stengel was perfect as a manager–five seasons, five pennants, five world championships. Billy Martin set a Series record with 12 hits in the Series, and Yogi Berra continued to be the Yankees leader on the field. He batted .297 and led the team with 27 homers and 108 RBIs. In the World Series, Berra batted .429 and drove in four runs.

But it was his intangibles that endeared him to Stengel, his catching, his ability to handle pitchers, his competitiveness and his stamina. Berra became a favorite of Stengel, who referred to his catcher as "my assistant manager."

Years later, asked to sum up Berra, the Ol' Perfesser offered another of his inimitable monologues. (In the interests of clarity, the Stengelese in the following paragraphs has been numbered; see end of chapter for an "English" language translation.)

"Yogi Berra worked for me a long time, and when he started, he had a wonderful career because he lived in St. Louis, which I was familiar with because I lived in Kansas City when I went to dental college and he was living in Kerry Patch (1) because all the Irish was there, then in come the Eyetalians like Graziola (2) and Berra and they commenced makin' more money because they worked in the factory and if it wasn't a factory they kept busy and everybody worked and they brought the beer in a bucket or whatcha call a pitcher that they filled because it was very hot in St. Louis like you wouldn't believe, next to hell, and the fellows was very tired in the factory and finally they got started with the ball club and most of the players like Howard (3) lived there and for 30-40 years they played ball in three or four parks (4) when the National League had it.

"Now Berra became very well known when the war commenced because Phil Rizzuto was in the Navy in Portsmouth and immediately Berra went and joined, and this is when I wasn't there, he wanted to sign up with the Yankees and he came to see the business man-

ager and if you went there you had to go through two or four secretaries, but he had four or five things that he could do which wasn't funny to me in my life with his antics. He was very nervous when he was there and young and now he has raised three kids that are taller than he is every one of them, when he had a way of walking around, you know, like a bear and they forgot that he could bat like Graziola did. And you could look it up that he went up there and he didn't care about signs if you tell him to bunt and he swung and hit some of them for home runs and you can't catch home runs.

"McDougald and Simmons everybody thought had peculiar stances (5) if you were a first year player in life they'd say how could you stand like that but I always thought he was graceful because few of them made good like Berra was a very good hitter and I thought he had a good year after he talked with people all over the country, they wanted to know, some of them, why you didn't get with Mr. Rickey and they didn't give ya a big bonus because he wanted to go back to Kerry Patch and say he got more than Graziola or at least as much (6).

Yogi Berra (at left) once said, "Bill Dickey learned me all his experiences." (UPI/Bettmann)

"In the World Series they put him in right field and when he saw he was in right field he used to have the best alibi guy which was DiMaggio and he would say, 'Isn't that so, Joe?' if he went to a banquet that he led the league in three or four departments he commenced partying because some of them owners were there and they took in outstanding people or an actor or singer not like New York which takes only baseball people (7) and they called on him to talk, but how ya gonna interview him about hitting the ball sideways on the golf course (8), now in time he got up to speak and Braven Dyer (9) said if you want to make that man talk you gotta ask him questions like how in the world did you sign so fast they thought you should hold out like Babe Herman used to say if you hold out they automatically pay you $1,000 to sign, but he signed at a banquet in New York because he thought he was the maitre d' he used to always be around Topping and Weiss (10) until they said why don't you come into the office and he said I do but you're never around and leading in three or four things how in the world can you sign the contract so soon and why wouldn't you hold out and he hemmed and hawed and he said, well he knew Del Webb was sitting there listening, and he said to tell you the truth I figured it out and I asked for $10,000 and they gave me $10,000 more than that.

"After that he talked about him with Brownie (11) who did wonderful in life and he even studied in spring training and now he's a big doctor with all them big doctors and he's done wonderful and everybody talked about the funnies (12) because they used to say if you owned a paper and you didn't use the funnies you couldn't sell the papers but it's not like that anymore and very seldom did you ever see Mr. Berra in a fight and with our pitchers they said he couldn't catch and handle pitchers and I think the greatest coach was Dickey (13) and he was wonderful against Cochrane and men who were real outstanding catchers if you owned them.

"One year he had stopped hitting, not stopped, but he had bad luck and he coulda led the league in home runs except he pulled the ball too much (14) they slowed up on him and I'd jump out and I'd say, 'Ohhhhh, it's foul but it will be a home run,' and he had beautiful brilliance with writers about why he hit bad balls for home runs you better not throw the ball over the plate to him. 'Yeah,' I said, 'I'd like to see 'em throw the ball over the plate, too, he'd do pretty good.'

"I always thought he worked good with young pitchers. That's why he could beat that Cleveland club 18 times without ever losing a game if you look it up. Now when you talk about Ford, he was the best pitcher we ever had for a lefthander, and they used to say he didn't think good and I said, 'Huh, huh,' but he hits good and he rearranged the Dodgers.

"When Reynolds pitched the no-hit game you must be pitching pretty good when Williams hits a pop fly and even if he got his toe stepped on, who would have thought he would do it again which only proves that

baseball must be honest because who would do it again except a guy who hits .110 and him one of the greatest hitters of all-time if you look it up and Del Webb with all his troubles because the market ain't so good and he said when he went and faced the Great Man above he hoped he got a second chance like that.

"Well, now, he was always a pleasant feller and he would never snitch on a ballplayer even when they got into some trouble in New York in a night club (15) that they had made a date 30 days ahead because it was a off day and they wuz takin' him out because it was Martin's birthday. Now it came up rain and we had to play but they still filled the engagement. I said, 'You was with them,' and he said, 'No, I went home early,' see he never snitched on anybody. He led a very good life off the field, I mean he liked a lot of people but he liked sports. You know, he thought they were really playing hard those women playing hockey (16), can you believe it?

"He had good instruction from Dickey and he got better. He's an awkward man, but he's fast. When we beat them in Brooklyn and they had all those good managers like Durocher and Dressen, he's the one went out and got the ball and they called him out, but he could go out and get the bunt. Another thing he did when he was playing, he never showed he was going crazy on the field, you never saw him tearin' up a uniform, did you? But I don't want to tell you too much about him because then you'll have 5,000 pages."

SAY WHAT?

A Footnote Translation of the Above

1. The section in St. Louis where Berra grew up, now called "The Hill," was known as Kerry Patch in earlier days when it was inhabited by Irish immigrants.
2. Joe Garagiola, Berra's childhood friend.
3. Former Yankees catcher, the late Elston Howard, was also a native of St. Louis.
4. The St. Louis Browns joined the American League in 1902 and left in 1954. The St. Louis Cardinals have been in the National League since its inception, playing home games in several ball parks, including Sportsman's Park and Busch Memorial Stadium.
5. Former Yankee Gil McDougald and Hall of Famer Al Simmons were noted for their unorthodox hitting stances.
6. Berra was hurt when his pal, Joe Garagiola, was offered a contract by their home town team, the Cardinals, and Berra wasn't. When Berra signed with the Yankees, he insisted his bonus be for the same amount Garagiola got from the Cardinals.
7. The Los Angeles Baseball Writers annual dinner, unlike that in New York, is often attended by Hollywood celebrities.
8. ? ? ?
9. A former Los Angeles sportswriter.
10. The Yankees always had a World Series victory party in a Manhattan hotel, and it was Berra's custom to stay near team owner Dan Topping and General Manager George Weiss. As the drinks flowed and the elation built, Topping would invariably ask Berra, "How much do you want next year?" Berra would mention a figure and Topping would say, "OK, come in tomorrow and we'll draw up the contract." It was Stengel's contention that Yogi therefore got a better contract than he would have had had he waited.
11. Bobby Brown, Yankees third baseman who became a heart specialist and later President of the American League.
12. A reference to Berra's predilection for reading comics.
13. When Berra joined the Yankees, coach Bill Dickey, a Hall of Famer, was assigned to help Yogi improve his catching ability. Later, Berra would say, "Bill Dickey taught me all his experiences."
14. A reference to Berra's habit of repeatedly pulling balls foul into the right field seats in Yankee Stadium.
15. The famous Copacabana Incident in which several Yankees, out for a night on the town to celebrate Billy Martin's 29th birthday, got into a much publicized fight.
16. Roller Derby, presumably. Berra is an avid fan of all sports.

(UPI/Bettmann)

The Mick

7

The line of succession of Yankee superstars went from Babe Ruth to Lou Gehrig to Joe DiMaggio to Mickey Charles Mantle.

Born in Spavinaw, OK, and raised in Commerce, his father, Elvin, known as Mutt, was a fanatical baseball fan who named his eldest son after his favorite player, Mickey Cochrane, and taught the boy to switch-hit. As a teenager he was a local sensation in both football and baseball. Scout Tom Greenwade spotted him on a sandlot and signed him for the Yankees.

After a brilliant minor league record he came to New York in 1951, but was sent back to the minors, so discouraged he threatened to quit baseball until his father told him, "If that's all the guts you have then quit . . . and come back to work in the mines with me."

Mantle eventually did visit his father in the Oklahoma lead and zinc mines, but it was as a member of the Yankees with his teammate Cliff Mapes.

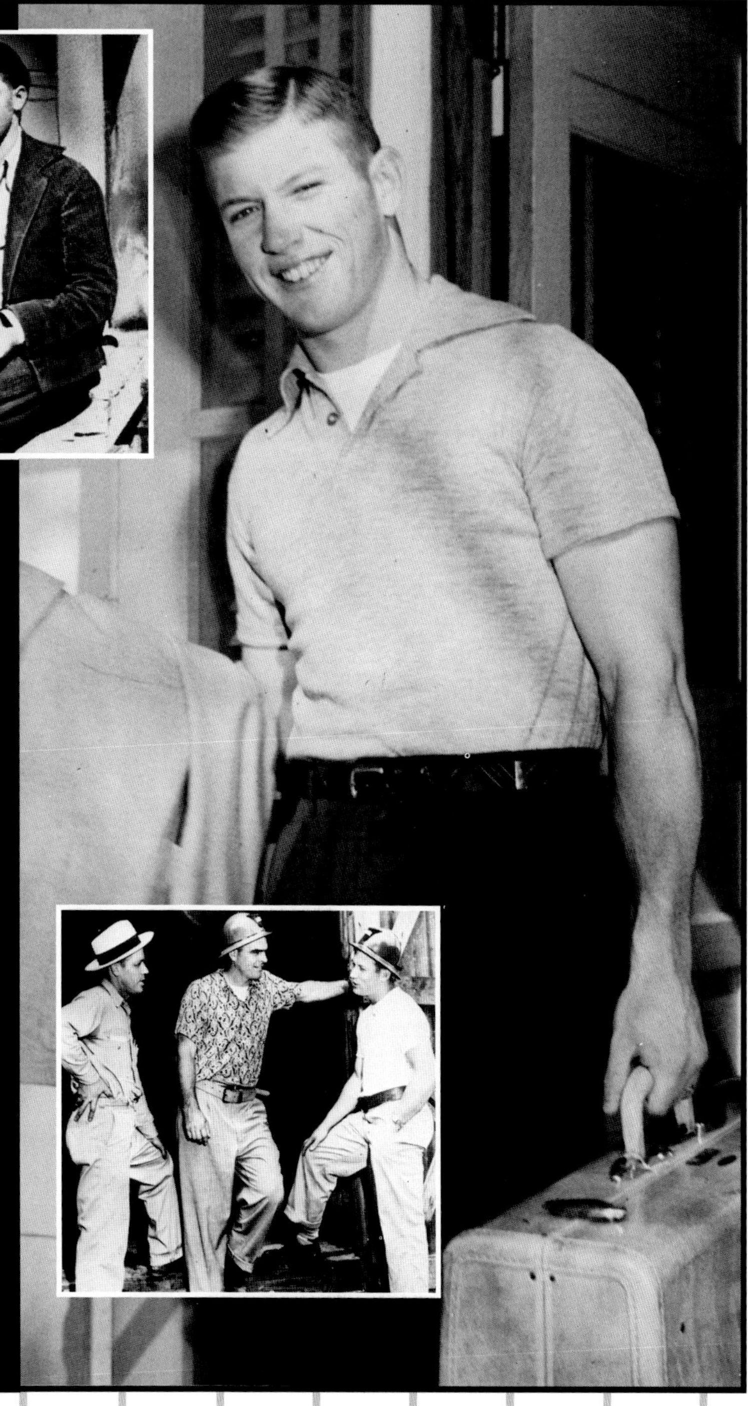

(all photos: New York Yankees Archives)

As a 19-year-old rookie, Mantle faced the legendary Bob Feller in Yankee Stadium in 1951. (UPI/Bettmann)

In 1954, the Yankees won 103 games, more than they had won in each of their previous five straight world championship seasons, and finished second to end their remarkable title streak.

The Cleveland Indians, with 23-game winners Bob Lemon and Early Wynn, 19-game winner Mike Garcia, 15-game winner Art Houtteman, and 13-game winner Bob Feller, and with American League batting champion Bobby Avila and home run and RBI champion, Larry Doby, won a record 111 games and finished eight games ahead of the Yankees.

But 1954 was the breakthrough year for Mickey Mantle. While he still had not corrected his penchant for strikeouts, leading the league with 102, he batted .300, belted 27 homers, knocked in 102 runs and at last attained the stardom that had been predicted of him since he joined the Yankees as a 19-year-old phenom.

Born in a two-room house in the heart of the zinc and lead mines in Spavinaw, Oklahoma, Mantle soon showed rare ability as an athlete. Although he came from football country, Mantle's father discouraged his son from playing football. Mantle's dad, called "Mutt" by his friends, was an avid baseball fan. He named his first son "Mickey" after his favorite player, Hall of Famer Mickey Cochrane of the Detroit Tigers. He taught the boy to be a switch-hitter. And he frequently took his son to the nearest major league city, St. Louis, some 300 miles away, to watch the Cardinals play.

Mantle was discovered by Yankees scout Tom Greenwade and signed on the day he graduated from high school. He received an $1,100 signing bonus, plus $400 for the balance of the 1949 season to play for Independence in the Class D Kansas-Oklahoma-Missouri League, a 17-year-old scatter-armed shortstop with the physique of a blacksmith and the power to match.

After 89 games at Independence, he moved up the following season to Joplin in the Class C Western Association, where, converted to the outfield, he attracted attention by tearing up the league with 26 homers, 136 RBIs and a league-leading .383 average.

It wasn't common for a player out of a Class C league to be invited to the major league camp for spring training, but Mantle's numbers and his power and speed could not be ignored. The Yankees asked him to join them for spring training, 1951, in Phoenix, Arizona. His reputation preceded him and he was being touted as the next great Yankees superstar; Babe Ruth, Lou Gehrig and Joe DiMaggio all rolled into one.

Curiosity about the young phenom brought hordes of reporters to Phoenix and Casey Stengel regaled them with stories about this terrific teenager who could not miss being one of the great players in the history of the game.

Mantle did not disappoint the writers. Perhaps because of the rarefied Arizona air, he hit dozens of eye-popping home runs in batting practice and displayed such awesome power that he was placed on the Yankees roster and taken east with the big team.

Once he got to New York, Mantle's problems surfaced. There were too few home runs and too many strikeouts, five in a row in one doubleheader against the Red Sox. Then on July 13, in Detroit, came the words Mantle feared most:

"Casey wants to see you."

Mantle went to the manager's office and there was the gnarled old man with the craggy caricature of a face, tears welling in his eyes.

"This is gonna hurt me more than you," Stengel said, "but..."

"No, skip, it's my own fault," Mantle said.

"Aww...it ain't nobody's fault. You're 19, that's all. I want you to get your confidence back, so I'm shipping you down to Kansas City."

Dejected and discouraged, Mantle found things no better in Kansas City. The home runs were few and far between. The strikeouts mounted. Frustrated, Mantle reached out for the one person he knew would understand, who would boost his confidence, stroke him. He placed a call to the Eagle-Picher mines in Oklahoma and asked for Mutt Mantle.

"I'm not hitting, dad," he said. "I just can't play any more."

"The hell you can't. Where are you staying?"

"I'm at the Aladdin Hotel."

"OK, I'll be there."

Mutt Mantle drove five hours from Oklahoma to Kansas City to be with his son. Expecting compassion, sympathy and a pat on the back, Mickey got anger and defiance instead.

Pete Sheehy, who saw them all from Ruth to Mattingly in his 60 years as Yankees clubhouse man, was the one who assigned Mantle number 7. (New York Yankees Archives)

"I tried as hard as I could, dad" he said. "And what for? Where am I headed? I tell you it's no use. That's all there is to it. I'm not..."

"Now you shut up," Mutt Mantle shouted. "I don't want to hear that whining. I thought I raised a man, not a coward. If that's all the guts you have, then quit. Pack your things and come back and work in the mines with me."

The words were just the right ones. Within minutes, Mickey was pleading with his father, begging him to let him stay, to give him another chance. Almost immediately, things changed for young Mantle. His bat came alive. The strikeouts still came, but not as frequently. In 40 games, he batted .361 with 11 homers, 50 RBIs and only 30 strikeouts, and he was on his way back to New York.

When he first made it to New York, he had been given uniform No. 6 by veteran clubhouse man, Pete Sheehy. When he returned from Kansas City, Sheehy changed the number, "for luck," he said. Sheehy assigned Mantle No. 7.

Back with the Yankees, Mantle's hitting improved. Including his terrible start, he played 96 games for the Yankees in his rookie season, batted a respectable .267 with 13 homers and 65 RBIs, and helped the Yankees win the third of their string of five consecutive world championships.

In his first World Series, Mantle batted first and played rightfield, with orders from Stengel to "take everything you can get over in center, the Dago's heel is hurting pretty bad."

In the fifth inning of Game 2, Willie Mays lofted a high, lazy fly ball to right center. Heeding Stengel's instructions, Mantle drifted over to make the catch. But he heard DiMaggio shout, "I got it."

Mantle slammed on the brakes and as he did, his spikes caught in a drainage ditch, tearing up his right knee. He fell to the ground in a heap. The pain from his knee was excruciating. It was the start of what would be a career-long problem with his knees. Mantle was through for the season.

Mantle showed steady improvement over the next two seasons and had his "coming out" season in 1954. After that, it was an explosion. Mickey Mantle was finally worthy of being the successor to Joe DiMaggio. In 1955, he led the league with 37 homers, knocked in 99 runs and batted .306.

Not since Boston's Ted Williams in 1947 had a player led his league in batting average, home runs and RBIs in the same season. Not since Williams in 1942 had a player led the major leagues in all three categories. In 1956, Mantle batted .353 (eight points higher than Williams; 25 points higher than the National League champion, Hank Aaron); he slugged 52 home runs (20 more than runner-up Cleveland's Vic Wertz; 9 more than the National League champion, Duke Snider, and the 11th highest single season total in history); he drove home 130 runs (two more than Detroit's Al Kaline; 21 more than the National League champion, Stan Musial). Mantle was only the 12th player in baseball history to win his league's Triple Crown of hitting; and only four other players ever led the major leagues in all three categories.

Mantle suffered his first of many serious injuries in Game 2 of the 1951 World Series when he caught his cleats in a drainage ditch and injured his right knee. He collapses at the feet of Joe DiMaggio who made the catch of Willie Mays' fly ball. (UPI/Bettmann)

If the 1956 season belonged to Mickey Mantle, the 1956 World Series belonged to Don Larsen, the unlikeliest of heroes. Larsen had come to the Yankees in one of the biggest trades in baseball history. It involved 18 players and was completed over a 13-day period.

On November 18, 1954, Larsen came from the Baltimore Orioles along with pitcher Bob Turley and shortstop Billy Hunter for six players, including Gene Woodling and catcher Gus Triandos. That was the forerunner of a trade on December 1 in which the Yankees received three more players from the Orioles and sent five more players to Baltimore.

In two seasons, Larsen had won 10 games and lost 33. With the Yankees in 1955, he was 9-2 and in 1956 was 11-5, but he was hardly the pitcher who figured to make baseball history. Larsen started Game 2 of the World Series in Brooklyn, but was knocked out in the second inning, so it was a surprise when, with the Series tied at two games each, Casey Stengel announced that Larsen would be his pitcher for Game 5.

It was Monday, October 8, a beautiful sun-splashed autumn day in New York as 64,519 fans

Mantle homered from both sides of the plate in one game 10 times. (UPI/Bettmann)

jammed into Yankee Stadium. The Dodgers pitcher was Sal "The Barber" Maglie, who had won 23 games for the New York Giants in 1951. Now, 39 years old, Maglie had been picked up in midseason by the Dodgers from the Cleveland Indians. He proceeded to win 13 out of 18 decisions, including a no-hitter, and help pitch the Dodgers to their fourth National League pennant in five years.

Maglie had been the winning pitcher in the Series opener, beating Whitey Ford, 6-3. And he showed immediately in Game 5 that he was on his game again, retiring the Yankees in order in each of the first three innings. Larsen, meanwhile, had also faced nine batters without allowing a baserunner.

The Yankees broke through for a run in the fourth on Mantle's home run just inside the rightfield foul pole, then scored another in the sixth on a single by Andy Carey, a sacrifice and an RBI single by Hank Bauer. The Dodgers still had not had a hit, or a baserunner, through six innings.

Up to that game, there had been 307 World Series games played and there never had been a no-hitter

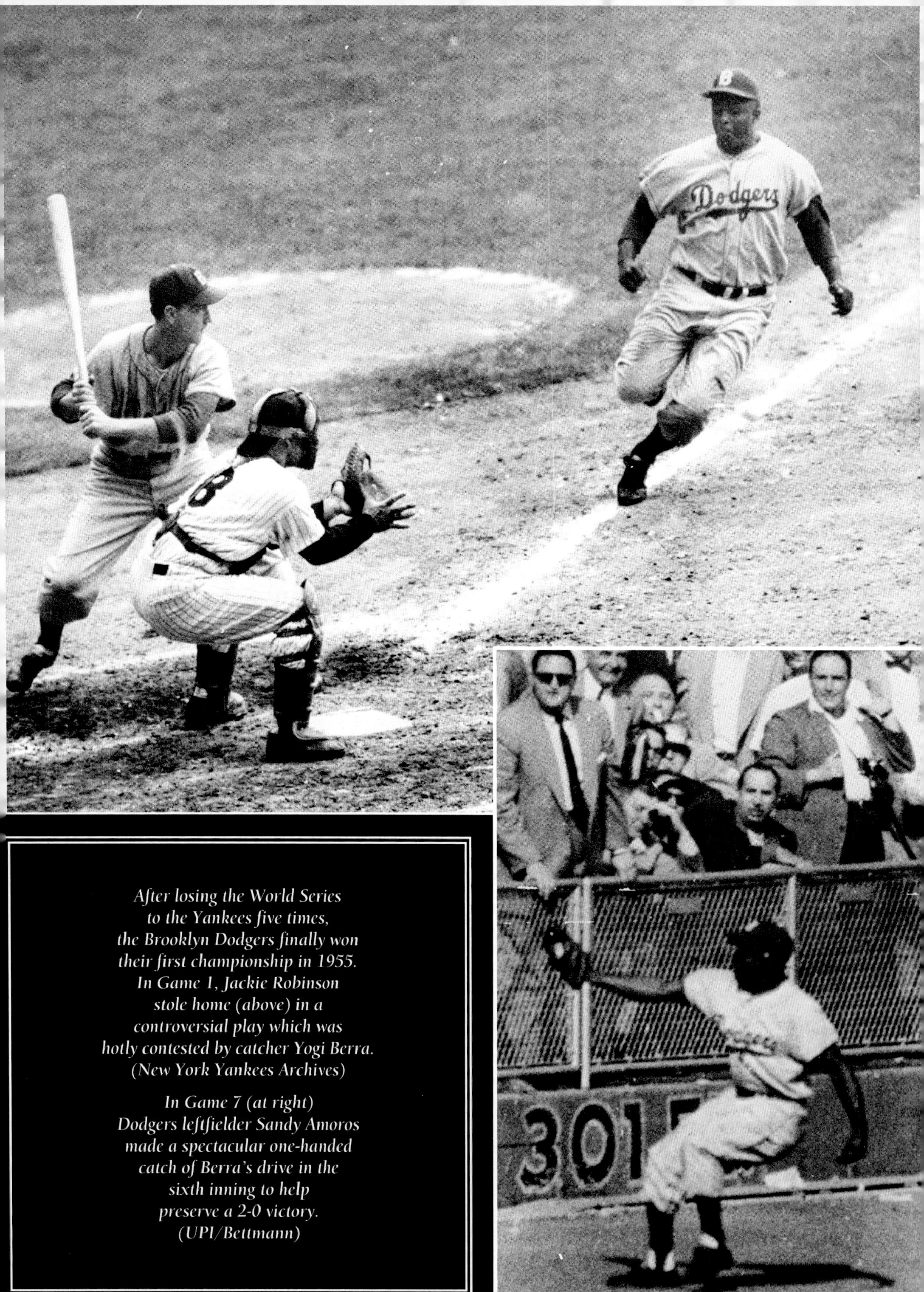

After losing the World Series to the Yankees five times, the Brooklyn Dodgers finally won their first championship in 1955. In Game 1, Jackie Robinson stole home (above) in a controversial play which was hotly contested by catcher Yogi Berra. (New York Yankees Archives)

In Game 7 (at right) Dodgers leftfielder Sandy Amoros made a spectacular one-handed catch of Berra's drive in the sixth inning to help preserve a 2-0 victory. (UPI/Bettmann)

The Yankees regained the World Championship from the Dodgers in 1956 with the help of the most spectacular pitching performance in World Series history. In Game 5, journeyman Don Larsen, who won only 11 games during the regular season, pitched the only no-hitter ever in the World Series and embellished the achievement by making it a perfect game. After Dale Mitchell struck out for the final out catcher Yogi Berra leaped into Larsen's arms and his teammates swarmed onto the field to congratulate the unlikely hero.

(background photo: New York Yankees Archives, all others UPI/Bettmann)

FIVE MANTLE HOME RUNS TO REMEMBER

Mickey Mantle hit 536 home runs during the regular season—one for every 15.1 at-bats—and 18 more in the World Series—one for every 12.8 at-bats.

He hit his first home run in Chicago off Randy Gumpert on May 1, 1951, and his last off Jim Lonborg in Yankee Stadium on September 20, 1968. In between, he hit some memorable home runs. Some won games. Some were unforgettable mammoth shots.

Here are 5 Mantle home runs to remember:

April 17, 1953—The granddaddy of all Mantle home runs from all accounts by longtime Mantle-watchers. It came in Washington's Griffith Stadium.

"For some reason," Mantle said, "I always hit well in Washington, even though it was not a good hitter's park. The fences were deep and the Senators had some good pitchers through the years, like Pedro Ramos and Camilo Pascual."

The Senators' pitcher this day was Chuck Stobbs, a left-hander. Mantle always said he believed he was a better hitter left-handed, but that he had more power from the right side. This blast proved it. The ball cleared the leftfield bleachers and flew out of the park.

"They said it went 565 feet," Mantle said. "I don't know about that, but I know I hit it good. Red Patterson, our public relations director, told the writers he went down and found out where the ball landed and he measured the distance and it was 565 feet. Red got a lot of publicity out of that, but to tell you the truth, I don't think he ever left the press box.

"The other thing I remember about that home run is that Billy Martin was on third base and he went back to the bag to tag up. I never did let him forget that. Here I hit the ball clear out of the ballpark and he went back to tag up."

May 30, 1956—Mantle hit two this day, one in each game of a doubleheader against the Senators, the first off Pascual, the second off Ramos, Nos. 140 and 141 of his career.

Ramos was one of Mantle's favorite characters, first as an opponent who was constantly challenging Mickey to a foot race, later as a teammate.

In a previous meeting between the two teams, a Senators player was hit by a pitch. In those days, that meant pay back against the first Yankees hitter in the next inning. Ramos was the pitcher and it happened that the first Yankees hitter in the following inning was Mantle, who expected the obligatory payback. It hit him in the middle of the back.

The following day, an apologetic Ramos sheepishly approached Mantle at the batting cage.

"Mee-kee," Ramos said in his Cuban accent, "I no want to heet you. They make me do it."

"That's all right, Pete," Mantle said. "You got to do what they tell you. But the next time you hit me, I'm going to drag a bunt down the first base line and run up your back."

The next time they met was Memorial Day. Mantle faced Ramos in the second game and hit what he describes as "the hardest ball I ever hit left-handed." It hit the roof in rightfield and witnesses estimated that, unimpeded, it might have traveled between 550 and 600 feet.

The following day, Ramos again approached Mantle.

"Mee-kee," he said. "I would rather have you run up my back than have you heet a ball like that off me."

June 16, 1962—This was No. 383 in Cleveland against Gary Bell, who served up more Mantle home runs than any other pitcher, eight. Mantle had missed a month with another injury and had just been activated for the doubleheader against the Indians. But he was not in the starting lineup.

It was the top of the ninth, the Yankees trailed

by two runs and had two runners on base with the pitcher due up. A pinch hitter was in order, but would it be HIM?

Manager Ralph Houk motioned to Mantle and Mickey hobbled to the plate on weakened knees. Bell fired nothing but fastballs, no doubt figuring the month's layoff had affected Mantle's timing.

Mickey took two balls and swung feebly at two other pitches. Then came the fifth consecutive fastball. Mantle swung and made contact, the ball soaring into the rightfield seats. The crowd, more than 72,000, was on its feet, cheering and screaming and pounding their hands together in spite of themselves. Their beloved Indians had fallen behind, but they had witnessed an unforgettable moment, and a remarkable feat of courage.

May 22, 1963—This is the one that came closest to going out of Yankee Stadium (inset photo). It was hit off Bill Fischer of Kansas City and it hit the top of the facade in rightfield, inches away from being the first ball ever to sail out of the Stadium. And it almost made a liar out of veteran baseball writer Dan Daniel.

Daniel answered readers' questions weekly in the New York World-Telegram & Sun. The most frequently asked question was, "Has a fair ball ever been hit out of Yankee Stadium?" To which, Daniel would repeatedly answer annoyingly, "No, no, a thousand times no, a fair ball never has been hit out of Yankee Stadium."

Mickey Mantle came close. Inches away. From field level to the top of the third deck in old Yankee Stadium measured 108 feet and one inch. Mantle's ball made about 106 feet in height, and the ball was still rising when it hit the facade.

The next day, the great sports cartoonist Willard Mullin drew a cartoon depicting Dan Daniel on top of the facade, hammer in hand, nailing an additional 20 feet of boards to the facade. The balloon coming from Daniel's mouth said, "Nobody is going to make a liar out of me."

September 19, 1968—The one that put Mantle into third place on the all-time list at the time, behind Babe Ruth and Willie Mays. It came in Detroit, against Denny McLain.

Mantle was in the twilight of his career, struggling through an injury-filled season, his once great skills eroded by age and injury. He had already announced that the 1968 season would be his last. McLain had become the first pitcher in 34 years to win 30 games and was on his way to No. 31, with a six-run lead. McLain was a free spirit. He also was a great admirer of Mantle and he possessed a sense of history.

Late in the game, Mantle strode to the plate and McLain summoned catcher Bill Freehan halfway to the mound.

"This is probably his last time at-bat in Detroit," McLain said, loud enough for Mantle to hear. "Let's let him hit one."

Mantle was flabbergasted. When Freehan returned to his position behind the plate, Mantle said, "Hey, Bill, did I hear what I think I heard? He wants me to hit one."

"Yeah," Freehan said. "He's not going to work on you. He's just going to throw you fastballs."

Mantle wasn't sure McLain was sincere.

"Denny always was kind of flaky," Mantle said. "I thought he might be setting me up. But, sure enough, the first pitch came in, a batting practice fastball right down the middle. I was so startled, I couldn't pull the trigger. And McLain is standing on the mound with his hands on his hips as if to say, 'Hey, man, what are you looking at it for?'

"Now I knew he was serious. The next pitch came in, another fastball down the middle and I swung so hard, I fouled it off. One more time. Another batting practice fastball. This one I got into and drove it into the upper deck for my 535th home run to pass Jimmie Foxx on the all-time list.

"As I'm going around the bases and I pass third, I take a peek at the mound. McLain sees me looking at him and he gives me a wink."

In 1956, his greatest year, Mantle led the major leagues in home runs (52), RBI (130) and batting average (.353). (background: UPI/Bettmann; inset: New York Yankees Archives)

Mantle is met at home plate by Yogi Berra (#8) after launching one completely out of Griffith Stadium against the Washington Senators, April 17, 1953. It was estimated to have traveled 565 feet. (UPI/Bettmann)

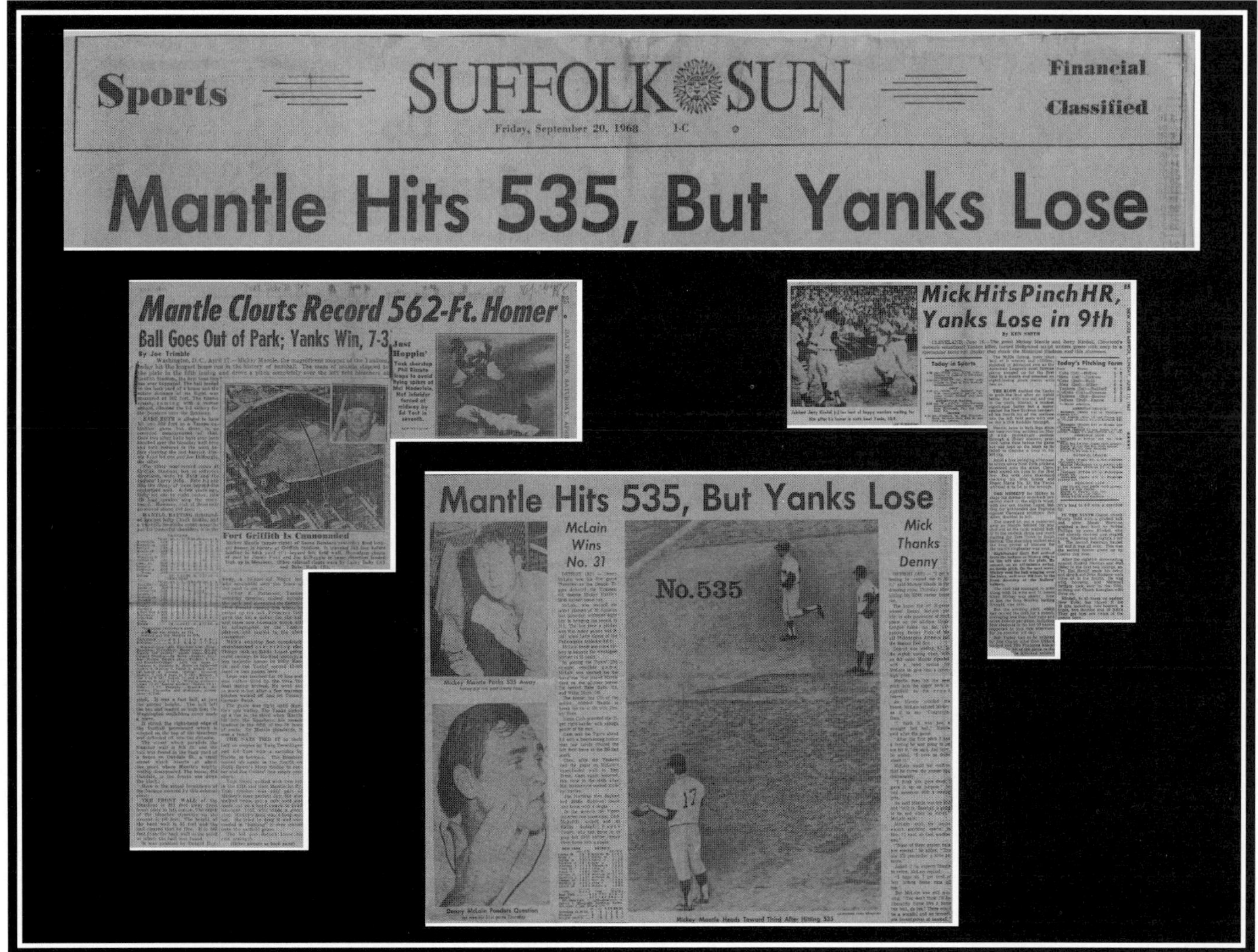

Sports — SUFFOLK SUN — Financial Classified

Friday, September 20, 1968 1-C

Mantle Hits 535, But Yanks Lose

Mantle Clouts Record 562-Ft. Homer

Ball Goes Out of Park; Yanks Win, 7-3

Fort Griffith Is Cannonaded

Mick Hits Pinch HR, Yanks Lose in 9th

Mantle Hits 535, But Yanks Lose

McLain Wins No. 31

Mick Thanks Denny

No.535

pitched. A Perfect Game was unthinkable. But no-hitter was on everyone's mind in Yankee Stadium as Larsen went out to pitch the seventh.

In the Dodgers fifth, Mantle protected the no-hitter by making a one-handed running catch of a drive by Gil Hodges for the second out. After the inning, Mantle went to the water cooler for a drink. Larsen ambled by and calmly said, "Hey, Slick, wouldn't it be something if I pitched a no-hitter."

Mantle chased Larsen away.

In the seventh inning, Jim Gilliam grounded to short, PeeWee Reese flied to center and Duke Snider flied to left.

In the eighth, Jackie Robinson grounded back to Larsen, Hodges lined to third and Sandy Amoros flied to deep center.

In the ninth, with the crowd going wild with every pitch, Carl Furillo flied to right, Roy Campanella grounded to second and veteran Dale Mitchell was sent up to pinch hit for Maglie. He took ball one, then strike one. He swung and missed for strike two, then fouled one off into the leftfield stands. Larsen then wound up to deliver his 97th pitch. Mitchell tried to check his swing. Umpire Babe Pinelli of the National League pumped his right arm. Strike three! A Perfect Game for Don Larsen.

The Yankees went on to win the World Series in seven games, avenging their loss to the Dodgers in the 1955 Series.

Larsen would remain with the Yankees until he was traded to Kansas City in 1960. He would move around to six other teams and finish with a career record of 81-91. But for one day, this tall right-hander from Michigan City, Indiana, known more for his nocturnal adventures than his pitching, would achieve something that has never been duplicated.

For three consecutive seasons, Mickey Mantle had batted .300, but the strikeouts continued and with each one, Mantle became more infuriated. He threw bats, smashed helmets and attacked water coolers. His pal, Billy Martin, no less competitive or even-tempered, did likewise. This caused Casey Stengel to sit down his two hot heads for a fatherly talk.

"Look," Stengel said, "strikeouts are a part of the

Mantle rounds third base after hitting #535 off of Detroit's Denny McLain. The blast vaulted him into third place on the all-time home run list. (UPI)

game. You're going to strike out. That's OK. I don't want you to throw things or punch things. You might get hurt, or you might hurt one of your teammates. When you strike out, just laugh it off."

That gave the mischievous Martin an idea.

"Hey, Mick," he said. "Let's try it. The next time you strike out, just laugh it off. And I'll do the same thing."

So they did. Mantle would strike out and go back to the bench laughing.

"Ha, ha, ha, imagine that, I struck out again."

Martin did likewise. After striking out, he'd place his bat gently in the bat rack and say, "Ha, ha, ha, how about that guy striking me out with a hanging curve ball? Ha, ha, ha."

This went on for several days until Stengel had had enough. He watched Martin strike out and return to the bench laughing and snapped. "OK, that will be enough of that crap."

Mantle followed up his triple crown year with another outstanding season in 1957. He batted .365, but was beaten out for the batting title by Ted Williams. He hit 34 homers, and drove in 94 runs although injuries kept him out of 10 games. The Yankees, augmented by rookies Tony Kubek and Bobby Richardson, won their third straight pennant.

Mantle's star was in its brightest phase in the second half of the decade of the '50s. He had replaced DiMaggio as the idol of Yankees fans and with his newfound stature came recognition and celebrity. He hooked up with Billy Martin and Whitey Ford to form a close, if unusual, trio of revelry–Mantle, the country boy from Oklahoma; Martin, the tough kid from the other side of the tracks in Berkeley, California; and Ford, the street-wise kid from New York.

A wife and kids on Long Island prevented Ford from always joining his buddies on their nocturnal forays, but Mantle and Martin didn't miss a beat...or a night spot. They were regulars at some of the poshest pubs in town.

It was their penchant for fun that would break up their chummy clique.

In honor of Billy Martin's 29th birthday, May 16, 1957, several Yankees decided to go out for a night on the town. The group included Mantle, Yogi Berra, Hank Bauer, Johnny Kucks and Whitey Ford and their wives, and Martin and his date. The evening began with dinner at Danny's Hideaway, one of the favorite haunts of Mantle, Martin and Ford. After dinner, they went to the Copacabana night club where Sammy Davis, Jr., was appearing.

The Yankees' party found themselves seated next to a group made up of members of a bowling team. The group was loud, crude, insulting and slightly intoxicated. They made racial remarks about Davis and used language in front of the Yankees wives that the players found offensive.

Hank Bauer, a tough ex-Marine, spoke first, asking the bowlers to quiet down so his party could enjoy the show. There were words and the next thing anyone knew, one of the bowlers was laying on the floor, under a table, his face bloodied and busted up.

Employees of the Copa hustled the Yankees and their wives out the door, but the news hit the next day's newspapers in big, bold headlines:

YANKEES IN COPA FIGHT

The six Yankees were summoned to the office of general manager George Weiss, a stern man who had little tolerance for any actions that caused embarrassment to the Yankees name. The players were docked to pay for the damage and most of them figured that was the end of it. Except Martin.

"I'm outta here, Mick," Martin told Mantle. "Weiss is going to trade me. He never liked me. He's been waiting for an excuse to trade me and now he's got it."

Sure enough, less than a month later, on June 15, Martin was traded to Kansas City.

Martin had been with the Yankees for parts of six previous seasons and in each one, they had won the pennant. He had played in five World Series with the Yankees and they won four. With Martin gone was it just a coincidence that the Yankees lost the 1957 Series to the Milwaukee Braves in seven games? But they avenged that defeat the following season, coming back from a three games to one deficit to the Braves to sweep the last three games and win their seventh world championship in 10 years.

The Yankees showed signs of slipping in 1959. Injuries reduced Mantle's home runs and RBI numbers to 31 and 75 and the Yankees won only 79 games and finished third, 15 games behind the Chicago White Sox. In an effort to remedy the situation, the Yankees pulled off a blockbuster trade on December 11, 1959. They sent old heroes Hank Bauer and Don Larsen to Kansas City along with promising youngsters Marv Throneberry and Norm Siebern for shortstop Joe DeMaestri, first baseman Kent Hadley and a young left-handed power hitter named Roger Maris.

Maris, born in Hibbing, Minn., and raised in Fargo, North Dakota, had caught the Yankees eye when he belted 28 homers for Cleveland and Kansas City in 1958. He had the perfect Yankee Stadium stroke, but

AT BAT 12 POS. 3B
BALL 2 STRIKE 2
OUT 0

there was no way to predict what was to come.

Maris made an impact immediately. His first season as a Yankee was a portent of things to come as he battled teammate Mantle for the league home run championship. Mantle won the title with 40, one more than Maris, who led the league in RBIs with 112 and was voted the league's Most Valuable Player.

The Yankees returned to the top of the American League, finishing eight games ahead of the Baltimore Orioles, then engaged the Pittsburgh Pirates in one of the most bizarre World Series ever played. Because the Series started in Pittsburgh, Stengel held Whitey Ford, his best pitcher, out of Game 1, preferring to save him for Game 3 in Yankee Stadium.

After the teams split the first two games, Ford beat the Pirates in Game 3 on a four-hit shutout. Ford pitched again in Game 6 with the Yankees down, three games to two. Again, he pitched a shutout, this time a seven-hitter to force a decisive seventh game. Had he pitched Game 1, Ford might have had three starts in the Series. Instead, he was finished after Game 6. And having pitched two complete games, he couldn't even be used in relief in Game 7, which turned out to be one of the most memorable World Series games of all-time.

The Yankees led 7-4 going into the bottom of the eighth, when the Pirates rallied for five runs. Down to their final three outs, the Yankees scored two in the top of the ninth to tie, 9-9. But in the bottom of the ninth, Pirate second baseman Bill Mazeroski hit Ralph Terry's second pitch over the left field wall to give the Pirates their first world championship in 35 years.

To the Yankees and their fans, there was no question that the better team lost the 1960 World Series. While the Pirates won their four games by scores of 6-4, 3-2, 5-2 and 10-9, the Yankees won their three games by scores of 16-3, 10-0 and 12-0. The Yankees scored 55 runs, the Pirates 27. The Yankees also set Series records with 91 hits, 27 extra base hits and a team batting average of .338 and still lost.

"It was the only time in my career I cried after a game," Mantle later admitted.

Stengel was under fire for having blown the Series by holding Ford out of the first game, and he was three months past his 71st birthday. Still, there was no reason to expect anything negative when the Yankees summoned the press to the Savoy Hilton Hotel on Fifth Avenue on the morning of October 18, 1960. Likely, it was simply to announce a contract extension for the old man. After all, he had won another pennant. In 12 seasons, he had won 10 pennants and seven world championships and he had a team that looked strong enough to repeat in 1961.

But there were other factors at work, including Stengel's age and the belief that he was slipping. Waiting in the wings was coach Ralph Houk, who had managed successfully in the Yankees minor league system and whose time had come. If the Yankees didn't lock him up, Houk was certain to go elsewhere.

Public Relations director Bob Fishel called for the attention of the press, then introduced co-owner Dan Topping, who walked to the microphone.

"Casey Stengel has been, and deservedly so, the highest paid manager in baseball history," Topping began. "Casey Stengel has been, and is, a great manager. He is being well rewarded with $160,000 to do with as he pleases."

"Do you mean he's through, resigned?" came a voice from the crowd.

Now, Stengel was on his feet, inching toward the microphone. "Now wait a minutes for crissakes and I'll tell ya," he shouted.

"Now I wasn't fired, I was paid up in full. Mr. Webb and Mr. Topping have started a program for the Yankees. They needed a solution as to when to discharge a man on account of age. My services are no longer required by this club and I told them if this was their idea not to worry about me."

"Were you fired?" came a voice from the back of the room.

"Resigned, fired, quit, discharged, use whatever you damn please. I don't care. You don't see me crying about it."

Hours after most of the reporters had left to file their stories, Stengel remained talking with many of his old friends and said somewhat wistfully, "I commenced winning pennants when I came here, but I didn't commence getting any younger."

And with that, a brilliant chapter in the history of the New York Yankees was brought to a close, and another was about to begin.

FACING PAGE: *In 1960, the Yankees lost the World Series to Pittsburgh and Casey Stengel was replaced as manager by Ralph Houk. It was also the year Roger Maris (foreground) arrived and joined Mickey Mantle (in centerfield) to help continue the Yankees dynasty into the '60s. (New York Yankees Archives)*

On October 20, 1960 the Yankees announced the signing of Ralph Houk as their new manager and co-owner Dan Topping hoped Houk would keep the club's championship lights burning well throughout the '60s. (New York Yankees Archives)

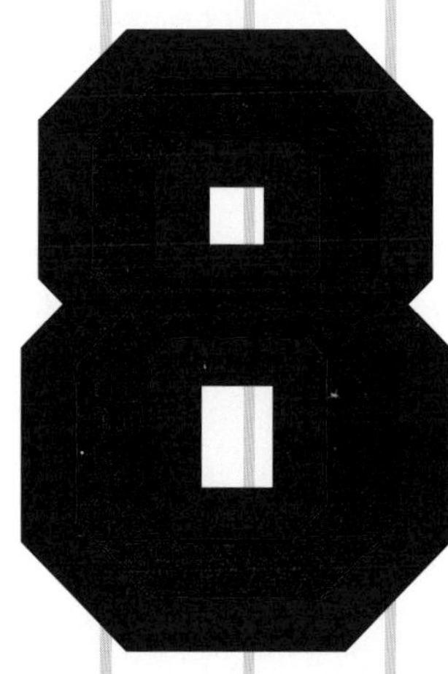

To succeed the venerable Casey Stengel as manager, the Yanskees chose Ralph George Houk, who knew what was expected of him. Any 71-year-old could win a pennant. His job was to return the Yankees to the pinnacle of the baseball world by not only winning the 1961 American League pennant, but the world championship, as well.

Houk, 41, was eminently qualified for the job. He had been in the Yankees organization as player, minor league manager and coach for 23 years, minus four years in military service. Houk was an attractive managerial prospect and several teams inquired of the Yankees about his availability, which might have hastened the decision to force Stengel out.

His playing career had been spectacularly mediocre. He spent parts of eight seasons with the Yankees, among that graveyard of catchers playing behind Yogi Berra. In those eight seasons, Houk appeared in 91 games, came to bat 158 times, had 43 hits, no home runs, 20 RBIs and a lifetime batting average of .272. All those years sitting and observing from the bench helped him hone his knowledge of the game, and he was a born leader of men.

During World War II, Houk served as a Ranger with the 9th Armored Division, earning decorations and a battle field commission to the rank of Major.

When his playing career ended, the Yankees made him manager of their farm team at Denver in the class AAA American Association. He finished third in his first season, second in his second season and second again in his third season, during which he led the Denver Bears to the American Association playoff championship and victory in the Little World Series.

In 1958, he was brought back to New York to serve as Stengel's first base coach. Houk earned a reputation for toughness during a train ride returning from the 1958 World Series victory in Milwaukee. A celebration was taking place on the train and one of the players, relief pitcher Ryne Duren, a little over exuberant, thought it would be fun to smash Houk's ever present cigar in his face. Houk didn't appreciate the humor and decked Duren. From that point on the word was out, you don't mess with the "Major."

One of Houk's first moves in 1961 was to switch Roger Maris (at left) and Mickey Mantle in the batting order. Maris would now bat third and Mantle fourth. (New York Yankees Archives)

One of Houk's first moves was to bring in his old teammate and friend, Johnny Sain, as pitching coach. Sain was from the old school, a believer that a pitcher's arm is more durable than most people think. He advocated more work for pitchers, not less, and was a strong exponent of starting pitchers working every fourth day, instead of the current trend of four days off between starts.

Houk agreed with Sain's view and decided to implement the new plan. One night, while

LEFT: *The pressure often plagued Maris in his chase of Babe Ruth's record. On September 24 in Boston he failed to hit a home run against the Red Sox and was stuck at 59. Teammate Bob Cerv (at left) and broadcaster Phil Rizzuto try to console the slugger. (UPI/Bettmann)*

BELOW: *By mid-summer of '61 Mantle and Maris were the scourge of the American League. (UPI/Bettmann)*

ABOVE: *Although competing for the same record, Mantle and Maris were close friends who shared an apartment in Queens. (UPI/Bettmann)*

Mantle (below) grabbed the early lead in the home run race, but Maris (right) caught and passed him in mid-August. (New York Yankees Archives)

Maris admires home run number 60, which tied Babe Ruth on September 26 against Baltimore's Jack Fisher.
(New York Yankees Archives)

Moved by manager Ralph Houk to a four-day rotation, Whitey Ford enjoyed his greatest season in 1961 with a record of 25-4. (UPI/Bettmann)

attending a New York Knicks basketball game at Madison Square Garden, Houk ran into Whitey Ford. While Ford was the ace of the Yankees' staff, averaging 15 victories in the previous eight seasons, he had never won 20 games.

"What do you think about starting every fourth day instead of every fifth?" Houk asked.

"I'd love it," Ford replied.

Houk would make another change that would have a powerful impact on the Yankees season. He switched the batting positions of Mickey Mantle and Roger Maris.

Since he became established as the Yankees leader and best player in 1952, Mantle had batted in the No. 3 position in the batting order. Houk consulted with his star, telling him he wanted him to bat in the cleanup spot with Maris taking over the third position. Mantle, Houk reasoned, would do his customary damage in any spot in the batting order, and batting fourth would afford him greater opportunity for driving in runs. Maris, on the other hand, would benefit by having Mantle batting behind him. He would be assured of getting better pitches to hit.

Houk had inherited from Stengel an outstanding team comprised of seasoned veterans who had been through the baseball wars and won championships, such as Mantle and Maris, Yogi Berra, Whitey Ford and Bill "Moose" Skowron; and excellent young players in Tony Kubek, Bobby Richardson, Clete Boyer, Elston Howard, Bill Stafford and Ralph Terry. The team had everything, power, pitching and defense.

"But," said Houk, "when we started playing games in spring training, we couldn't win. I was beginning to wonder what I had gotten myself into."

His veteran players assured him they would be ready when the bell rang. It rang on April 11 against the Minnesota Twins in Yankee Stadium. The Yankees lost, 6-0.

They then won their next five, lost three straight, then won eight out of nine. Through the months of June and into July, the Yankees battled neck-and-neck with the Detroit Tigers, each taking a turn at leading the league. Finally, on July 18, the Yankees moved into first place to stay, winning the pennant by eight games.

But almost overshadowing the pennant race was the assault by Mantle and Maris on the most exalted, most time-honored, most cherished of all baseball records, Babe Ruth's 60 home runs in a season, established 34 years earlier, in 1927, and believed to be (with Joe DiMaggio's 56 game hitting streak) one record that would last forever.

Maris didn't exactly come flying out of the chute in the 1961 season. He just sort of sneaked up on the home run list, giving no omen of what was to come. He didn't hit his first home run until the Yankees' 11th game. By the time he hit his second, six games later, Mantle, his more popular and more respected teammate, had hit eight.

From 1957 to 1965 the Yankees boasted one of baseball's best doubleplay combinations, second baseman Bobby Richardson (at left) and shortstop Tony Kubek, seen here turning two in the 1960 World Series. (New York Yankees Archives)

In mid-May, Maris' home run bat started smoking and the home runs came in bunches. He hit 10 in 14 games, but it wasn't until he hit No. 14, in the Yankees' 44th game on June 2, that he drew even with Mantle. At that point, the newspapers paid more attention to the terrific tandem, hailing the M&M Boys, than they did to any assault on Ruth's record.

Through the months of June and July, Mantle and Maris were on fire, a dynamic duo of power, their individual and friendly rivalry inspiring each other. At the All-Star break, Maris had 33 homers, Mantle 29.

But Mantle was on a roll in July and early August. When he belted three in a doubleheader against the Twins on August 6, it gave him 43 for the season, putting him 24 games ahead of Ruth's pace, but only two home runs ahead of Maris.

On the day after Mantle's three-homer binge, Maris bunted for a base hit, raising eyebrows, but winning a game. Was this any way to chase Babe Ruth?

"I guess that shows you he's not greedy," said manager Houk. "He must not have been thinking of the record. He must have been thinking of winning."

Said Maris: "I told you this game isn't all made up of home runs. Bunts count, too. If they're going to play back, I'm going to bunt. You put a man on third base and I don't care if I have the hottest bat in the league. My job is to try to score him."

As the home run race heated up, so did the emotions of those in the game. Oldtimers questioned the worthiness of Mantle or Maris to displace Ruth from his home run throne. Even Commissioner Ford C. Frick threw his asterisk into the ring.

Frick was an old baseball writer from Ruth's day and a great friend and admirer of the Bambino. His admiration bordered on idolatry and colored his thinking. Fearful that Mantle or Maris would break Ruth's record, Frick took a controversial stand as if on a one-man crusade to protect and perpetuate the Ruth image and record.

Noting that because of expansion the American League schedule had been increased to 162 games, eight more than in Ruth's day, Frick handed down an autonomous ruling. Should any player exceed Ruth's record of 60 home runs in a season, it would be noted with a "distinguishing mark" that the usurper did so in an expanded season.

Frick never used the word "asterisk," but some baseball writers did and it took hold.

Oldtimers cheered Frick's decision. Rational men scorned it on the premise that a season is a season.

61

Home run Number 61 came on the final game of the season on October 1 against Boston's Tracy Stallard in the fourth inning. (UPI/Bettmann)

A modest hero (left), Maris had to be pushed onto the field by his teammates for a curtain call after his historic home run. (UPI/Bettmann)

ABOVE: *The Yankees' three catchers in 1961, Yogi Berra (left), Elston Howard (center) and Johnny Blanchard (right), combined for 64 home runs. As a team, the Yankees' 240 home runs set a major league record. (UPI/Bettmann)*

BELOW: *Elston Howard was a Yankee for 12 seasons and won the AL's Most Valuable Player Award in 1963. He later coached and worked in the Yankees' front office. (New York Yankees Archives)*

Ford was dubbed the "Chairman of the Board" by his batterymate Elston Howard (at right). (New York Yankees Archives)

Many observers regarded Clete Boyer as one of the greatest defensive third basemen in the game's history, the equal of Hall of Famer Brooks Robinson. (New York Yankees Archives)

The controversy raged heatedly throughout the summer, with Mantle and Maris innocent bystanders.

On August 13, Maris completed a four-game series in Washington in which he went on a home run-a-game diet to draw even with Mantle at 45, 16 games ahead of Ruth. The possibility of breaking the record was mentioned to Maris.

"Don't ask me about that bleeping record," Roger exploded. "I don't want to talk about it. All I'm interested in is winning the pennant."

Clete Boyer (above), one of three brothers to play in the major leagues, spent eight years in Pinstripes and later became a Yankee coach. (New York Yankees Archives)

After winning 25 games in the regular season, Whitey Ford (right) started Game 1 of the 1961 World Series and broke a Series record for consecutive scoreless innings (32) held by Babe Ruth. (UPI/Bettmann)

On September 2, Maris hit two homers against the Tigers, his 52nd and 53rd. Mantle, at 48, suffered a pulled muscle in his left forearm. Although he refused to sit, it cost him some power and, perhaps, a home run or two.

Eight days later, the count was Maris 56, Mantle 53, both still with a legitimate chance at catching Ruth within the 154-game limit prescribed by Frick (they had nine games left to reach 154) or in 162 games. Within days, Mantle's chances had vanished. Suffering with the flu, he went to a doctor for a flu shot and apparently was injected with a contaminated needle. He developed an abscess in his hip, where he had been shot, that caused him excruciating pain and left him sidelined for several days.

Mantle would hit just one more home run for the remainder of the season and he would leave Maris to carry the ball alone.

"I'm finished, Rog," Mantle told his friend. "I can't make it. It's up to you."

Of all the players who could have been tapped to challenge baseball's most cherished, most legendary and most revered record, Roger Maris was among the least likely. He never sought the spotlight, didn't want it and didn't know how to handle it when he got it.

Maris was a simple man of simple tastes and a simple lifestyle. He was a devoted family man, not a flamboyant man-about-town, a private person, not a celebrity, a blue-collar baseball player, not a poster-boy hero.

In some ways, chasing Ruth's exalted record chipped away at Maris' popularity rather than enhanced it. To many, he was unworthy to stand alongside the great Babe, an ingrate, an upstart, a pretender to the great man's throne, a player who had come into the season with a lifetime batting average of .257 and 97 home runs in four seasons.

Ruth, and the record, would have been better served had Maris' teammate, Mickey Mantle, challenged it, or Willie Mays or Ted Williams or Henry Aaron.

But Maris was the chosen one, and the pressure on him was so intense, it caused patches of his hair to fall out.

Maris hit home run No. 58 in Detroit in the Yankees' 152nd game, leaving him three games in which to tie Ruth's record under Frick's edict (there had been a tie earlier in the season which would be

The Yankees received a big boost in 1962 when Tom Tresh, seen here being congratulated by Mickey Mantle, Elston Howard, and Joe Pepitone after hitting a grand slam, was named the AL's Rookie of the Year. (New York Yankees Archives)

replayed and would count as part of the 154-game schedule). The Yankees played a doubleheader in Baltimore on September 19. Maris came to bat nine times. He walked once and singled, but was victimized by a stiff wind from Hurricane Ethel blowing in from right field that held up a couple of his drives.

There was one game left in the Frick deadline and Roger needed two home runs to tie Ruth, three to break the record.

"You'd be almost a Houdini if you did it," Maris said.

He was no Houdini, but Maris gave it a shot. He leaned into a Milt Pappas fastball in the first inning. On a normal night, it would have been out, but the stiff wind was still whipping in from rightfield and it held the ball up at the fence.

In his second at-bat, Maris got into another fastball, driving it through the wind, into the rightfield seats.

"As I went around the bases," Maris said later, "I was thinking, 'That's 59.' I had two, maybe three more shots at it."

When he batted a third time, the pitcher was Dick Hall. Maris struck out. In his fourth at-bat, he had two shots at No. 60. One was a long drive that had the distance, but hooked foul. The other was another tremendous drive that was knocked down by the wind and caught at the fence.

There was one more chance in the ninth inning. Maris would be the Yankees' third hitter, but Orioles manager Luman Harris had brought in the veteran knuckleballer Hoyt Wilhelm to pitch the inning. Maris would rather face the toughest left-hander in the league than a knuckleballer. He took a strike, then tried to check his swing. The ball hit his bat and trickled back to the mound.

Maris had failed to hit 60 home runs in the prescribed 154 games plus one tie, but it wasn't over.

"My season is 162 games," he said.

It would be five games before he would hit his next

RIGHT: *A mainstay for the Yankees in the late '50s and early '60s was Bill "Moose" Skowron who hit 28 home runs in 1961.*

BELOW: *Kubek was Rookie of the Year in 1957. He retired after the 1965 season at the age of 28 and later became a successful broadcaster.*

BELOW RIGHT: *Richardson was a Yankee for 12 seasons and also retired prematurely at age 31. In 1962, he led the American League with 209 hits. (all photos: New York Yankees Archives)*

The 1961 World Series was the second of five consecutive appearances the Yankees would make in the Fall Classic to start the decade. (New York Yankees Archives)

BANKERS
TRUST
AUTOMATS
402FT
36

homer, connecting against Jack Fisher of the Orioles for No. 60 in the third inning of the Yankees' 159th game. He had tied Ruth, even if it would not be officially recognized. Still, he had hit as many home runs in one season as any player in major league history.

The fanfare for Maris' tremendous feat was relatively subdued. The *Associated Press* account said, "Roger Maris blasted his 60th homer of the season Tuesday night, but it came four official games too late to officially tie Babe Ruth's 34-year old record in 154 games."

Ralph Terry, who threw the pitch that Bill Mazeroski hit to beat the Yankees in the 1960 World Series, came back two years later in Game 7 of the 1962 Series and beat the San Francisco Giants. (New York Yankees Archives)

The day after tying the record, Maris went to manager Ralph Houk's office.

"I'm beat, Ralph," Roger said. "I need a day off."

"You can't take a day off," Houk pleaded. "You're going for the record."

"I can't stand it any more," Maris said.

"What should I tell the press?" Houk asked.

"Tell them I went fishing."

Maris sat out game No. 160, and failed to hit a home run in game No. 161. That brought him to the final game of the season, still tied with Ruth, officially or unofficially. One game remaining to become baseball's all-time single season home run champion.

It was a bright, sunny, early fall Sunday afternoon. The Boston Red Sox were in town and Tracy Stallard, a hard-throwing right-hander, was pitching for Boston; the kind of pitcher Maris usually blistered.

In his first at-bat, Stallard fooled Maris with a changeup and Roger popped it softly into leftfield. He came to bat again in the fourth. Phil Rizzuto was on the air, on WPIX, channel 11. This was his call:

"Here comes Roger Maris. They're standing up, waiting to see if Roger is going to hit No. 61. Here's the windup...the pitch to Roger...Way outside, ball one (Boos). The fans are starting to boo....Low, ball two. That one was in the dirt. And the boos get louder. Two balls, no strikes on Roger Maris. Here's the windup...fastball...HIT DEEP TO RIGHT...THIS COULD BE IT....HOLY COW....HE DID IT...61 HOME RUNS...They're fighting for the ball out there. Holy cow...another standing ovation for Roger Maris."

Veteran baseball observers compared the '61 Yankees with their 1927 and 1939 forebears, both of whom have their supporters for the designation, "Baseball's Greatest Team."

With their combined total of 115 home runs, Maris and Mantle hit more homers than any two teammates in history, eight more than Babe Ruth and Lou Gehrig smacked in 1927. Maris led the league with 142 RBIs and won his second consecutive Most Valuable Player award. Mantle knocked in 128 runs.

In addition, Skowron hit 28 homers and the three catchers, Elston Howard, Yogi Berra and Johnny Blanchard, combined for 64 homers. Howard batted .348 and the Yankees set an all-time record with a team total of 240 homers. Ford, pitching on his four-day rotation, had his greatest season, a record of 25-4.

The Yankees met the Cincinnati Reds in the World Series and beat them in five games despite injuries to two key players. Mantle, still suffering with the abscess in his hip, missed the first two games. He started Game 3 and was hitless in four at-bats, then had to leave Game 4 in the fourth inning and never got back in the lineup.

Ford pitched a two-hit shutout in Game 1 and was forced to leave after five innings of Game 4 with an injured foot. When he left, Ford had recorded 32 consecutive scoreless innings in World Series competition, breaking the record Babe Ruth established as a Boston Red Sox pitcher of 29.2 consecutive scoreless innings.

The question in 1962 was what could the Yankees do for an encore. Certainly, it was too much to expect Maris to even come close to his 1961 numbers, and he didn't, slipping to 33 homers and 100 RBIs. Mantle, injured much of the season, hit 30 homers and drove in 89 runs in only 123 games, which earned him his second Most Valuable Player award. Ford fell off to 17-8.

But the Yankees got help from some unexpected quarters. Rookie Tom Tresh played shortstop in place of Tony Kubek, who was in military service, and had 20 homers and 93 RBIs and was named American League Rookie of the Year. Ralph Terry won 23 games to assume Ford's position as ace of the pitching staff. And the Yankees finished five games ahead of the Minnesota Twins to win their third straight pennant.

The 1962 World Series, against the San Francisco Giants, was one of the most memorable ever, only partly because heavy rains in San Francisco caused a four-day hiatus between Games 5 and 6.

Going into Game 6, the Yankees led, three games to two, but veteran Billy Pierce stymied the Yankees on a three-hitter and beat Whitey Ford to force a sudden death seventh game. It would be one of the most dramatic games in World Series history, Terry against veteran right-hander, Jack Sanford.

Neither team scored in the first four innings, then in the top of the fifth, the Yankees loaded the bases with none out. Giants manager Alvin Dark elected to play his infield in, rather than cut the run off at the plate, and the Yankees scored when Tony Kubek, back from military duty, hit into a double play.

The score remained 1-0 Yankees going into the bottom of the ninth. Pinch hitter Matty Alou led off with an infield hit. Terry then struck out Felipe Alou and Chuck Hiller and faced the aging, but still dangerous Willie Mays, who ripped a line drive into the right-field corner. When the ball was hit, it looked like it would rattle around in the corner long enough for Alou to score, but Maris, showing his defensive brilliance, cut the ball off and quickly fired a perfect strike to second baseman Bobby Richardson, whose equally quick relay home held Alou at third.

Maris' 62nd home run of 1961 was a Game 3, ninth inning blast at Crosley Field off Bob Purkey. (UPI/Bettmann)

The play that saved the '62 Series.In the ninth inning of Game 7, Maris made a quick recovery of Willie Mays' double in the rightfield corner and fired the ball to second baseman Bobby Richardson, whose relay throw to catcher Elston Howard held the tying run, Matty Alou, at third base. (New York Yankees Archives)

With the awesome Willie McCovey, a powerful left-handed hitter due up, manager Ralph Houk paid a visit to the mound. But he decided to stay with his starter, Terry, victim of Bill Mazeroski's Series-winning home run two years before.

McCovey threw a scare into the Yankees, and thrilled the Candlestick Park crowd, by hitting a long drive over the rightfield fence, but foul. On the next pitch, McCovey hit a bullet, headed for rightfield. When it left the bat, it looked like a hit that would score two runs and give the Giants the game and the Series. But the ball stayed low enough for second baseman Richardson to reach up and make the catch, preserving the Yankees 1-0 victory and giving them their second consecutive world championship.

The Yankees showed amazing resourcefulness to win their fourth straight pennant in 1963. With injuries severely curtailing Mantle (65 games, 15 homers, 35 RBIs) and Maris (90 games, 23 homers, 53 RBIs), other veteran Yankees and some newcomers stepped up as the Yankees won 104 games and finished 10 games ahead of the Chicago White Sox.

Skowron had been traded to the Los Angeles Dodgers for pitcher Stan Williams. In Skowron's place, Joe Pepitone hit 27 homers and drove in 89 runs. Kubek returned to reclaim his shortstop position, moving Tresh to the outfield to hit 25 homers and knock in 71 runs. Elston Howard, now the full-time catcher as Yogi Berra was giving in to age, belted 28 homers and drove in 85 runs.

Whitey Ford returned to his 1961 form, winning 24 and losing 7. Two newcomers to the pitching staff, Jim Bouton and Al Downing, combined for 34 wins, 21 of them for Bouton.

The Yankees and Dodgers, who had met five times in the World Series when the Dodgers were in Brooklyn, met again in the 1963 World Series for the first time since the Dodgers moved to Los Angeles. It was a Dodger team built on pitching, with a Big Three of Sandy Koufax, Don Drysdale and Johnny Podres, who combined for 58 victories, and Ron Perranoski, who won 16 games in relief and saved 21 others.

Koufax, who was 25-5 with a 1.88 ERA, 11 shutouts and 306 strikeouts in the regular season, set the tone in the World Series, beating Ford, 5-2 in Game 1 and striking out a record 15 batters. Podres, who was the winning pitcher in the seventh game of the 1955 Series, the only time the Dodgers beat the Yankees, won Game 2. Drysdale pitched a three-hitter to beat Bouton, 1-0, in Game 3.

Down three games to none, the Yankees knew they were up against it as Ford faced Koufax in Game 4 in Dodger Stadium. Both left-handers pitched brilliantly. Going into the bottom of the seventh, the score was tied, 1-1, the two runs scoring on home runs by Mickey Mantle for the Yankees and Frank Howard for the Dodgers.

In the bottom of the seventh, Jim Gilliam led off with a grounder to third baseman Clete Boyer, who fired across the diamond to first baseman Pepitone. But the ball got past Pepitone for a three base error and Willie Davis followed with a sacrifice fly for what would be the winning run.

Later, Pepitone would say he lost the ball in the white shirts of the fans sitting in the box seats behind third base. Nevertheless, the way Koufax was pitching, the Yankees probably weren't going to score another run against him, and with Podres, Drysdale and Koufax, again, scheduled to work the next three games, the four-game sweep by the Dodgers probably merely accelerated the inevitable.

In his first three years, Ralph Houk was almost perfect as a manager. Three seasons, 309 wins, three pennants, two world championships. It would be difficult to improve on his record and Houk wasn't about to tarnish what he had achieved. When the Yankees asked him to take off his uniform and fill their vacant General Manager's chair, Houk readily accepted. But who would replace him? Who could possibly fill so large a void?

The Yankees decided there was one perfect candidate, one of the most popular players in the team's long and glorious history, whose illustrious career was drawing to a close. One Lawrence Peter Berra. The man called "Yogi."

After winning pennants in each of his first three seasons as Yankees manager, Ralph Houk was promoted to General Manager in 1964. (New York Yankees Archives)

After a Hall of Fame career, Yogi Berra was selected by the Yankees to succeed Ralph Houk as manager in 1964.
(New York Yankees Archives)

"It Gets Late Early"

The first time Yogi Berra walked into the Yankees' clubhouse, Pete Sheehy, the team's veteran clubhouse manager who had been there since Babe Ruth's day, took one look at the squat, round-shouldered, burly, gnome-like kid wearing a sailor's suit that seemed two sizes too large and exclaimed, "Who the hell is that?"

The year was 1945. Berra was a Yankee farmhand, signed out of high school. After one season in the minor leagues, he had been drafted into the Navy and was serving in nearby New London, Connecticut, so he decided to pay a visit to Yankee Stadium.

He was born Lawrence Peter Berra to Italian immigrants in St. Louis. To his friends, he was Larry. To his relatives, he was "Lawdie." He became "Yogi" one summer afternoon. A bunch of kids from the section in St. Louis known as "The Hill" had gone to a movie. There was a travelogue about India featuring a Hindu fakir called a yogi, who sat with his arms folded and his legs crossed and a look of solemnity and sadness on his face. One of the kids decided the fakir looked like their pal, Lawdie. From that day on, Lawdie Berra was Yogi Berra.

Young Yogi was a terrific baseball player. He and his pal, Joey Garagiola, were the best in the neighborhood, which is why it was a surprise to all, and a disappointment to Yogi, that the hometown Cardinals signed his pal Joey to a contract for a bonus of $500 and bypassed Yogi.

Young Yogi with his pals from "The Hill" section of St. Louis. That's our hero third from left in the middle row. (New York Yankees Archives)

It was the commander of the local American Legion Post who wrote a letter to the Yankees telling them of this kid, Larry Berra, who could hit and throw and field. The Yankees sent bullpen coach John Schulte, a St. Louis resident, to look at the kid. Schulte liked what he saw and recommended that the Yankees sign Berra. But Yogi wouldn't sign unless he got the same bonus as his pal Joey received from the Cardinals, $500, no more, no less.

The Yankees sent Berra to their Norfolk farm team in 1943. He appeared in 111 games, batted .253, hit 7 home runs and drove in 56 runs. In back-to-back games, he knocked in the remarkable total of 23 runs. Years later, when he was asked how he was able to drive in 23 runs in two games, Berra replied, "Every time I came to bat, there were men on base."

Upon his discharge from the Navy, Berra was sent to the Yankees' powerhouse Newark farm team in the International League, which had spawned so many great Yankee stars. There, he batted .314 with 15 homers and 58 RBI in 77 games, which earned him a promotion to the Yankees for the final two weeks of the 1946 season. In 22 at bats with the Yankees, Berra batted .364 and the team

A rare photo of a young Yogi with the legendary Babe Ruth less than two months before his death in 1948. (UPI/Bettmann)

decided he was to be their catcher of the future.

He was awkward and unpolished, but he had wonderful natural gifts, an eagerness to improve, a willingness to work and he could hit, even if he did sometimes swing at balls over his head or in the dirt: Swing at them and hit them for line drives. The Yankees turned him over to coach Bill Dickey, the Hall of Fame catcher, with instructions to mold him into a major league catcher. Or as Berra said, "Bill Dickey is learning me all his experiences."

Berra learned his lessons well. Soon, he was the Yankees' regular catcher on his way to being a star and one of baseball's most unforgettable characters. He even was outdoing his pal, Joe Garagiola, who made it to the Cardinals in 1946 and batted .316 in the World Series.

In recognition of Berra's accomplishments, when the Yankees went to St. Louis late in the 1947 season, the folks from "The Hill" gave him a night. Berra was thrilled and flattered. He also was frightened to death. It meant he'd have to make a speech.

It must have been someone with the Yankees possessed of a weird sense of humor who roomed Berra with third baseman Bobby Brown, a young man from Fort Worth, Texas, to whom baseball was merely a sideline. He was studying to be a doctor.

Berra got his opportunity to manage the Yankees when Ralph Houk (at left) was promoted to become the team's general manager. (New York Yankees Archives)

Legend has it that they would spend evenings on the road sitting in their room, reading. Brown would read his huge medical tomes. Berra would be voraciously absorbing the latest comic books. One night, according to legend, as Berra turned the last page of his comic, Brown closed his copy of Gray's Anatomy with a thud, and a sigh.

"How did yours come out?" Berra inquired.

Through the '50s, there was no finer catcher in major league baseball than Yogi Berra. In seven seasons, he batted .290 or better. For 10 consecutive seasons, he had at least 20 home runs. Five times he knocked in more than 100 runs, nine times 90 or more. Three times, in 1951, 1955 and 1956, he was named Most Valuable Player of the American League. And when he retired, he was the all-time leader in World Series games played, at bats, hits and doubles, second in runs and RBIs, third in walks and home runs.

He was strong, consistent and durable. In a six-year stretch from 1950 through 1955, he caught at least 140 games five times. And he was smart. Casey Stengel called him, "My assistant manager."

In addition to all of the above, there was no Yankee of his time, or any time, who was more popular with the fans and the press. So it was only natural that Berra would be chosen as manager to succeed Ralph Houk in 1964.

No matter that he had no managerial experience. As Yogi himself once remarked, "You observe a lot by watching." He had a veteran team of proven winners and stars, made up of players who were not only his teammates through the wars, but his friends. Players like Mantle, Ford, Maris, Boyer, Kubek, Howard, and Richardson would not take advantage of him. And they would play hard for him.

What had not been considered was that many of those Yankees stars had passed the age of 30. Their bodies breaking down more easily, their skills eroding ever so slightly, the Yankees were coming back to the field in the American League. They started slowly in 1964, losing four of their first five games, struggling to get over .500, standing 25-21, in fourth place, six games behind the Chicago White Sox on June 10.

Everybody said it was just a matter of time, that it

The Cardinals' Tim McCarver scores in the '64 Series as the ball gets away from catcher Elston Howard.

Phil Linz (above) tooted the harmonica that became the '64 Yankees rallying point in their drive for their fifth consecutive pennant.

Brooklyn-born Joe Pepitone (left) replaced Moose Skowron as Yankees first baseman in 1963 and hit 159 home runs in seven full seasons in Pinstripes.

(All photos: New York Yankees Archives)

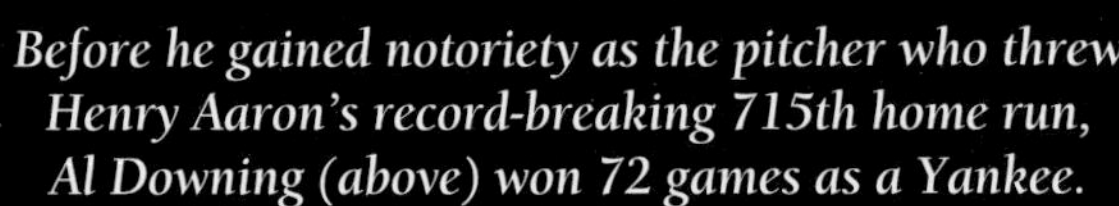

Before he gained notoriety as the pitcher who threw Henry Aaron's record-breaking 715th home run, Al Downing (above) won 72 games as a Yankee.

Hall of Famer Bob Gibson beat the Yankees twice in the '64 Series. He also broke a few bats along the way as Bobby Richardson can attest (below).

In 1963 and '64, Jim Bouton (top right) won 39 games for the Yankees.

Rookie Mel Stottlemyre (bottom right) joined the Yankees in August of 1964 and his nine victories helped the club win the pennant. (All photos: New York Yankees Archives)

In spring training, 1964, Yogi managed against his mentor Casey Stengel, then leading the Mets. (UPI/Bettmann)

Yankee Stadium was the scene of a World Series for the fifth straight year in 1964. (New York Yankees Archives)

takes warmer months for a veteran team to get it in gear, that the Yankees would turn it on and win going away, as usual. In fact, they did put on a spurt in June, winning seven straight, 13 of 15, to take over first place on June 22. But they then lost four straight to lose the lead to the Baltimore Orioles.

The Yankees remained inconsistent through the early part of July, jockeying with the Orioles for first place, but moved into the lead on July 26 and held it until August 7, when they were shut out by the Orioles.

On August 10, the team trailed the Orioles by 2 1/2 games as they headed for Chicago, where disaster struck. The White Sox swept the four-game series, and the Yankees had fallen 6 1/2 games out of first place.

It was Sunday, August 13, and the bus was outside Comiskey Park waiting for the Yankees to shower and dress and board the bus for the trip to the air-

Catcher Elston Howard leaps high for a late throw as the Cardinals' Curt Flood scores. (New York Yankees Archives)

port. One by one, the Yankees climbed aboard, most of them with their heads hanging down, embarrassed at being swept by the White Sox, dejected at the prospect of their fifth straight pennant slipping from their grasp.

Berra was already on the bus, sitting in the front seat, the "manager's seat," when shortstop Phil Linz came aboard. Linz was a blithe spirit, fun-loving and flaky. He had purchased a harmonica and some learner's sheet music and for the past week or so, he had been practicing on his harmonica. He saw no reason why he shouldn't practice while waiting for his teammates to board the bus, so he pulled out his sheet music and started playing "Mary Had A Little Lamb."

Berra was from the old school. When you lose, you don't play music, you don't sing, you don't laugh. When you lose, you sit quietly and pretend you're attending a funeral.

"Hey, Linz," Berra shouted to the back of the bus. "Take that harmonica and stuff it."

"What did he say?" Linz asked Mickey Mantle.

"He said to play louder," Mantle said.

So Linz played louder, at which point, Berra rose from his seat and headed for the back of the bus.

"I said to take that harmonica and stuff it," said a now angry Berra, angrier than most Yankees ever had seen him.

With that, Linz said, "Do it yourself," and flipped the harmonica to Berra, who swiped at it, knocking it into Joe Pepitone's leg. All hell broke loose. Pepitone began limping around the bus, claiming injury to his leg. Linz was shouting at Berra, who was shouting back at Linz. Mantle retrieved the harmonica and began tooting it.

"That's it for our manager," Mantle said. "From now on, I'm the manager. Here's the signal for the bunt...toot...Here's the signal for a steal...toot, toot."

By now, everybody on the bus was laughing, including Berra, and that was that. The incident was over as quickly as it started...until the next day, when it hit the papers.

It wasn't a major incident in any case, more humorous than serious. It ended quickly, but in some ways it served to clear the air and loosen the tension and it has been called a rallying point in the season.

In fact, the Yankees lost the first two games in Boston and fell six games out of first place on August 22, their low point of the season.

Then the Yankees won three straight, followed that with a four-game winning streak and a five-game streak. On September 16, the Yankees beat the

After winning the AL pennant and losing the World Series to the Cardinals in seven games, Yogi Berra was fired. (New York Yankees Archives)

Angels to move a half game out of first. The following day, they beat the Angels again to take over first place by percentage points. They then won their next nine for an 11-game winning streak to open a four-game lead with eight games to play.

But the Orioles refused to quit. They cut the lead in half and going into the final three games of the season against the Indians, the Yankees lead was two games. They beat the Indians on Friday night and again on Saturday, clinching their fourth consecutive pennant on the next-to-last day of the season.

Maybe it was the Harmonica Incident, maybe not. Maybe it was their manager's laid back, ever-optimistic approach. Maybe it was a last hurrah for a lot of veteran players. Maybe it was the big lift they got from a young right-hander named Mel Stottlemyre, who came up from Richmond on August 11 and won nine games in the stretch. Whatever the reason, Berra had won the pennant in his first season as a manager and the Yankees got set to face the St. Louis Cardinals in the World Series.

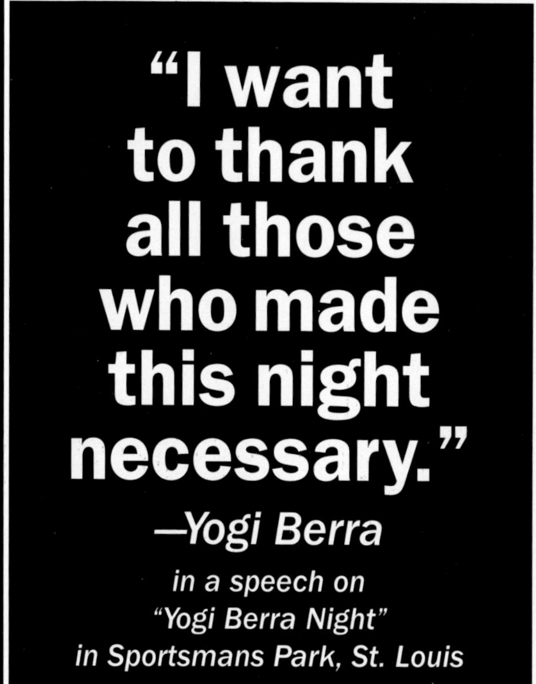

The Cards had come through in one of the closest pennant races in history, after the Philadelphia Phillies had blown a six and a half game lead in the final two weeks. Going into the final two games of the season, four teams, the Cardinals, Phillies, Cincinnati Reds and San Francisco Giants, had a chance to win the pennant. But the Cardinals won, rallying around their beleaguered manager Johnny Keane, who most of the season had been rumored to be on the verge of being replaced by Leo Durocher.

The Cardinals and Yankees split the first two games of the 1964 World Series in St. Louis and returned to New York for the middle three games. In Game 3, Mantle hit the first pitch of the bottom of the ninth, a knuckleball by ace Cardinals reliever Barney Schultz, into the rightfield seats to give the Yankees a dramatic 2-1 victory and a 2-1 lead in the Series.

But the Cardinals won the next two games and returned to St. Louis needing to win one out of two to take the world championship. Jim Bouton won Game 6 for the Yankees and it came down to the sudden death seventh game, Cards' ace right-hander Bob Gibson against the rookie, Stottlemyre.

The Cardinals struck for three in the fourth, forcing the Yankees to play catch-up. Stottlemyre was removed for a pinch hitter in the fifth and the Cards scored three more in the bottom of the fifth . The Yankees got three in the sixth off a tiring Gibson, pitching with only two days' rest. The Cards made it 7-3 with a run in the seventh.

In the top of the ninth, Gibson was running out of gas. Clete Boyer homered with one out to make it 7-4. Phil Linz homered with two out to make it 7-5. Cardinals' manager Keane stayed with an obviously spent Gibson, who got Bobby Richardson on an infield pop for the final out.

The Yankees had lost the World Series for the second straight year, but they had won five consecutive American League pennants and Berra had shown, as a rookie manager, the ability to rally an injury-riddled team from adversity.

On the plane ride back from St. Louis to New York, General Manager Ralph Houk slipped into the seat next to his manager and said, "Mr. Topping wants to see you in his office tomorrow morning at 10."

Berra had no negative thoughts, no premonitions about the request, although he did think it strange that the owner of the team wanted to see him on the morning after the Yankees had lost the seventh game of the World Series. Berra assumed it was to talk about his contract for 1965. But why couldn't that wait a day or two?

Dutifully, Berra awoke early the next day and reported to the Yankees' office at 745 Park Avenue, New York City.

Later that day, the Yankees called a press conference. It seemed a routine thing. The press figured it was being assembled to be told that Berra had been hired for 1965. Maybe for 1966 and 1967, as well, probably at a substantial pay raise. They were hardly prepared for what they heard.

Yogi Berra would not be back as manager of the New York Yankees in 1965. No successor was named.

YOGI'S 20 BEST BERRAISMS

His theory on golf:
"Ninety percent of the putts that fall short don't go in."

About a popular restaurant:
"Nobody goes there any more, it's too crowded."

Sizing up the pennant race:
"It ain't over 'til it's over."

On the shadows in leftfield at Yankee Stadium in the fall:
"It gets late early out there."

Asked for the correct time:
"Do you mean now?"

When a sportscaster presented him with a check made payable to "Bearer" when he appeared on a pre-game show:
"You know me over 20 years and you still don't know how to spell my name."

Explaining his collection of sweaters in a variety of colors:
"The only color I don't have is navy brown."

When coach Joe Altobelli turned 50:
"Now you're an old Italian scallion."

When Billy Martin locked his keys in his car:
"Ya gotta call a blacksmith."

After he and wife Carmen watched the movie, "The Magnificent Seven," with Steve McQueen:
"He made that movie before he died."

To the clubhouse man after a workout on a hot, humid day:
"Hey, Nick, get me a diet Tab."

To a sportswriter complaining that the hotel coffee shop charged $8.95 for a breakfast of orange juice, coffee and English muffins:
"That's because they have to import those English muffins."

Jim Bouton had asked Yankees public relations director Bob Fishel for a ticket to the opening game of the 1964 World Series in St. Louis. As the bus was about to leave for the airport, a breathless Fishel appeared with a manila envelope and told Bouton, "You're lucky, this is the last one." Said Berra:
"You mean they're out of them envelopes already?"

To a young player who was emulating the hitting style of a veteran player without much success:
"If you can't imitate him, don't copy him."

When asked what he does on the afternoon of a night game:
"I usually take a two-hour nap, from one to four."

Upon seeing a well-endowed blonde woman:
"Who's that, Dag-wood?"

Why he refused to buy new luggage:
"I only use it for traveling."

When someone refused his invitation to go deep sea fishing because he gets sea sick:
"What, on water?"

On his recognizability:
"Most everybody knows me by my face."

Disputing the veracity of much of the above:
"I really didn't say everything I said."

New York Yankkees Archives

To replace Yogi Berra as Yankees manager in 1965, General Manager Ralph Houk chose Johnny Keane, the man who beat Berra with the Cardinals in the 1964 World Series. (New York Yankees Archives)

Dismantled

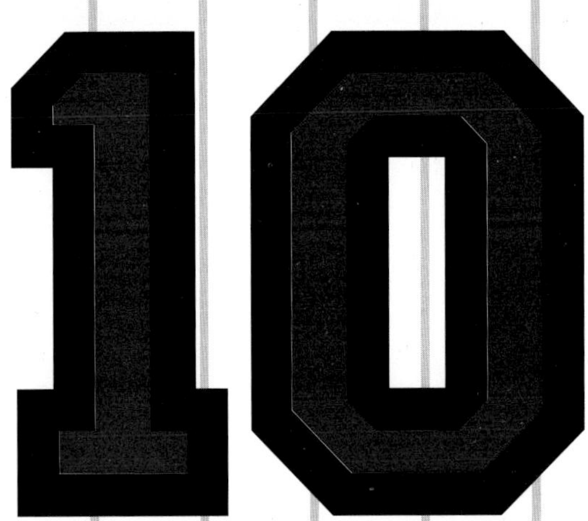

The Yankees' choice to replace Yogi Berra as their manager for the 1965 season was a curious one, none other than Johnny Keane, the man who guided the St. Louis Cardinals to their World Series victory over the Yankees.

Keane had been under fire by Cardinals president, Branch Rickey, for most of the 1964 season. Rumors abounded that Rickey wanted to bring the veteran Leo Durocher in to take over the team, but when the Cardinals got hot in August and September, Rickey backed off. To his surprise, and embarrassment, Keane's Cards won the National League pennant, then the World Series.

When Rickey went to Keane, hat in hand, with a generous offer to continue as manager of the Cardinals, Keane said, in effect, thanks, but no thanks.

There was speculation, never proven, that the reason Keane could be so independent was that he had already agreed to take over as manager of the Yankees. According to the theory, the Yankees decided in August that Berra would not return to manage in 1965 and, having made that decision, entered into a secret agreement with Keane.

Shortly after Keane was introduced as the new manager another curious development unfolded. On November 2, 1964, Dan Topping and Del Webb announced the sale of the Yankees to CBS.

Starting with the 1965 season, the Yankees embarked on the most unsuccessful period in their history since their early Highlanders/Yankees, pre-Ruthian days. They were to go 12 years without winning a championship, their longest drought since the 18 years at the franchise's start. Attendance would dwindle steadily to its lowest total since before World War II, failing to reach 1.2 million in seven consecutive seasons, from 1966 through 1972.

Keane took over an aging and injury-riddled team, the one bright spot was Mel Stottlemyre who won 20 games. (New York Yankees Archives)

In fairness to Keane, he inherited a team that was aging, breaking down physically and past its prime years. Playing on knees weakened by a series of operations and past his 33rd birthday, Mickey Mantle appeared in only 122 games, batted .255, hit 19 homers and drove in 46 runs. Roger Maris, suffering with a mysterious hand injury, played in only 46 games, had 8 homers and 27 RBIs. Elston Howard batted .233, Tony Kubek batted .218 and announced his retirement at the end of the season, a few days before his 29th birthday. Jim Bouton, a 21-game winner only two years

Wracked with pain for two seasons from his injuries, Mickey Mantle decided to hang up his number 7 after the 1968 season. June 8, 1969 at Yankee Stadium was Mickey Mantle Day and the man who played more games and had more at-bats than any Yankee ever said his last good-bye to the fans. (New York Yankees Archives)

MM-7

before, slipped to 4-15 after a bitter holdout.

There were few bright spots. Mel Stottlemyre won 20 games. Tom Tresh led the team in home runs with 26 and RBIs with 74. The Yankees won 77 games and lost 85 and finished sixth, their lowest standing in 40 years. While Keane may not have been at fault, his failure was vindication for Berra.

Keane lasted only 20 games into his second season. When he could win only four of them, he was fired and Ralph Houk was persuaded to put the uniform back on and take over as manager. While the players were happy to have the Major back as their leader, their performances failed to reflect their pleasure as they won only 70 games in 1966 and finished last in the 10-team American League.

Bobby Murcer, seen here with manager Johnny Keane broke in with the Yankees as an 18-year-old by appearing in 11 games in 1965. (New York Yankees Archives)

It was obvious the end was near for Mantle (23 homers, 53 RBIs) and Whitey Ford (2-5), and wholesale changes were needed, a complete overhaul for a team that had suddenly grown old together.

On November 29, 1966, Clete Boyer was traded to the Atlanta Braves for promising outfielder Bill Robinson and Chi Chi Olivo. Twelve days later, Roger Maris was traded to the St. Louis Cardinals for third baseman Charlie Smith. On August 1, 1967, with the Yankees destined to finish ninth, Elston Howard was traded to the Red Sox, lending his veteran leadership to their American League championship.

On May 30, 1967, Whitey Ford, suffering with a circulatory problem on his left side, retired after having won just two games in each of the past two seasons.

Mickey Mantle, moved from the outfield to first base to save his legs, struggled through pain-wracked seasons in 1967 and 1968. He reported to spring training for the 1969 season, but decided to retire, foregoing another $100,000 contract.

On June 8, 1969, the Yankees paid homage to the man who played more games and had more at bats than any player in Yankee history. He also finished his career third on the team's all-time list in runs, third in hits, fifth in doubles, ninth in triples, second in home runs, fourth in RBIs, ninth in batting average and eighth in stolen bases. The Oklahoma phenom had indeed been a worthy successor to the great DiMaggio. On "Mickey Mantle Day," his familiar uniform No. 7 was officially retired.

On June 15, 1969, Tom Tresh was traded to the Detroit Tigers for Ron Woods. On December 4, 1969, Joe Pepitone was dealt to the Houston Astros for Curt Blefary.

By 1970, a new cast of young players had moved in to take up residency in Yankee Stadium. Gene Michael was the regular shortstop, Roy White the leftfielder, Bobby Murcer the centerfielder, and the catcher was a squat, somewhat irascible youngster from Canton, Ohio, named Thurman Munson, who batted .302 and was named American League Rookie of the Year. With the arrival of expansion, the league's split into two divisions and the Yankees enjoyed their greatest success in six years in 1970, finishing second to the Baltimore Orioles in the American League East.

It was short-lived success, however, and equally short-lived hope that a resurgence was at hand. In 1971, with basically the same cast as the previous season, the Yankees won 11 fewer games than the year before and finished with a record of 82-80, fourth in the six-team division.

The 1972 season did not bring any significant improvement (a second straight fourth place finish), but it did bring to New York from Boston a player who would make a monumental contribution toward returning the Yankees to baseball's pinnacle. In a trade viewed by Red Sox fans with almost as much disdain as the one that sent Babe Ruth to the Yankees a half century earlier, the Red Sox sent left-handed relief pitcher Sparky Lyle to New York in exchange for Danny Cater, a journeyman first baseman.

In his first season in New York, Lyle gave Yankees fans a preview of things to come by winning 9 games and saving 35.

After eight years in which the Yankees finished

Twenty games into the 1966 season, Keane was fired and Ralph Houk moved out of the front office and back to the field. It didn't take long for him to realize the frustrations of managing a team in decline. (New York Yankees Archives)

Suffering with a circulatory ailment in his left side and having won only four games in two years, Whitey Ford announced his retirement May 30, 1967, leaving Mickey Mantle as the lone figure of the Yankee dynasty. (New York Yankees Archives)

higher than second just once and saw their attendance fall below one million customers for the first time in 27 years, CBS decided it was not suited for the baseball business. The network was losing money. It was, basically, an absentee owner. And it had people running the Yankees who had no previous experience in the baseball business. Consequently, its Board of Directors handed down orders to find a buyer for the team.

Their search took them to Cleveland, to a young entrepreneur, businessman and sportsman named George M. Steinbrenner III. As a boy, Steinbrenner had starred as a multi-sport athlete at Culver Military Academy and Williams College. Later, he would serve as an assistant football coach at Northwestern and Purdue.

His first fling at sports ownership was with the Cleveland Pipers of the American Basketball League, where he hired John McLendon to become the first black to be a head coach in a major sports league.

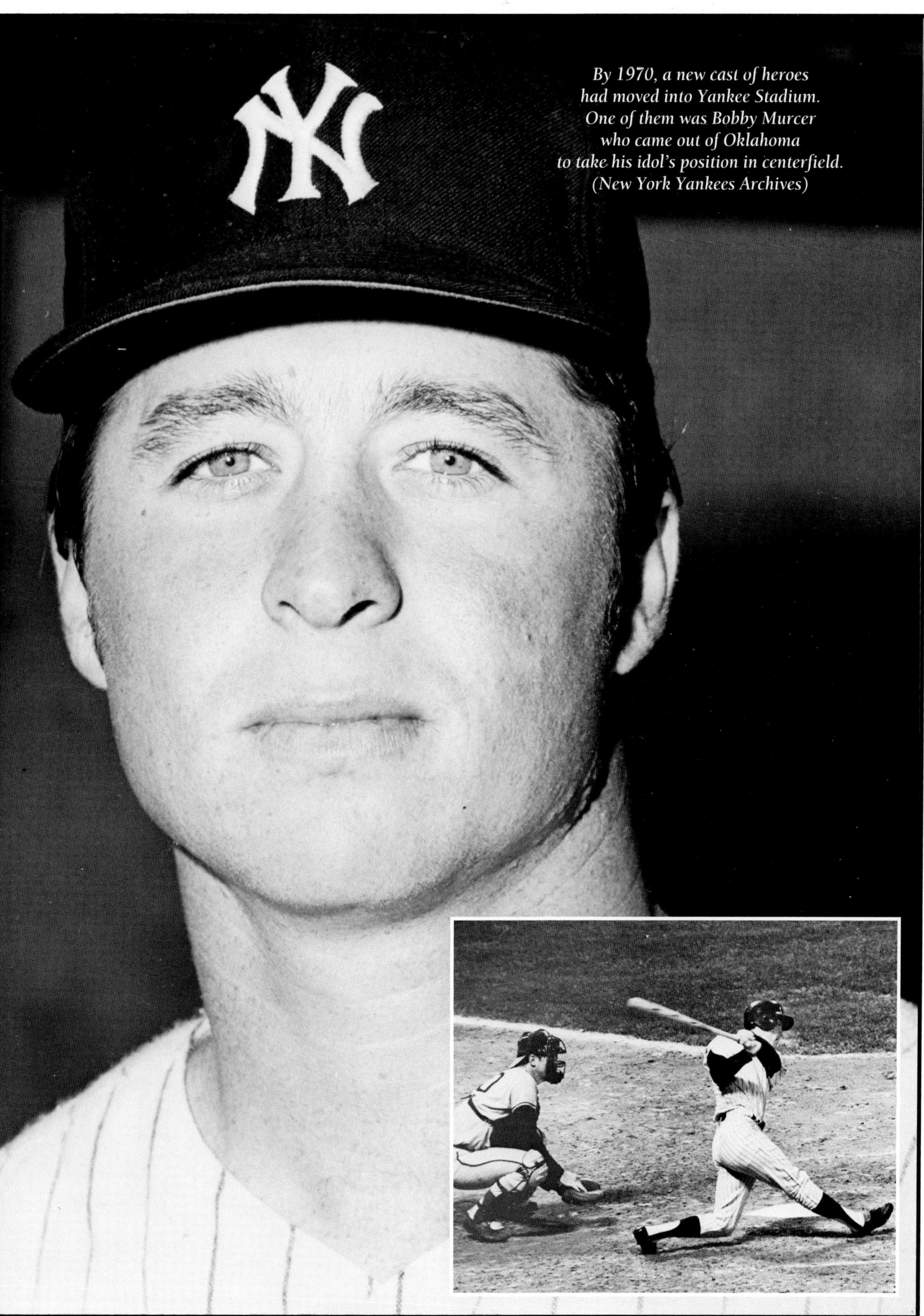

By 1970, a new cast of heroes had moved into Yankee Stadium. One of them was Bobby Murcer who came out of Oklahoma to take his idol's position in centerfield. (New York Yankees Archives)

The Yankees' number one draft choice in 1968 was a squat catcher from Kent Sate named Thurman Munson. Two years later he was the American League's Rookie of the Year. (New York Yankees Archives.)

Switch-hitter Roy White came to the Yankees in 1965 and stayed for 15 years, long enough to help the team win three consecutive pennants in the late '70s. (New York Yankees Archives)

A half century after they acquired Babe Ruth from the Red Sox, the Yankees made another important transaction with Boston when they acquired relief pitcher Sparky Lyle who became the ace of manager Houk's bullpen. (New York Yankees Archives)

Shortstop Gene Michael (at left) was purchased from the Dodgers after the '67 season and teamed with second baseman Horace Clarke. (New York Yankees Archives)

He entered the family business, Kinsman Marine, which carried iron ore, coal and grain on the Great Lakes, and built it into the American Shipbuilding Company and in a short time tripled its revenues with $200 million in annual sales. In 1970, *Fortune* magazine named Steinbrenner one of the nation's 12 "Movers and Shakers."

It was through a friend, Gabe Paul, the longtime baseball executive then serving as President and General Manager of the Cleveland Indians, that Steinbrenner learned that CBS was looking to sell the Yankees. Recognizing it as an opportunity of a lifetime, Steinbrenner put together a group of businessmen, mostly from Cleveland, and headed up a limited partnership that purchased the Yankees from CBS.

On January 3, 1973, at Yankee Stadium, George M. Steinbrenner III and Michael Burke, the man selected by CBS to operate the Yankees, met the press to announce that a 12-man group headed by two "general partners," himself and Steinbrenner, had purchased the Yankees for $10 million in cash, $3.2 million less than CBS had paid for the team, $5 million less than its intrinsic value as calculated by National Economics Research Associates.

"It's the best buy in sports today," Steinbrenner said. "I think it's a bargain. This is a dream come true. The Yankees are the greatest name in sports."

"The Yankees are the greatest name in sports."
– George M. Steinbrenner III, upon being introduced as the new managing general partner of the Yankees.

It's right for you!
Always a hit!

A New Era

An era was coming to an end with the final game of Yankee Stadium as we knew it. This photo is of the final game played in the old Stadium on September 30,1973. The old ballpark was to undergo a facelift and re-open in 1976. The Yankees would spend their next two years at Shea Stadium in Queens. (New York Yankees Archives)

The Yankees landed the left-handed, power-hitting third baseman they long had coveted when they acquired Graig Nettles from the Cleveland Indians on November 27,1972. (New York Yankees Archives)

On November 27, 1972, the Yankees pulled off a six-player trade with the Cleveland Indians that would have a long-range effect on Yankee fortunes. They dispatched four young players, John Ellis, Jerry Kenney, Rusty Torres and Charlie Spikes, to Cleveland for catcher Jerry Moses and Graig Nettles, a left-handed-hitting third baseman with an ideal Yankee Stadium stroke who had hit 71 home runs in three seasons with the Indians.

Shortly after George Steinbrenner took over, long-time baseball executive, shrewd and experienced Gabe Paul, left the employ of the Indians to join the Steinbrenner Yankees team as a limited partner, President and General Manager. Steinbrenner and Paul wasted little time overhauling their team.

The first deal in the Steinbrenner regime came just 13 days after he assumed command. On January 20, 1973, the Yankees acquired veteran outfielder Johnny Callison from the Chicago Cubs for relief pitcher Jack Aker. Four days short of three months later, with the season 10 days old, the Yankees purchased the contract of slugger Jim Ray Hart from the San Francisco Giants.

Steinbrenner was not the only newcomer to baseball in 1973 that would draw attention. The other was a rules change. The American League, acting independently and in opposition to the National League, adopted the designated hitter rule. Selected by Ralph Houk to be the Yankees' DH for their opener in Boston was Ron Blomberg, a popular and free-spirited Georgian. As it developed, the Yankees-Red Sox game in Boston was the earliest game scheduled for opening day, so Blomberg would be making history as baseball's first DH.

When that fact became known, writers covering the Yankees in spring training approached Blomberg and asked him how he felt about being the first designated hitter in baseball history.

"I don't know," he said. "I've never done it before."

The Yankees opened the 1973 season with four consecutive losses and on June 1 were a break-even team at 24-24, but in second place only two games behind the Detroit Tigers. Sensing a chance to finish first in a mediocre division, and recognizing the team's need for pitching, Steinbrenner instructed Paul to find some quality, experienced starting pitching. Two deals were consummated on the same day, June 7. Sam McDowell, a 20-game winner for the Indians three years earlier when he was regarded as the hardest thrower in the game, was purchased from San Francisco; Pat Dobson, a 20-game winner for the Baltimore Orioles two years before, was obtained from the Atlanta Braves in a trade for four prospects.

Before the season ended, the Yankees would add Mike Hegan, Duke Sims and Wayne Granger as the renovation continued, but they would again finish fourth for the third straight season, at 80-82. Steinbrenner knew there was still a great deal of work to be done.

The first order of business was to find a new manager, Ralph Houk having submitted his resignation on the final day of the season. As would become his style, Steinbrenner went after the best man for the job and settled on Dick Williams, who had won a pennant in Boston and had just won three consecu-

Another Yankee made history on opening day of the 1973 season in Boston when Ron Blomberg became baseball's first designated hitter. He walked with the bases loaded. (New York Yankees Archives)

The Yankees continued to bolster their roster by acquiring Lou Piniella (above/below) from Kansas City before the '74 season. Piniella was AL Rookie of the Year in 1969 and was later a major contributor to four Yankee championships. (New York Yankees Archives)

Ralph Houk resigned as manager after the 1973 season and was replaced by Bill Virdon (above) who began his minor league career as a Yankee in the early 1950s. (New York Yankee Archives)

In their first season at Shea Stadium, the 1974 Yankees stayed in contention for the AL East title until the next to last day of the season. Lou Piniella (at bat above) hit .305 that season, fourth best in the league. (New York Yankees Archives)

Fans and sportswriters were outraged when the Yankees traded four pitchers to Cleveland to acquire Chris Chambliss three weeks into the '74 season, but his production soon quieted those opposed to his arrival. (New York Yankees Archives)

A trade of All-Stars sent Bobby Murcer to San Francisco and brought Bobby Bonds to the Yankees for the 1975 season. Above is Bonds stealing second base against the Tigers. Check out Detroit shortstop Gene Michael. (New York Yankees Archives)

One of baseball's first big free-agent signings came at an unprecedented New Year's Eve signing in 1974 when Jim "Catfish" Hunter became a Yankee. (New York Yankees Archives)

While the Yankees were finishing their two-year stint at Shea, the renovation of Yankee Stadium (above) was nearing its completion. (New York Yankees Archives)

tive American League pennants and two straight world championships for Oakland. Williams was having problems with A's owner, Charles O. Finley, and was eager to leave Oakland.

Williams never got to manage the Yankees. Commissioner Bowie Kuhn ruled that Williams still had a valid contract with the A's. Kuhn suggested that if the Yankees and A's could agree on a deal, Williams would be free to leave Oakland.

As compensation for signing Williams, Finley demanded the Yankees' two best prospects, pitcher Scott McGregor and outfielder Otto Velez. The Yankees refused.

"We're not going to trade away our crown jewels," Paul said.

So the deal was voided and the Yankees began the search for another manager.

The search ended with Bill Virdon, who had managed the Pittsburgh Pirates to a division title in 1972, but lost to Cincinnati in the National League Championship Series. The following year, with his Pirates in second place, Virdon was fired after 136 games. The Pirates finished third.

Ironically, Virdon had originally signed with the Yankees, but he never made it to New York as a player. In 1954, he was traded to the St. Louis Cardinals along with two other minor leaguers for Enos Slaughter. Virdon went on to have a distinguished career with the Pirates, and played for them in the 1960 World Series against the Yankees. It was a ground ball off the bat of Virdon in the eighth inning of Game 7 that took a bad hop, hit Tony Kubek in the throat, and got the Pirates started on a five-run rally that turned a 7-4 Yankees lead into an 8-7 Pirates advantage.

As a footnote to history, Virdon would be the only

YANKS!

The Yankee faithful on Bat Day, June 2, 1973
(New York Yankees Archives)

By August 1, 1975, the Yankees had slipped into third place. Bill Virdon was replaced by longtime fan favorite Billy Martin. (New York Yankees Archives)

manager of the Yankees never to manage a game in Yankee Stadium. In August of 1972, the Yankees had entered into a deal with the City of New York to refurbish Yankee Stadium. The renovation began following the 1973 season and would not be completed until 1976. For the 1974 and '75 seasons, the Yankees played their home games at Shea Stadium as co-tenants with the New York Mets.

The Yankees' roster improvement continued in 1974. Before the start of the season, they had acquired shortstop Jim Mason and outfielder Elliott Maddox from Texas. Three weeks into the season, they pulled off a controversial trade with the Indians. The Yankees sent four pitchers, Fritz Peterson, Tom Buskey, Steve Kline and Fred Beene, to the Indians for first baseman Chris Chambliss and pitchers Dick Tidrow and Cecil Upshaw.

Fans and baseball writers were outraged. That a team, in desperate need for pitching, would trade away half its staff was mind-boggling. But Tidrow won 11 games and Rudy May arrived from the California Angels on June 15 to win eight more. With Pat Dobson and George Medich each winning 19, the Yankees stayed in contention in the American League East until the next-to-last day of the season when they lost to the Milwaukee Brewers and the Orioles won to clinch the division.

For winning 89 games, nine more than the previous season, and guiding the Yankees to their highest finish in four years, Virdon was named American League Manager of the Year.

More changes were forthcoming the following

year. Twenty days after the end of the 1974 season, the Yankees pulled off a spectacular trade of stars with the San Francisco Giants. They sent to the West Coast the most popular Yankee, Bobby Murcer.

In exchange for Murcer, the Yankees received Bobby Bonds, an electrifying player who two seasons before had missed by one home run becoming baseball's first 40-40 man (40 homers, 40 stolen bases).

The Yankees, or more properly Steinbrenner, pulled off the biggest coup on New Year's Eve. Writers were roused out of their homes, from parties, rounded up from midtown celebrations for a major press conference in the team's temporary offices near Shea Stadium. The purpose of the press conference was to announce the signing of Jim "Catfish" Hunter as a free agent for the princely sum of $2.5 million for five years.

It was headline news throughout the country. Hunter, considered the best pitcher in the game, just 28 years old and a 20-game winner in each of the previous four seasons (25-12 in 1974) had obtained his freedom from the Oakland Athletics and had become a free agent. In the first major courting of the free agent era, the Yankees won out over several other clubs for Hunter's services.

Coming off their surprising second-place finish of the previous season and adding an explosive offensive performer like Bonds and a solid pitching leader like Hunter, had Yankees fans excited about their team's prospects of ending an 11-year pennant drought. But the Yankees lost six of their first seven games in 1975, struggled through April and spent most of the month of May in fifth or sixth place in the American League East.

They climbed over the .500 mark on June 5 and even managed to pull into first place for a brief stay at the end of the month. But by August 1, they had fallen into third place, just two games over .500 and 10 games behind the Red Sox after beating the Indians at Shea Stadium. After the game, the writers were asked to assemble in a room near the Yankees clubhouse and were told that Virdon was no longer manager of the Yankees.

The man hired to replace Virdon was none other than Yankee hero Billy Martin, Battling Billy, who had been the guts of those championship Yankees teams of the '50s. After leaving the Yankees in 1957, and finishing his playing career in 1961, Martin scouted for the Minnesota Twins from 1962 through 1964, became the Twins third base coach in 1965, then embarked on his managerial career with Denver in the American Association in 1968. A year later, he returned to the Twins as manager and led them to their first division championship.

Martin was fired after his successful rookie season as Minnesota manager. He resurfaced as manager of the Detroit Tigers in 1971 and finished second. In 1972, he led the Tigers to a division championship, but was dismissed on September 1, 1973, with his team in third place. A week later, he was hired to manage the Texas Rangers for the final 23 games of the season. The Rangers finished sixth. The following year, with Martin there from the start of spring training, the Rangers finished second.

On July 21, 1975, Martin was let go by the Rangers. Twelve days later, he was hired to replace Bill Virdon as manager of the Yankees.

In his first full season with the Yankees as manager, Billy Martin brought his baseball brilliance and feistiness to a club on the verge of winning a championship.
(New York Yankees Archives)

Billy Ball

The hiring of popular Billy Martin to manage the Yankees was greeted enthusiastically by Yankees fans. As a player, Martin was a great fan favorite. He was fiery. He was feisty. He was combative. And he was a winner; a blue-collar player, a symbol for the average working guy, the perpetual underdog who usually finished on top.

As a player, Martin was at his best in big games. He was a Yankee for all or parts of seven seasons, and the Yankees won seven pennants and five world championships. In 28 World Series games, he hit five home runs, drove in 19 runs and batted .333, 76 points higher than his lifetime regular season average.

As a manager, he was close to genius, improving

The first game at renovated Yankee Stadium, Opening Day 1976. (New York Yankees Archives)

Bobby Bonds' stay in New York was not long, but he was used to acquire leadoff hitter Mickey Rivers (inset) and pitcher Ed Figueroa, who would later become the first native Puerto Rican to win 20 games. (New York Yankees Archives)

A Yankee for over a decade, Roy White (above) finally got a chance to play for a pennant winner in 1976 as he led the league in runs scored (104).

On the same day they acquired Rivers and Figueroa from California, the Yankees also picked up 21-year-old Willie Randolph (left) from the Pirates. Randolph went on to play an All-Star caliber second base for the next 13 years. (New York Yankees Archives)

The 1976 season was an exceptional one for Munson.
He batted .302, was second in the league in RBIs with 105 and was named Most Valuable Player.
(Focus On Sports)

Always a big game pitcher, Catfish Hunter started and won Game 1 of the 1976 American League Championship Series against Kansas City. (New York Yankees Archives)

teams immediately by his very presence. When Martin arrived for the final 56 games of the 1975 season, the Yankees were in third place, which is where they finished. But Martin brashly vowed a new beginning for 1976, confident he would improve the team once he had the opportunity to implement his unique style in spring training.

The 1976 season also marked the Yankees' return, after a two-year absence, to Yankee Stadium, following a major renovation. Befitting their new ballpark, the Yankees continued to overhaul their roster. Three off-season trades were to have a major impact on the team's fortunes, not only for 1976, but for years ahead.

On November 22, 1975, the Yankees sent pitcher Pat Dobson to the Cleveland Indians for outfielder Oscar Gamble, who would hit 17 home runs and drive in 57 runs while seeing limited duty. Then at baseball's annual winter meetings, the Yankees pulled off two blockbuster trades on the same day, December 11.

In one, Bobby Bonds was sent to the California Angels for centerfielder Mickey Rivers and pitcher Ed Figueroa. In the other, the Yankees swapped George Medich to the Pittsburgh Pirates for pitchers Dock Ellis and Ken Brett, and a gifted if untested second baseman from Brooklyn named Willie Randolph.

Rivers moved into the leadoff spot in the batting order, where he batted .312, rapped out 184 hits,

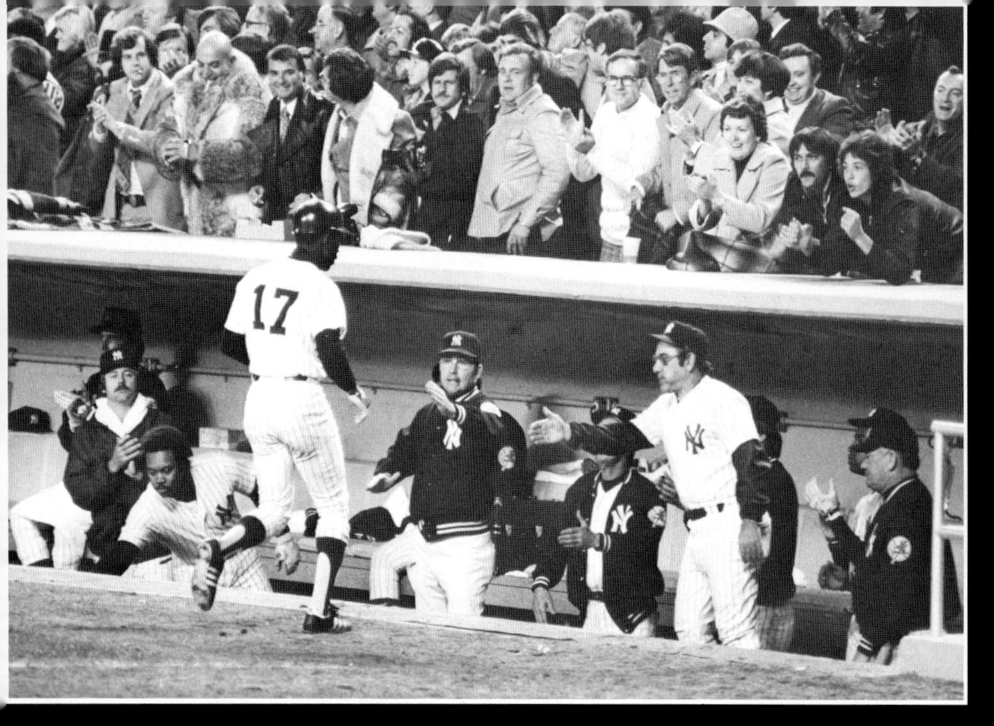

Mickey Rivers (left) was a catalyst for the Yankees' championship series victory. In five games he batted .348 and scored five runs.

In Game 3 of the '76 ALCS, Chris Chambliss (below) singled and homered, drving in three runs. It was a sign of things to come. (New York Yankees Archives)

Game 5 1976 ALCS

The detonation.

The exultation.

The celebration.

(background: UPI, insets AP)

After only four years, owner George Steinbrenner made good on his promise to bring New York a pennant. *(New York Yankees Archives)*

stole 43 bases, scored 95 runs and drove in 67. Randolph batted .267, stole 37 bases and gave the Yankees the sort of defense at second base they hadn't had since the days of Bobby Richardson. Figueroa became the Yankees biggest winner with 19 victories (two years later, he would become the first Puerto Rican-born pitcher to win 20 in the major leagues), and Ellis won 17 games, his highest win total in five seasons.

Steinbrenner and Paul continued their retooling during the season. On May 18, the Yankees obtained veteran Carlos May from the Chicago White Sox to serve as a left-handed pinch hitter, and on June 15, they pulled off a 10-player trade with the Baltimore Orioles, the Yankees' chief rival in the American League East. Going for all the marbles, the Yankees parted with prospects Scott McGregor, Tippy Martinez and Rick Dempsey, along with Rudy May and Dave Pagan, in order to acquire veteran pitchers Ken Holtzman, Doyle Alexander and Grant Jackson. For the Yankees, the future was now.

If winning a championship right now was the goal, the trade was a huge success. The Yankees had not been in the World Series in a dozen years and

The 1976 World Series featured baseball's top two catchers in Munson and Cincinnati's Johnny Bench and they did not disappoint. Bench batted .533 and was named Series MVP. Munson held up his end by hitting .529. (top: New York Yankees Archives, bottom: Lou Requena)

(New York Yankees Archives)

they figured they had waited long enough. Alexander and Holtzman won 19 games between them. Jackson was 6-0 in relief. That was more than enough to justify the trade as the Yankees finished 10 1/2 games ahead of the Orioles.

Newcomers Rivers and Randolph and veteran Roy White served as table setters for the power hitters– Graig Nettles, who led the league with 32 homers and knocked in 93 runs, Chris Chambliss, who drove in 96, and Thurman Munson, who batted .302 and finished second in the league in RBIs with 105, and was named American League Most Valuable Player.

Happy days were here again as the Yankees drew more than two million customers to Yankee Stadium for the first time in 26 years and prepared to meet the Kansas City Royals in the American League Championship Series.

The Yankees got the jump on the Royals by winning Game 1 of the best-of-five playoff, 4-1, in Kansas City. Catfish Hunter, who always excelled in big games, did it again, limiting the Royals to five hits.

The Royals rebounded to win Game 2, but the Yankees were confident as they returned to Yankee Stadium for the final three games of the series. As a prelude of things to come, Chambliss homered and drove in three runs in the Yankees' 5-3 victory in Game 3, leaving them one victory away from their 30th pennant.

It would prove to be an elusive victory as the Royals evened the series at two games apiece by winning Game 4, 7-4, despite two home runs by Nettles. That left it up to a sudden death fifth game, October 14, in Yankee Stadium.

Dennis Leonard started for the Royals against Ed Figueroa, who was touched up for two runs in the first. But the Yankees knocked Leonard out in the bottom of the first to tie the score. The Royals got a run in the second, but the Yankees came back with two in the third and two in the sixth to take a 6-3 lead.

The Stadium crowd was beginning to buzz with anticipation, sensing that the end was near and another World Series in the Bronx was at hand. But George Brett spoiled the fun by crashing a three-run homer in the eighth to tie the score, 6-6.

It stood that way going into the bottom of the ninth with the game in the hands of relievers, Dick Tidrow for the Yankees, Mark Littell for the Royals. Chambliss, hero of Game 3, was the first batter Littell would face in the bottom of the ninth. He threw one pitch. Chambliss swung mightily and sent a high, towering drive to rightfield.

The ball soared into the night, then disappeared over the wall. Yankee Stadium was bedlam. Pennant-starved revelers swarmed all over the field. Chambliss, hopped and skipped and ran around the bases, clutching his cap against souvenir-hunters, dodging and side-stepping bodies on his journey, then finally arriving home and landing on the plate with both feet to score the run that won the game and the pennant.

The Yankees hardly had time to savor their dramatic victory. The next day, they were on their way to Cincinnati, to take on the powerful Big Red Machine of Johnny Bench, Joe Morgan, Pete Rose and Tony Perez, defending world champions, in the World Series.

The Yankees never knew what hit them. Perez had three hits, Morgan homered and Don Gullett pitched a five-hitter and the Reds won Game 1.

In Game 2, the Reds scored three in the second off Hunter, but the Yankees came back to tie going into the bottom of the ninth when Perez singled home Ken Griffey for the winning run in a 4-3 victory.

Back in Yankee Stadium for Game 3, the Reds won again, 6-2, as Dan Driessen cracked three hits including a home run. Down to their last chance, the Yankees were destroyed by Bench, who belted a two-run homer in the fourth and a three-run homer in the ninth for a 7-2 Reds win and a four-game sweep of the Series.

Bench batted .533 for the Series, with two homers and six RBIs and overshadowed his counterpart, Munson, whose .529 average normally would have earned him rave reviews.

In the post-Series interview room, where the stars of the game and the managers met the press, Reds' manager Sparky Anderson took the podium and, as is his wont, waxed rhapsodic about his catcher.

"Don't embarrass nobody," Anderson said, "by comparing him to Johnny Bench."

Standing off to the side was Thurman Munson, disappointed at having played on the losing side, but proud that he had done his utmost to help his team. He bristled at Anderson's words, which he would never forget or forgive for the rest of his life.

The Yankees had had a great season. Munson had had a great season and a spectacular World Series, but in that moment, listening to Sparky Anderson, the Yankees catcher vowed that next year things were going to be different.

(Focus on Sports)

"Reggie... Reggie... Reggie!"

The centerfield flag pole in Yankee Stadium, upon which had been adorned the greatest array of championship banners known to the world of sports, had been barren these dozen years. The elegant, stately ballpark, which had been draped in bunting for a series of endless summers, had endured 12 starkly drab autumns. Then, in the fall of 1976, it came alive once again with the sounds and shouts of victory.

Billy Martin had brought his feistiness, his intensity and his tradition for success back home in a triumphant return.

Already in place was the indomitable spirit of Thurman Munson, the quiet efficiency of Chris Chambliss, the youthful exuberance of Willie Randolph, the defensive wizardry of Graig Nettles, the high octane energy of Mickey Rivers, the veteran professionalism of Roy White, the fiery temperament of Lou Piniella, the cocky swagger of Sparky Lyle and the consummate class of Catfish Hunter.

The Yankees would win their first pennant since 1964, but they would be dismembered in the World Series by the Cincinnati Reds juggernaut in a disappointing four-game sweep.

Clearly, the job was not yet complete. Yankees never did settle for second best, and they wouldn't rest until they brought another world championship to the Bronx. There was still work to be done, pieces to be fit into the puzzle.

The missing piece was put in place exactly one month and eight days after the final game of the 1976 World Series. On November 29, 1976, the Yankees signed Reggie Jackson to a lucrative five-year, free agent contract.

Jackson was clearly the class of the free agent field, the dominant power hitter of his time. He had led the American League in home runs twice. Five times he had hit more than 30 homers, with a high of 47 in 1969 as a 23-year-old slugger with the Oakland Athletics. Four times he had knocked in more than 100 runs in a season.

As far back as the fall of 1975, Jackson had given strong indications that he wanted to play for the Yankees, and would jump at the opportunity if it ever presented itself. Sitting in the third base stands in Fenway Park prior to the final game of the 1975 American League Championship Series between Oakland and Boston, Reggie told a group of baseball writers, "If I played in New York, they'd name a candy bar after me."

> **"If I played in New York, they'd name a candy bar after me."**
>
> ***—Reggie Jackson***

After the 1975 season, Jackson was traded from Oakland to Baltimore, where he would have to play one year before becoming eligible for free agency. His 27 home runs and 91 RBIs helped the Orioles finish second in the American League East, but he watched the Yankees win the division by 10 1/2 games and waited for his time to come.

The Orioles made a strong bid to resign Jackson. Other teams came in with tempting offers. But George Steinbrenner pursued Jackson relentlessly, squiring him around town and extolling the Yankee tradition and the benefits of playing in New York. Jackson rejected other offers for more money to sign with the Yankees.

Some members of the Yankees hierarchy had campaigned for the signing of Jackson's teammate, outfielder Joe Rudi, regarded as a more well-rounded player. But Steinbrenner opted for box office, home run power and a track record for winning, which proved to be the wise choice.

Prior to the '77 season, George Steinbrenner courted and won the biggest free-agent prize of the decade when he inked Reggie Jackson to a five-year deal. At the press conference to announce his signing, Jackson was greeted by coaches (from left to right) Elston Howard and Yogi Berra and new teammates Thurman Munson and Roy White. (UPI/Bettmann)

Reggie Jackson and New York was a match made in heaven, but Jackson's Yankees tenure got off to a rather rocky start. In spring training, Jackson submitted to an interview by a writer from a national sports magazine and was quoted as making some regrettable off-the-record remarks that cast aspersions on catcher and captain Thurman Munson.

It would take weeks, even months, for Jackson to live down his ill-chosen remarks and to repair the damage they had done. He did it by smashing 32 home runs, driving in 110 runs, stealing 17 bases and playing hard.

But controversy would follow Jackson throughout his first season as a Yankee. On June 17 in Boston, a Saturday afternoon, manager Martin perceived that Jackson loafed on a ball hit to right field. Martin ordered Paul Blair to go to rightfield and replace Jackson, who was stunned when he realized what was happening.

When he reached the dugout, Jackson appealed to Martin for an explanation. There were words between the two, heated words, and coaches Yogi Berra and Elston Howard had to keep the manager

The 1976 AL MVP and the 1975 AL home run king join forces in the spring of 1977. (New York Yankees Archives)

Yankee greats of past and present meet at Fort Lauderdale Stadium in the spring of '77. (UPI/Bettmann)

from physically attacking his rightfielder.

Reggie survived the incident. So did Billy. It might even have been the turnaround in the Yankees' season, although it wasn't until more than two months later that the Yankees took over first place to stay. They beat the White Sox, 8-3, in Chicago, ran off nine victories in 10 games and won their second consecutive division title by $2\frac{1}{2}$ games over the Orioles.

Relative calm came to the Yankees for the remainder of the season, but, then, for the 1977 Yankees, even calm was relative. Nettles led the team with 37 homers, five more than Jackson. Munson batted .308 and drove in 100 runs. Nettles knocked in 107, Chambliss 90. Rivers was fourth in the league with a .326 average.

Defensive specialist Paul Blair came from Baltimore and played a prominent role in the Yankees' drive to the World Championship. (New York Yankees Archive)

The Yankees charged into the playoffs against the Kansas City Royals, and more controversy.

In Game 1 at Yankee Stadium, Hal McRae, John Mayberry and Al Cowens homered, the Royals knocked Don Gullett out in the second inning and beat the Yankees, 7-2. The Yankees tied the series at one game apiece on Ron Guidry's three-hitter, but lost Game 3 in Kansas City as Dennis Leonard pitched a four-hitter.

Down two games to one, the Yankees rebounded to tie the series with Sparky Lyle pitching five and one-third innings of scoreless relief (he had pitched two and one-third innings the day before) and Mickey Rivers slashing four hits.

With the best-of-five series tied at 2-2, Martin gambled. Against left-hander Paul Splittorff, Martin benched Jackson, who had been 1-for-14 in the first four games, and started Cliff Johnson as designated hitter.

The Yanks trailed, 3-1, going into the top of the eighth, when Martin called on Jackson as a pinch hitter and Reggie delivered an RBI single that cut the deficit to one run. Jackson's big hit gave the Yankees the lift they needed and they rallied for three in the top of the ninth for a 5-3 victory. Mickey Rivers

Sparky Lyle reached his apex in 1977 as he became the first American League reliever to win the Cy Young Award. (New York Yankees Archives)

knocked in the winning run, Lyle pitched in his third straight game, a scoreless inning and a third, and was the winner for the second straight game.

Jackson's big pinch hit had given the Yankees the impetus they needed to come from behind and win their 31st American League pennant, and it was to set the tone for even greater heroics to come.

Reggie Jackson would take center stage in the World Series against the Los Angeles Dodgers, Mr. October in his finest hour. The two teams split the first two games in New York. In Los Angeles, the Yankees won Game 3 behind Mike Torrez. It wasn't until Game 4 that Jackson asserted himself. He doubled, homered and knocked in two runs in support of Ron Guidry as the Yankees beat the Dodgers, 4-2, to take a commanding three games to one lead.

With a chance to wrap up the championship in Los Angeles, the Yankees were pounded, 10-5, to send the Series back to New York. In his last at-bat, Jackson belted his second homer of the Series off Don Sutton. It was a meaningless blast, but served as a portent of things to come.

On the night of October 18, in Yankee Stadium, Reggie Jackson put on the greatest display of power hitting in World Series history, a performance unequaled by any player, including the fabled Babe Ruth, himself.

The Dodgers pushed across two runs in the first against Mike Torrez. The Yankees tied it in the second on a home run by Chris Chambliss, scoring Jackson, who had walked ahead of him.

Another Reggie, the Dodgers' Smith, put LA ahead with a solo shot in the third. Then Jackson took command. With Munson on base in the fourth, Jackson jumped on Burt Hooton's first pitch and drove it on a searing line into the first row of seats in rightfield.

As he circled the bases, the television camera focused on his face and Jackson looked into the camera and mouthed, "Hi, mom," twice. Then he ducked into the jubilant Yankees dugout and the first one to greet him was Billy Martin, and the manager patted the slugger on the cheek.

In the fifth, it was Reggie again. A single by Mickey

The furor in Fenway. (UPI/Bettmann)

Reggie Jackson throws out Cleveland's Bruce Bochte at the plate in a key game late in September. (UPI/Bettmann)

Rivers, a force play and Munson's fly ball brought Jackson up batting against Elias Sosa with one on, two out. Again, he hit the first pitch and ripped a carbon copy line drive home run into the rightfield seats to make it a 7-3 game.

The redoubtable, irrepressible Jackson, who set World Series records for total bases (25) and runs scored (10), would get another chance at history. And he would not blow it. Leading off the eighth against knuckleballer Charlie Hough, Jackson again jumped at the first pitch and drove it to centerfield, a monster shot that landed halfway up the stands, some 450 feet away.

Jackson had put his indelible stamp on the World Series. He had hit three home runs in one game, on three consecutive pitches. He had hit home runs in four consecutive at-bats, five for the Series in his last nine official at-bats.

The Yankees had won their first world championship in 14 years. The centerfield flag pole in Yankee Stadium would be barren no longer.

Long after the game and the obligatory champagne had been splashed throughout the winners' dressing room, the Yankees still were feeling the exhilaration and excitement of winning the World Series. And Jackson still was basking in the glow of his remarkable performance. It was as if he didn't want to go home, he just wanted to stay in the ballpark and savor the night.

Hours after the final out, Jackson still was dressed in his uniform. Most of the players had departed, but Jackson sat in the manager's office.

Lyle and Munson celebrate the Yankees' 1977 ALCS victory over the Royals in Kansas City. Lyle won two of the three games in the best-of-five series. (UPI/Bettmann)

"Reggie...

Reggie...

Reggie!"

#2

Reggie Jackson's three home runs in Game 6 of the 1977 World Series.

(All photos are UPI/Bettmann)

#3

LEFT: *Reggie jumps into the arms of Billy Martin after hitting his third home run. (UPI/Bettmann)*

BELOW: *A home plate collision in the 1977 World Series between Munson and Steve Garvey. (New York Yankees Archives)*

OPPOSITE PAGE: *In his only season in Pinstripes, right-hander Mike Torrez was an important part of the Yankees' World Championship, winning 14 games in the regular season and two games in the World Series. (New York Yankees Archives)*

EW YO
1

ABOVE: *(from left) Pitchers Ed Figueroa, Don Gullett and Ken Holtzman enjoy their victory champagne. (New York Yankees Archives)*

Manager and hero celebrate the Yankees' first World Series championship since 1962. (UPI/Bettmann)

"I hit three home runs tonight," he said. "Do you realize that? Three home runs."

"Yeah," Martin said, "and you broke my record (for extra base hits in a World Series) and that tees me off."

With that, both men, who had battled so many times during the season, began to laugh in unison.

"Billy Martin," Jackson said. "I love the man. I love Billy Martin. The man did a hell of a job this year. There's nobody I'd rather play for."

"Next year," Martin said, "is going to be super."

"Weak is the man who cannot accept adversity," Jackson said. "Next year, we're going to be tougher, aren't we, skip?"

"You bet we will," Martin said. "We'll win it again next year."

"Yes, we will," Jackson said. "We'll win because we have a manager who's feisty and I'm feisty and we're going to be tougher next year. I'll go to the wall for him and he'll go to the wall for me and if anybody clashes with us, they're in trouble."

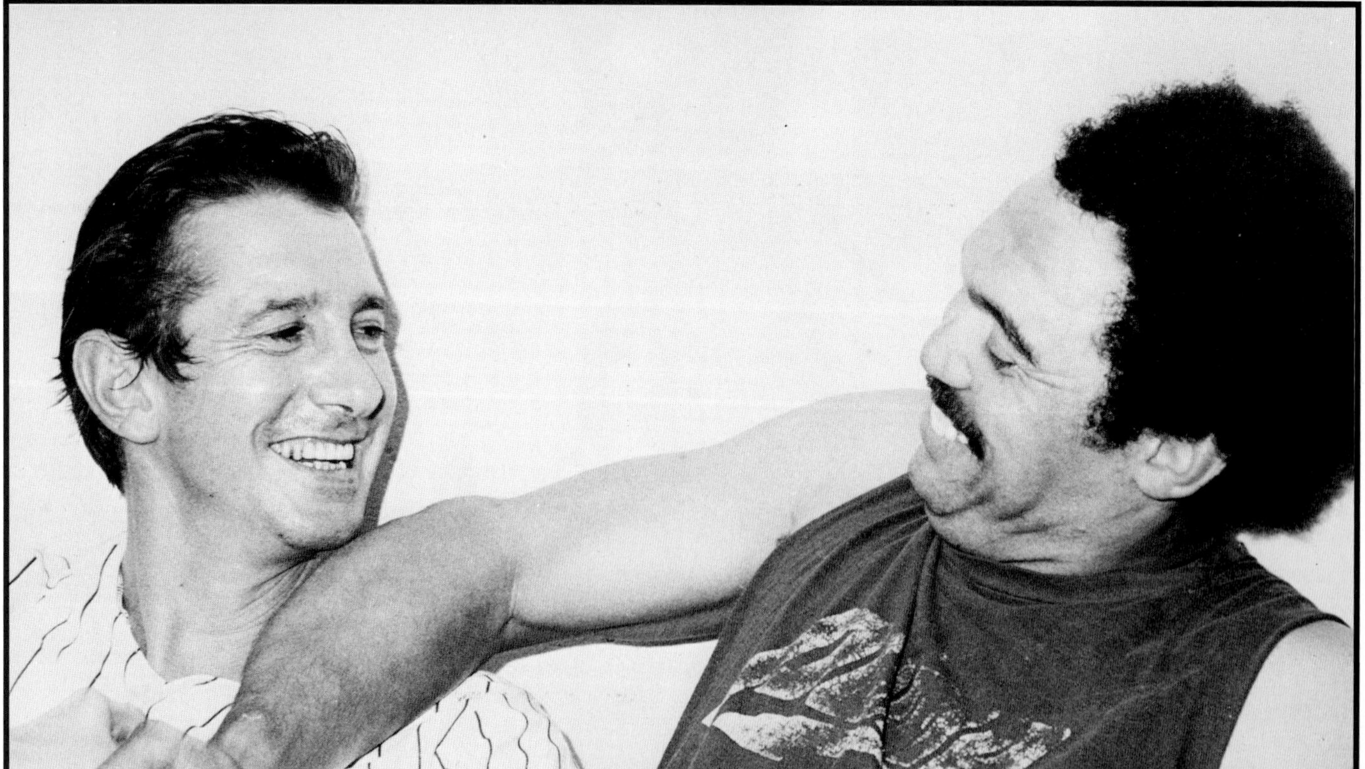

ABOVE: *The 1977 victory parade in downtown Manhattan was led (left to right) by Yankees general manager Gabe Paul, New York City mayor Abe Beame, owner George Steinbrenner, and manager Billy Martin.*

LEFT: *A beaming Billy Martin basks in the fans' adulation.*

BELOW: *Happy days are here again.*

(all photos: New York Yankees Archives)

The Yankees opened the 1978 season by asking Mickey Mantle and Roger Maris to raise their 1977 World Championship flag, their first since 1962. (New York Yankees Archives)

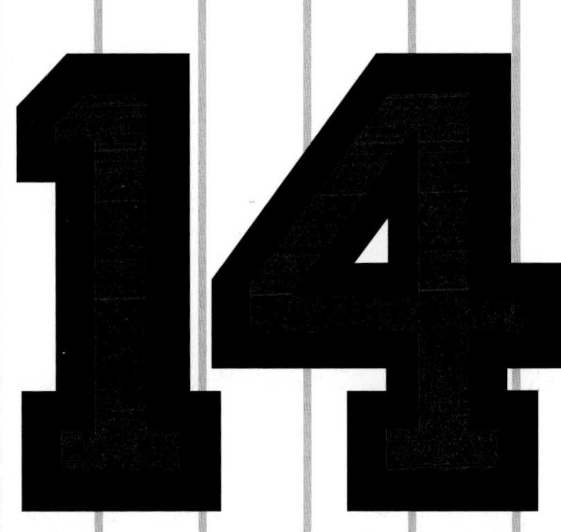

Comeback

There would be a second consecutive world championship for the Yankees in 1978, but it would not come easily. It would be won in dramatic fashion, with perhaps the greatest comeback in baseball history, and Reggie Jackson would be a major contributor to that comeback.

After 88 games, the Yankees, crippled by injuries, stood at 47-41, in fourth place, 13 games behind the rampaging Red Sox. In the offseason, the Yankees had added another free agent, fireballing Rich "Goose" Gossage, considered at the time to be baseball's premier bullpen stopper.

With the White Sox in 1975, Gossage led the American League in saves with 26. But the following season, he became a starter and struggled to a 9-17 record, then was traded to the Pittsburgh Pirates. Back in the bullpen, Gossage saved 26 games for the Pirates in 1977, then opted for free agency and came to New York.

Gossage was expected to be the addition the Yankees needed to win a second consecutive world championship, but they already had Sparky Lyle as their stopper and hindsight now tells us that two stoppers in one bullpen can be an embarrassment of riches.

A new addition to the '78 Yankees was fireballing reliever Rich "Goose" Gossage. (New York Yankees Archives)

Besides the bullpen dilemma and the injuries, most of the key Yankees were experiencing a severe drop-off in production from 1977, with the exception of pitchers Ron Guidry and Ed Figueroa. The Yankees also got excellent production from some of their lesser known players, substitutes who filled in and did the job in place of injured starters.

Figueroa became the first native born Puerto Rican to win 20 games in the major leagues, posting a record of 20-9 and an earned run average of 2.99. Bench players such as Brian Doyle, Paul Blair, Jim Spencer and Jay Johnstone would make important contributions. And Guidry would emerge as the best pitcher in the game and almost single-handedly keep the Yankees competitive.

Guidry set one club record by winning his first 13 decisions and another when he struck out 18 California Angels on June 17 in Yankee Stadium. He would put together one of the greatest seasons in baseball

In one of the greatest seasons ever by a pitcher, Ron Guidry, with a record of 25-3 an ERA of 1.74, nine shutouts and 248 strikeouts, won the '78 Cy Young Award. (New York Yankees Archives)

history, a record of 25-3, an earned run average of 1.74, 16 complete games, 248 strikeouts and a league-leading 9 shutouts. His winning percentage is the third best in baseball history, the best for a 20-game winner. His strikeouts and shutouts also were team records.

Trouble hit the Yankees on a western trip in July. Jackson was suspended by Martin for what the manager deemed insubordination when the slugger ignored a bunt sign. Jackson returned to the team in Chicago on July 23, but did not play. The Yankees won their fifth straight and packed for the trip to the next stop on their journey, Kansas City. During the trip, controversy and the pressure of the season overcame Billy and he resigned while the team was in Kansas City. Bob Lemon, who had been Martin's pitching coach in 1976 and who was a close friend and former Cleveland Indians teammate of Yankees president Al Rosen, was brought in to replace Martin.

To replace Billy Martin the Yankees chose Hall of Famer Bob Lemon, whose steadying hand guided the Yankees to one of the greatest comebacks in history. (New York Yankees Archives)

But just five days later, during the annual Old Timers Day ceremonies at Yankee Stadium, a capacity crowd was startled to hear veteran public address announcer Bob Sheppard say..."the manager for 1980, and hopefully for many years to come... NUMBER ONE... BILLY MARTIN."

With that, Martin ran onto the field in his Yankees uniform to tumultuous applause.

Steinbrenner decided to bring him back, a decision that was greeted with some skepticism in the press, but with overwhelming approval by the fans.

Who is to say the Yankees would not have staged their dramatic second-half comeback in 1978 had Martin remained as manager? He had, after all, won five straight games up to his resignation, cutting the Red Sox lead from 14 games to 10. The fact is we'll never know if the Yankees would have come back under Martin. What we do know is that they did come back under Lemon.

In dramatic fashion on Old Timers Day 1978 the Yankees announced that Billy Martin would follow Bob Lemon as manager. (UPI/Bettmann)

Billy with Yankees heroes Joe DiMaggio, Whitey Ford and Roger Maris on Old Timers Day '78. (New York Yankees Archives)

As the Yankees turned to Guidry, Guidry turned to third baseman Graig Nettles whose defensive wizardry frustrated the Dodgers with several brilliant plays (opposite page: New York Yankees Archives; this page, top photo AP; bottom photo UPI)

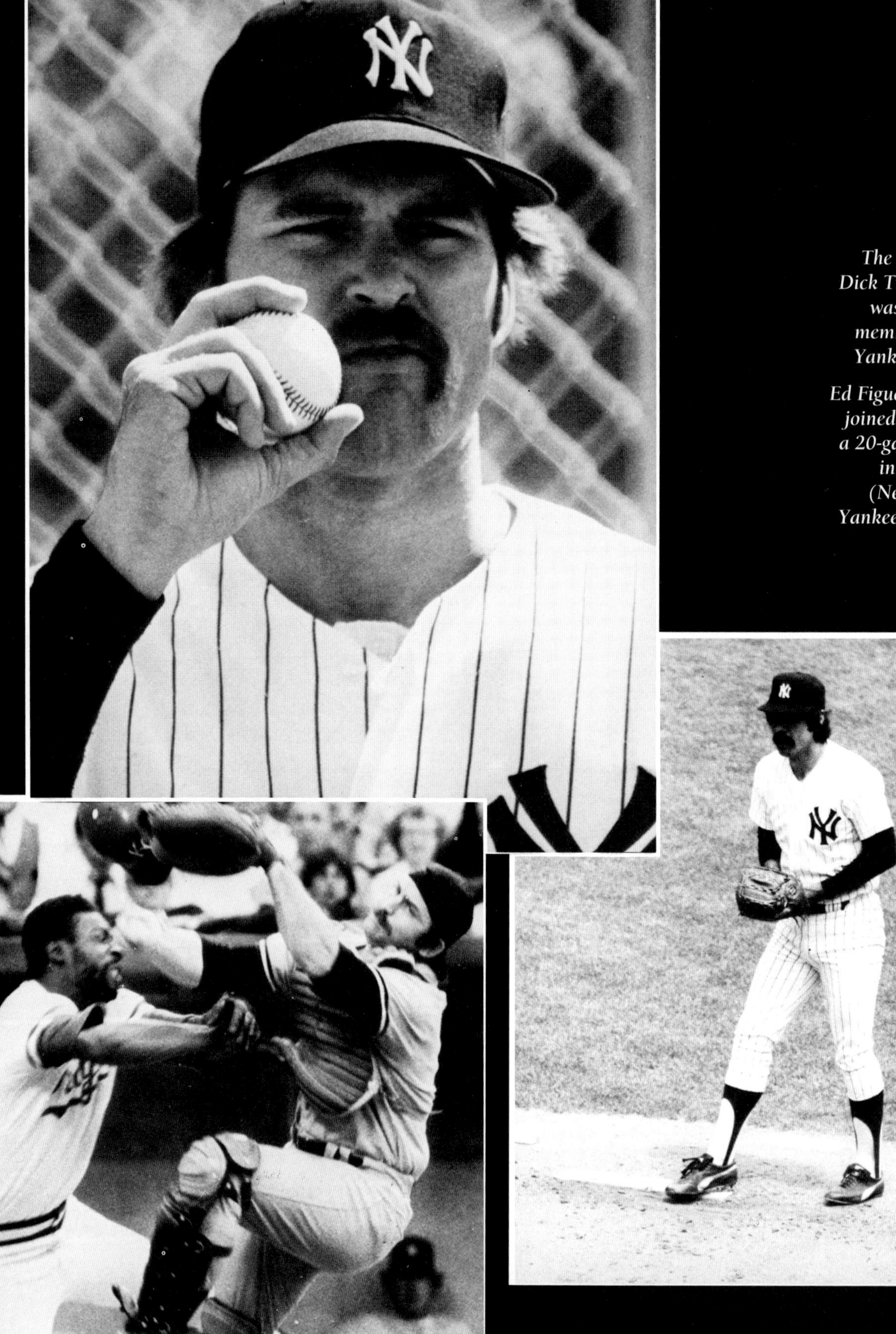

The versatile Dick Tidrow (left) was a vital member of the Yankees' staff.

Ed Figueroa (below) joined Guidry as a 20-game winner in 1978. (New York Yankees Archives)

Kansas City's Willie Wilson (left) is thrown out at the plate after a violent collision with Thurman Munson in Game 2 of the 1978 ALCS. (UPI)

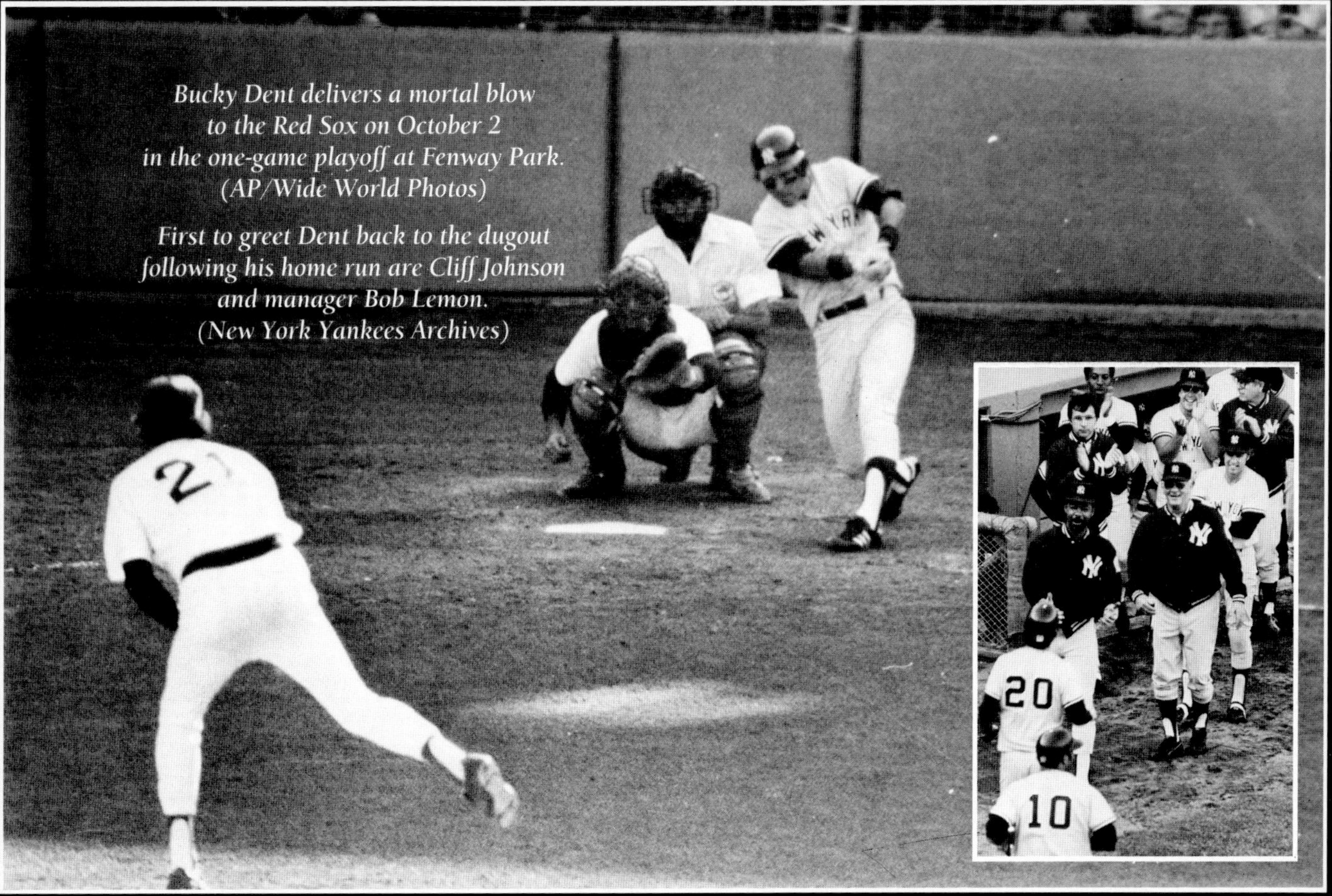

Bucky Dent delivers a mortal blow to the Red Sox on October 2 in the one-game playoff at Fenway Park. (AP/Wide World Photos)

First to greet Dent back to the dugout following his home run are Cliff Johnson and manager Bob Lemon. (New York Yankees Archives)

Munson blasts his famous home run to the bullpen off Doug Bird to win Game 3 of the ALCS and is congratulated by Graig Nettles and Bucky Dent. The Yankees won the series in four games. (UPI/Bettmann)

The Yankees dominated the second half of the season. A wave of injuries hit the Red Sox, while the Yankees' walking wounded of the first half returned in the second half. Slowly, the Yankees cut into the Red Sox lead and when they went into Fenway Park

TOP: *In Game 5 at Yankee Stadium,the Dodgers jumped out to a 2-0 lead in the third, both runs scored by Dave Lopes. (Focus On Sports)*

ABOVE: *In Game 4, the Yankees' defensive brilliance continued with this fourth-inning catch by number 6, Roy White, who beat Dent and Nettles to the play. (AP)*

RIGHT: *Leftfielder Lou Piniella saved the Yankees further damage with this spectacular catch off Steve Yeager in the third inning. (AP)*

ABOVE: *After the first two games in Los Angeles, the Yankees returned home to the thrilling sight of another World Series in Yankee Stadium. (New York Yankees Archives)*

BELOW: *Down two games to none, the Yankees turned to 25-game winner Ron Guidry in Game 3. (Focus On Sports)*

The Yankees tied the Series in Game 4 when Lou Piniella (above) hit a two-out, 10th-inning single to score Roy White (opposite page top) with the winning run. Piniella is mobbed by teammates (opposite page bottom) after the clutch hit. (AP)

for a four-game series on September 7, they trailed by only four games.

The Yankees swept the four games in Boston to draw even, and punished the Sox by outscoring them in the four games, 42-9. The Yankees continued to surge and opened a 3 1/2 game lead on the Red Sox with 15 games to play.

Then the Red Sox showed their heart, coming back to trail by one game with seven to play. The Yankees reeled off six straight. So did the Red Sox. They came to the final day of the season with the Yankees one game in front. All they needed to do was win their game and the division championship would be theirs.

But the Indians beat the Yankees, 9-2, and the Red Sox won, forcing a tie and necessitating a one-game playoff, in Boston, on Monday, October 2.

It was a game for the ages, one of the most memorable in baseball history. Ron Guidry, 24-3 to that point, started for the Yankees, former Yankee Mike Torrez for Boston. For six innings, Torrez was masterful, holding the Yankees scoreless. Going into the seventh, the Red Sox led, 2-0.

Bucky Dent completed a once-in-a-lifetime post-season by batting .417 with seven RBIs and being named Series MVP. (New York Yankees Archives)

To pitch the Series clincher in Los Angeles, the Yankees sent veteran Catfish Hunter (above) to the mound. (Focus On Sports)

Goose Gossage's two scoreless innings of relief for Hunter nailed the Game 6 victory (right). (Focus On Sports)

The Yankees put two runners on base with two outs and Bucky Dent due up. The crowd expected a pinch hitter. Lemon stayed with Dent, the rock solid shortstop who had joined the Yankees the year before in a trade with the Chicago White Sox. On Torrez' second pitch, Dent swung and fouled one off his foot and began limping around the batter's box as the trainer, Gene Monahan, called time and went to the plate to spray pain killer on the foot.

In the on-deck circle, Mickey Rivers noticed that Dent had cracked his bat. He summoned the bat boy to bring out another bat, one of Rivers'. Mickey handed it to Dent.

On Torrez' next pitch, a fastball down the middle, Bucky Dent swung Mickey Rivers' bat, which connected with the ball and sent a towering drive to leftfield. It wasn't a jolt, but it didn't have to be. Not in Fenway Park. It was deep enough to land into the netting above the Green Monster for a three-run homer

Filling in for the injured Willie Randolph, Brian Doyle batted .438 in the '78 World Series. (New York Yankees Archives)

and it turned the game around. Rivers walked and Munson doubled him home to make it 4-2 Yanks, and in the eighth, Jackson homered for a 5-2 lead.

But the Red Sox would not die. They scored two in the eighth and rallied in the ninth, putting two men on with one out and their best hitters, Jim Rice and Carl Yastrzemski, coming to bat. Goose Gossage, pitching his third inning in relief of Guidry, got Rice on a heart-stopping drive to deep right, which Lou Piniella caught a few steps in front of the fence. That brought up the veteran Red Sox hero, Yastrzemski, with a chance to be an even greater hero.

Throwing nothing but his blazing, 98-mile per hour fastball, Gossage got Yaz to hit a high, twisting pop to third base, which Nettles gloved and in the same motion leaped into the air in triumph. The Yankees had won the American League East title in the Great Comeback of 1978.

There still was work to be done. For the third straight year, the Yankees engaged the Kansas City Royals in the American League Championship Series. And for the third straight year, the Yankees prevailed, this time in four games. The turning point came in Game 3, with the series tied, 1-1. George Brett almost singlehandedly beat the Yankees with three home runs, the third off Gossage in the top of the eighth with one on to give the Royals a 5-4 lead. But in the bottom of the eighth, Thurman Munson drove a tremendous two-run homer into the bullpen in left-center to give the Yankees a 6-5 victory.

Guidry and Gossage closed it out in Game 4, a 2-1 victory on solo homers by Nettles and Roy White, and the Yankees had won their third consecutive American League pennant.

For the second year in a row, they met the Los Angeles Dodgers in the World Series. The Dodgers won the first two games in Los Angeles and it was time for still another Yankees comeback.

Back in Yankee Stadium, the Yankees turned once again to Guidry in Game 3. Thanks to the brilliant play of Nettles at third, Guidry beat the Dodgers, 5-1, for his 27th win of the season counting regular and post-season. Lou Piniella's RBI-single in the 10th inning of Game 4 scored White and gave the Yankees a 4-3 victory to even the Series at two games each.

The Yankees pounded out 18 hits to win Game 5, 12-2, then closed out their second straight world championship in Los Angeles by winning, 7-2. Catfish Hunter pitched seven innings for the win. Bucky Dent and Brian Doyle each had three hits. And Reggie Jackson, of course, accounted for the last two Yankees runs with a two-run homer in the seventh.

After Reggie Jackson's two-run homer in the seventh (background), the Yankees sensed the championship was theirs. (UPI/Bettmann)

Jackson and Guidry rejoice in the miracle of '78. (UPI/Bettmann)

In the first game of the 1996 ALCS, young Jeffrey Meier reaches out to catch the controversial home run by Derek Jeter as Orioles right fielder Tony Tarasco watches helplessly. The solo eighth-inning shot tied the score, and the Yankees finally won in the eleventh on a lead-off homer by Bernie Williams. (AP/Wide World)

Return to Glory

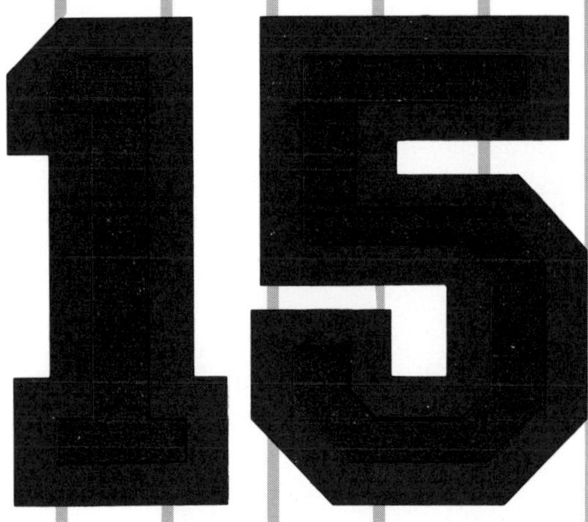

Three years after winning their last world championship, the Yankees returned to the World Series in a bizarre split season caused by another strike. When the 1981 season was interrupted by a players' walkout and resumed after a two-month cessation of play, the Lords of Baseball ruled that the season would be played in two parts. The division leaders at the time of the strike (the Yankees in the American League East) would face off against the division leaders in the post-strike schedule (the Milwaukee Brewers in the AL East) for the opportunity to advance to the championship series.

The Yankees defeated the Brewers, three games to

Pitcher Dwight Gooden is carried off the field by his teammates after pitching a no-hitter against the Seattle Mariners on May 14, 1996, at Yankee Stadium. The Yankees won 2-0. (AP/Wide World)

Rookie Mariano Rivera was virtually unhittable for two innings a game. He was the perfect setup man for closer John Wetteland during the 1996 season. (Focus On Sports)

two, and moved on to face the Oakland A's, who had eliminated the Kansas City Royals in three games to win the AL West.

The Yankees swept the A's, managed by Billy Martin of all people, in three games, and for the third time in five years, the 11th time in their history, were paired against the Dodgers for the world championship.

This time, it was the Dodgers who dominated and turned the Yankees around. After losing the first two games of the Series, the Dodgers rebounded to win the next four and beat the Yankees for only the second time in 11 World Series meetings.

Nevertheless, flushed with the intoxicating narcotic of success—three pennants and two world championships in five years—the Yankees fantasized about another dynasty to equal those of the thirties, forties and fifties. But they would go through 15 seasons and 13 managers before scaling the heights again.

In 1996 the Yankees had reached an impasse on contract talks with Buck Showalter, the young manager who had guided the team's resurgence through four seasons, giving him the longest tenure for a Yankees manager since Ralph Houk ended a seven-year run in 1973. When Showalter left to take over as manager of the expansion Arizona Diamondbacks, who would not begin play until the 1998 season, the Yankees were in the market for a new manager.

Several names surfaced as candidates, but ultimately George Steinbrenner settled on Joseph Paul Torre, a native New Yorker. The Brooklyn-born-and-raised Torre had 14 years of experience as a major league manager, all in the National League—five with the crosstown New York Mets, three with the Atlanta Braves, six with the St. Louis Cardinals. With only five winning seasons of 14 and a combined record of 894-1,003, his selection was not well-received by a critical media, who branded him a "chronic loser."

But Torre's easygoing, laid-back approach, his ability to communicate and his candidness with his players proved to be the perfect fit for a veteran team. His first order of business was to assemble an experienced coaching staff that included past Yankees heroes Chris Chambliss as batting instructor, Mel Stottlemyre as pitching coach and Willie Randolph, a holdover from the Showalter regime, as third base coach. Torre also brought in as his bench coach Don Zimmer, who had been the manager of the Red Sox during the Yankees' march to the 1978 world championship.

When the Yankees gathered for spring training, they welcomed several new faces in addition to Torre and his coaches. Although he never formally announced his retirement from baseball, the beloved Don Mattingly failed to report for spring training. In his place at first base was Tino Martinez, who had been obtained from Seattle, along with righthanders Jeff Nelson and Jim Mecir in a trade for third baseman Russ Davis and left-handed pitcher Sterling Hitchcock.

Other newcomers included lefthander Kenny Rogers, infielder Mariano Duncan and longtime Mets star Dwight Gooden, all signed as free agents; veteran

Bernie Williams slugs the game-winning home run against the Orioles in Game One of the 1996 ALCS. (Allsport)

outfielder Tim Raines, acquired from the Chicago White Sox; and catcher Joe Girardi, obtained from the Colorado Rockies for two minor league pitchers.

Also in camp were two promising rookies: hard-throwing righthander Mariano Rivera and 21-year-old Derek Jeter, whom the Yankees hoped would take his place in the long line of outstanding Yankees shortstops that extended from Roger Peckinpaugh to Mark Koenig to Frank Crosetti to Phil Rizzuto to Gil McDougald to Tony Kubek to Bucky Dent.

In his first game as the Yankees' shortstop, on a bitter cold day in Cleveland, Jeter quickly erased any uncertainty about his ability when he homered and made a spectacular over-the-shoulder catch in support of David Cone in a 7-1 victory. Sophomore Andy Pettitte won in Cleveland the following day, but the Yankees were wiped out in three games in Texas. They returned to Yankee Stadium for the home opener on April 11 and Pettitte, pitching in a driving snowstorm, beat the Kansas City Royals, 7-3.

But the Baltimore Orioles broke swiftly from the starting gate and, by April 17, they had opened a four-game lead on the Yankees.

Perhaps the defining moment for the Yankees came against Minnesota on April 28. For the third time in nine days, Mariano Rivera threw three scoreless innings against the Twins, prompting Twins manager Tom Kelly to proclaim, "That guy belongs in a higher league."

New faces (from left) Tino Martinez, Darryl Strawberry, Cecil Fielder, and Derek Jeter, shown here celebrating the defeat of the Orioles in Game Three of the 1996 ALCS, all contributed to the Yankees' championship season. (Allsport)

Baseball as ballet: Rookie of the Year Derek Jeter avoids Andruw Jones's slide to turn a double play in Game Two of the 1996 World Series against the Atlanta Braves. (Allsport)

In fact, there would be many defining moments for the Yankees in their march to destiny. Two days after Rivera stymied the Twins, the Yankees went to Baltimore, beat the Orioles, 13-10, and took over first place. The following night, they beat the Orioles again, 11-6, in 15 innings to keep Baltimore from reclaiming first place in the American League East. The Yankees would reside there for the remainder of the season.

On May 14, with the Yankees leading the Orioles by two games, Dwight Gooden, suspended for the entire 1995 season for violating his drug aftercare program, punctuated his comeback with the first no-hitter of his career, a 2-0 victory over the Seattle Mariners.

Torre had hit upon a formula for success that worked perfectly. He would hope to get six solid innings from his starting pitcher, then turn it over to Mariano Rivera, whose overpowering fastball made him practically unhittable for two innings. Rivera, in turn, would be replaced by the equally overpowering and practically unhittable John Wetteland, who would pitch the ninth inning.

Because of the Rivera-Wetteland tandem, the Yankees would finish the season with a record of 70-3 when leading after six innings, 79-2 when leading after seven innings and a staggering 86-1 when leading after eight innings. Rivera won eight games, saved five, had an earned run average of 2.09 and held batters to a combined .198 average. Wetteland led the American League with 43 saves.

At the All-Star break, the Yankees held a six-game lead over the Orioles. But looming in front of them, right after the beak, were four games against the Orioles in Camden Yards, four games that looked to determine the Yankees' fate. Were they flashes in the pan? Or in it for the long haul?

Darryl Strawberry was called up by the Yankees in July 1996; he hit .262 with 11 home runs and 36 RBIs, then belted 3 homers in the ALCS against Baltimore. (New York Yankees Archives)

Andy Pettitte was the ace of the Yankees pitching staff in 1996. The left-hander won 21 games in only his second major league season, and capped the year off with a dramatic shutout of the Braves in Game Five of the World Series. (Focus On Sports)

Tino Martinez was obtained in 1996 to replace a Yankees legend, Don Mattingly, at first base—and hit .292 with 25 home runs and a team-high 117 RBIs. He also led the league's first basemen in fielding. (New York Yankees Archives)

Wade Boggs rides a police horse around the field after the Yankees' 3-2 defeat of the Atlanta Braves in Game Six of the 1996 World Series. (AP/Wide World)

In the first game, Derek Jeter hit a two-run homer off Mike Mussina in the eighth inning to break a 2-2 tie and beat the Orioles, 4-2. The second game was rained out and played as part of a doubleheader the next day. The Yankees swept both games, by scores of 3-2 and 7-5, then completed their wipeout of the Orioles by wining the fourth game of the series, 4-1. The four-game sweep put them 10 games in front, enough of a cushion to withstand an Orioles drive that brought them within 2½ games of the Yankees on September 9.

The final showdown came at Yankee Stadium on September 18 when the Orioles came in for a three-game series trailing the Yankees by three games. Down 2-1 in the ninth, the Yankees tied the score on Bernie Williams' RBI single and won it in the tenth on an RBI single by rookie Ruben Rivera.

The Yankees won the second game of the series, and even though they lost the third game, they were in command. Six days later, on September 25, the Yankees crushed the Milwaukee Brewers, 19-2, to clinch the American League eastern division title.

Along the way, the Yankees executed two deals that would prove vital in helping them reach their ultimate goal. On July 7, Darryl Strawberry was recalled from Columbus. He had played 32 games with the Yankees in 1995, but was not offered a contract for the 1996 season. So eager was he to get another shot at the big leagues, Strawberry signed to play for St. Paul in the independent Northern League, the baseball rockpile, where he impressed the Yankees enough for them to re-sign him and send him to their class AAA International League farm team in Columbus.

On July 31, the Yankees sent outfielder Ruben Sierra

and pitching prospect Matt Drews to Detroit for veteran slugger Cecil Fielder, who had hit more home runs and driven in more runs than any player in the nineties. Fielder was the right-handed power hitter the Yankees desperately needed to balance their attack.

The 1996 season was not without its setbacks for the Yankees. On May 2, David Cone pitched a complete game victory over the White Sox, after which he complained that his pitching hand was cold and clammy. Several days later, an examination revealed that Cone had suffered a potentially life-threatening aneurysm in his shoulder that would keep him sidelined for four months.

On June 21, Joe Torre got word during a doubleheader sweep in Cleveland that his oldest brother Rocco had died of a stroke.

Six weeks later another brother, Frank, arrived from Florida and checked into Columbia Presbyterian Hospital to await a donor for a heart transplant. His heart was failing. Nine years Joe's senior, Frank had played for the Milwaukee Braves against the Yankees in the 1957 and 1958 World Series.

It was with conflicting emotions of elation over his team's triumph and concern for his brother's well-being that Joe Torre took his Yankees into postseason play in search of his dream.

First up were the Texas Rangers, who had beaten the Yankees seven out of 12 in the regular season. This would be a best-of-five series that minimized the margin for error. A Yankee Stadium crowd of 57,205 was rendered mute when Juan Gonzalez (who would later be named the AL MVP) belted a three-run homer and Dean Palmer added a two-run shot off David Cone in the fourth inning of the first game. The Rangers coasted to a 6-2 victory that left the Yankees needing three wins in four games to keep their dream alive.

Again, in Game 2, Gonzalez intruded on the dream. A solo shot in the second, then a three-run blast in the third off Andy Pettitte built a 4-1 Texas lead. But the Yankees slowly inched back, tying it at 4-4 in the eighth on a clutch RBI single by Cecil Fielder, who had earlier homered just as he had been acquired to do.

The two teams trudged laboriously into the bottom of the twelfth, the game looking for a hero, the Yankees looking for a break. It came with two outs and runners on first and second. A sacrifice bunt was fielded by the usually reliable Rangers third baseman Dean Palmer, whose throw sailed past first base and allowed Derek Jeter to score the winning run.

The series was tied, 1-1, but the Yankees had to play the balance of the series in hostile territory.

The Yankees needed another dramatic comeback to win Game 3. Down 2-1 in the ninth, they scored twice on Bernie Williams' sacrifice fly and Mariano Duncan's two-out RBI single for a 3-2 victory and two games-to-one lead in the series.

In Game 4 the Rangers once again jumped out to an early lead, sparked by Juan Gonzalez's fifth home run of the series. Down 4-0 in the fourth, the Yankees mounted their third straight comeback. Fielder's RBI single in the seventh and Bernie Williams' home run in the ninth gave the Yankees a 6-4 lead, and for the second straight game John Wetteland saved the victory.

The Yankees had cleared the first hurdle. There were two more remaining.

There is no advantage to having beaten a team 10 times in 13 meetings during the regular season, no handicap award for such dominance. The American League Championship Series starts from scratch. The Baltimore Orioles, unless their psyches were damaged by their inability to beat the Yankees all spring and summer, felt they had gained a reprieve in the fall. The best-of-seven AL Championship Series was a whole new ballgame…all seven of them.

Teams en route to championships often seem blessed by divine intervention, by supernatural powers that influence the outcome of games. Angels in the outfield…and in the infield…and in the dugout. In the case of the Yankees in Game 1 of the ALCS, it was not the occult but the schoolboy from New Jersey named Jeffrey Meier who helped them get the jump on the Orioles.

With the Yankees trailing by one in the eighth inning, Derek Jeter hit a high drive to right field. Orioles rightfielder Tony Tarasco, his back pressed to the wall, waited for the ball to descend into his glove. But young Jeffrey Meier, a 12-year-old angel in the right field seats, had come to Yankee Stadium with his trusty mitt. He reached over the railing into the area of play and snatched the descending sphere away from Tarasco.

"Me and the kid almost touched gloves," said Tarasco later. "It was a routine fly ball. In my mind, there is no way in the world I would have dropped it. Merlin must have been in the air."

Cecil Fielder, traded from the Tigers on July 31, was the right-handed power hitter the Yankees needed in 1996. He had 2 homers and 8 RBIs against Baltimore in the ALCS and then batted .391 against Atlanta in the World Series. (New York Yankees Archives)

The Orioles protested. Umpire Rich Garcia ruled the ball had cleared the fence. No interference. Home run. Tie Score. Three innings later, Bernie Williams led off the bottom of the eleventh with a home run off Randy Myers and the Yankees had taken the first game.

There had been so many late-inning heroics for the Yankees that it seemed shocking when they didn't come back. But they failed in Game 2. With the Orioles ahead 5-3 in the ninth, the Yankees put runners on first and second with one out and Cecil Fielder and Tino Martinez due up. Surely one of them would find the seats, or another bleacher cherub, for another dramatic Yankees victory. But Armando Benitez retired Fielder on a foul pop to first and Martinez on a fly to short right, and the series was tied going to Baltimore.

The magic was back for Game 3 in Camden Yards, proving that the occult, the supernatural, or whatever you'd like to call it will travel. The Yankees overturned a one-run Orioles lead with a four-run eighth, highlighted by Cecil Fielder's two-run homer off Mike Mussina. With the 5-2 triumph they forged ahead in the series, two games to one.

Once they had the lead, the Bombers' season-long dominance kicked in. They pounded the Orioles in Game 4. Bernie Williams slammed a two-run homer in the first. Darryl Strawberry, a solo homer in the second. Paul O'Neill, a two-run homer in the fourth. Strawberry again, a two-run homer in the eighth. Final score: New York 8, Baltimore 4. The Yanks were one win away from getting to the World Series for the first time in 15 years.

They wasted little time settling the issue, scoring six times in the third inning, including Jim Leyritz's solo homer and Cecil Fielder's three-run shot. They would be held scoreless the rest of the game and the Orioles would claw their way back, but John Wetteland came in to pitch the ninth, teased the Baltimore faithful by allowing a two-run homer by Bobby Bonilla, then choked off the Orioles to record his fourth save of the postseason and give the Yankees a 6-4 pennant-winner.

As Cal Ripken grounded to Derek Jeter at deep short and Jeter gunned his throw to first base for the final out, Joe Torre sat calmly in the Yankees' dugout, thinking that after 4,280 games as a player and a manger he was finally going to the World Series, thinking about his brother lying in a New York hospital bed waiting for a heart transplant. He silently crossed himself. Then he cried.

In order to scale the top of the mountain, the Yankees were going to have to defeat a formidable opponent. The Atlanta Braves, all the experts agreed, owned the best four-man pitching rotation in the game. They had wiped out the Los Angeles Dodgers in three games in the first round of the playoffs. Then, after falling behind the St. Louis Cardinals three games to one in the National League Championship Series, the Braves had come back with a vengeance, outscoring the Cardinals 32-1 in winning the final three games.

The Braves' mini-dynasty was in the World Series for the fourth time in five years (excluding the strike year, 1994). If they had a weakness, it wasn't readily apparent, and they were hotter than a Georgia heat wave.

Joe Torre hardly had time to revel in the elation of winning the pennant, or to enjoy the experience of being in a World Series for the first time, when he found his team down two games to nothing. The Braves marched triumphantly into Yankee Stadium and, with the swagger of champions, bludgeoned the Yankees 12-1 in Game 1 as teenage prodigy Andruw Jones homered twice and drove in five runs. In Game 2 the Yankees fell victim to the mastery of the incomparable Greg Maddux, losing 4-0.

After two games in their own ballpark, the Yankees found themselves heading for Atlanta down two games to nothing, a desperate position. Where was Jeffrey Meier when they needed him?

Yankees owner George Steinbrenner was concerned...and embarrassed. His manager reassured him.

"We'll be all right," Torre promised.

Was this just false bravado? Or did Torre know something that eluded everyone else?

What Torre knew was that the six days off between the final ALCS game and the first game of the Fall Classic had taken some of the edge off the Yankees, had slowed their momentum and rusted their skills.

What he knew was that 38 years earlier, the Milwaukee Braves (ancestors of the Atlanta Braves), of which his own brother Frank was a member, won the first two games, then lost the World Series to the Yankees. He had heard Frank's sad lament of the 1958 World Series all too often.

And what Joe Torre knew best was his team and what

John Wetteland led the league with 43 regular-season saves in 1996, then saved 4 World Series games for the Yankees. (New York Yankees Archives)

Jimmy Key struggled to a 12-11 record in 1996 but won the final Series contest against Atlanta. (New York Yankees Archives)

they were made of: their grit, their resolve, their heart, their pride and their professionalism.

In the third game, David Cone and Tom Glavine hooked up in a tense pitching duel through six pulsating innings. Cone yielded one run and Glavine two, one unearned. But when it was Glavine's turn to bat in the bottom of the seventh, manager Bobby Cox, needing a run to tie, opted for offense and sent former Yankee Luis Polonia up to pinch-hit for his pitcher.

Polonia reached on a walk, but the Braves failed to score, and with Glavine out of the game, the Yankees jumped on reliever Greg McMichael for three runs in the eighth, capped by Bernie Williams' two-run homer. The Yankees won the game, 5-2, and dodged a tomahawk.

"Everyone was talking about how great the Braves were, where their place in history was," said Cone after the game. "Well, if we get one more win, the Series goes back to New York."

The Yankees got that one win in Game 4. They got it in unbelievable fashion, so unbelievable that it left its mark on the Braves' psyche.

The Braves unloaded against Kenny Rogers early and led 6-0 after five innings. Considering the national stage, the position another loss would have put the Yankees in and the fact that they were in enemy territory, this was the mother of all Yankees comebacks in 1996.

They scored three in the sixth to halve the Braves' lead, but were held scoreless in the seventh. In the eighth, Braves manager Bobby Cox called on his closer, Mark Wohlers, he of the 100-mile-per-hour fastball and 39 saves during the regular season. With two on and two out, Wohlers fed Jim Leyritz a diet of fastballs until the count went to 2-2. Then he tried tricking Leyritz with a slider. The Yankees' backup catcher was ready. He jumped on the pitch and drilled it over the left-field wall to tie the game as 51,881 fans in Fulton County Stadium fell silent.

The Yankees pushed across two runs in the tenth to complete their comeback and win, 8-6, and the Series was tied at two games each. They would be returning to the friendly confines of Yankee Stadium.

But first there was the small matter of the pivotal Game 5 in Atlanta, a rematch of Game 1's starters. John Smoltz had shackled the Yankees bats and the Braves had pounded Andy Pettitte.

It was different this time, although Smoltz continued to stymie the Yanks. He held them to four hits and one run, a tainted run at that, through eight innings. In the fourth, Charlie Hayes hit a fly ball to right center fielder Marquis Grissom, momentarily blocking Grissom's view. Grissom dropped the ball for an error. One out later, Cecil Fielder doubled home Hayes for his 14th RBI of the postseason.

Pettitte, the 23-year-old lefthander who had won 21 games during the regular season, his second in the major leagues, pitched with the guts of Ron Guidry and the poise of Whitey Ford. He held the Braves scoreless until replaced by John Wetteland with one out in the ninth. Wetteland got the last two outs. The Yankees, one win away from the 23rd world championship in their history, were going home.

A day off was scheduled between Games 5 and 6, and Joe Torre, one win away from reaching his dream, got even better news. A donor had been found. His brother Frank would have his heart transplant on the day before the sixth game.

"Frank's an old baseball guy," said Joe. "He knew enough to have the surgery on the off-day." The surgery was a success. The next night, Frank Torre was propped up in bed, watching his kid brother managing Game 6 of the World Series.

In order to win and avoid a seventh game, the Yankees would have to beat the great Greg Maddux, who had shut them down in Game 2.

Like Frank Torre's surgery, Game 6 also was a success, a microcosm of the formula used so skillfully by the Yankees all season. They bunched four hits in the third for three runs. A double by Paul O'Neill, a triple by Joe Girardi, singles by Derek Jeter and Bernie Williams.

The Braves scratched a run off Jimmy Key in the fourth and threatened against Key in the sixth. Torre followed his season-long formula and went to his bullpen. David Weathers pitched an inning, Graeme Lloyd got one huge out and Mariano Rivera pitched two overpowering innings. Then, as he had done so often all season, Rivera turned it over to John Wetteland in the ninth.

Typical of Wetteland, he made it interesting. He put Yankee fans on the edge of their seats by giving up a double to Ryan Klesko and an RBI single to Marquis Grissom to make it a 3-2 nailbiter.

Then, on a 3-2 pitch, Mark Lemke popped to third base. The ball hung in the air for an eternity…then settled into the glove of Charlie Hayes.

The Yankees were World Champions again!

Tino Martinez's grand slam in the seventh inning of Game 1 of the World Series had Yankees' shortstop Derek Jeter in a celebratory mood. (AP/Wide World)

The Greatest?

The seeds that would blossom full-flower into a mind-boggling, record-setting 1998 season were sown on the night of October 6, 1997, in Cleveland's Jacob's Field. The Cleveland Indians beat the Yankees, 4-3, to win the American League Division Series, three games to two, and eliminate the Yankees from World Series contention.

Right then the Yankees, from owner George Steinbrenner to manager Joe Torre to his coaches and players, vowed that they would take the necessary steps, make the necessary commitment that would get them back to the World Series.

It was agreed by the powers-that-be that no wholesale changes were needed. Instead, there would be some tinkering designed to fortify some positions and sweep out those players who adversely affected team

A $12 million bust in his first season in the United States, Japan's Hideki Irabu contributed 13 victories to the Yankees during their record season.
(AP/Wide World)

The Imperfect Man, David Wells, pitched a Perfect Game—only the 13th in the history of modern baseball—against the Minnesota Twins on May 17, 1998. (AP/Wide World)

chemistry—what Branch Rickey called "addition by subtraction."

The nucleus of the team was kept basically intact—steady, reliable Tino Martinez at first base; Derek Jeter, the brilliant rookie of 1996 who was now entering his third major league season and rapidly improving to star status, at shortstop; the irrepressible, fiercely competitive Paul O'Neill in right field; the classy, silky-smooth, low-keyed Bernie Williams in center field; and veteran, cerebral Joe Girardi at catcher, augmented by Jorge Posada, a youngster with exciting potential.

And then there was the pitching staff: The anchor, David Cone, renowned as a "big-game pitcher" and a leader in the clubhouse, was a battle-tested veteran who would attempt to make yet another comeback from shoulder surgery; Andy Pettitte, who at the age of 25 had already won 51 major league games; Mariano Rivera, the skinny, flame-throwing relief pitcher thrust into the closer's role after 1996 World Series star John Wetteland signed as a free agent with the Texas Rangers, who had saved 43 games in 1997; flamboyant, eccentric, free-spirited David Wells, signed by the Yankees as a free agent the day after Wetteland signed with Texas and 11 days after Jimmy Key signed as a free agent with the Baltimore Orioles, who had won 16 games in 1997; and the already legendary Hideki Irabu, a star in the Japanese League who had been a $12 million bust his first season in New York.

The Yankees made four noteworthy additions in the months between the end of the 1997 season and the start of the 1998 season.

Eager to dispose of the miscast and underachieving pitcher Kenny Rogers and to add a potent bat to their lineup, the Yankees worked out a deal with the San Diego Padres that would send the lefthander to the West Coast in exchange for slugger Greg Vaughn. But when a chronic shoulder ailment caused Vaughn to fail the Yankees' physical, the deal was scrubbed. The Yankees then shipped Rogers to the Oakland Athletics for journeyman third baseman Scott Brosius.

It was a trade that raised some questions. Brosius had batted only .203 with 11 homers and 49 RBI for the A's in 1997. But the Yankees insisted he was plagued by injuries that caused him to miss three weeks of the season entirely and play at less than his physical best the remainder of the time. They pointed to his .304 average, 22 home runs and 71 RBI in 1996 as the true measure of his abilities.

Brosius was viewed as nothing more than a stopgap until Mike Lowell, a prized prospect, was ready to take over at third base.

"If he can hit .250 and give us good defense, I'll be satisfied," said manager Joe Torre of Brosius.

But Brosius gave Torre more than he hoped for—an average of .300, 22 homers and 98 RBI in the regular season. And he would save his best for October.

When the Vaughn trade was nullified, the Yankees looked for a bat in free-agent Chili Davis, a 39-year-old switch-hitter who had amassed 2,222 hits in a 17-year career. Injuries would reduce Davis to barely 100 at bats in the regular season, but he would make his contribution in the postseason.

As spring training drew near, the Yankees still felt they needed a second baseman and a leadoff hitter. On February 6, they satisfied both needs with one man—Chuck Knoblauch, a perennial All-Star and career .304

After spending eight years in the minor leagues, Shane Spencer came to the Yankees and astonished the baseball world by blasting 10 home runs in 27 games.
(AP/Wide World)

The low point in the Yankees' 1998 postseason came in Game 2 of the ALCS, henceforth to be known as "Knoblauch's brain lock." On a bunt play, the Indians' Travis Fryman was hit on the back by the catcher's throw. Instead of retrieving the ball, Knoblauch let it trickle away while he argued the call, allowing the go-ahead run to score. (AP/Wide World)

hitter in seven seasons with the Minnesota Twins. Knoblauch was obtained in a trade for four minor leaguers, a deal made possible because the Yankees had upgraded their farm system in recent years and had a surplus of young talent.

The final pieces of the Knoblauch trade were put together by their new general manager of three days, 30-year-old Brian Cashman. After five years as assistant general manager, Cashman had been elevated to the position when Bob Watson resigned the post for health reasons.

Cashman's biggest contribution to the Yankees' record-breaking season turned out to be not the deal he made, but the one deal he didn't make later in the season.

With their team set, the Yankees opened the season on April 1 in Anaheim and immediately laid an egg.

The Angels swept the two-game series. The Yankees went to Oakland and lost the first game of a two-game series, won the second, then lost again in the first game of a three-game series in Seattle.

After five games, the Yankees had a record of 1-4, and the New York tabloids were wondering if Torre's job was in peril. Perhaps that sounds unthinkable for a manager who had won 188 games and one World Series in two years, but these are the Yankees. Bob Lemon had been fired as manager 14 games into the 1982 season after guiding the Yankees to the World Series the season before. And in 1985, Yogi Berra was fired after only 16 games.

On April 7, before the second game of their three-game series in Seattle, Torre called a team meeting. David Cone spoke. So did Paul O'Neill. Torre preached aggressiveness. Cone called for unity. O'Neill implored his teammates not to wait for things to happen, but to go out and make them happen.

Chuck Knoblauch led off the game with a home run. Darryl Strawberry hit two. The Yanks won, 13-7. They won again the next night, then came back to New York for the home opener, a celebration of the 50th anniversary of Yankee Stadium.

Down 5-0 to the Oakland A's, the Yankees rallied for a 17-13 victory, their third straight. They pushed their winning streak to eight and charged into first place, where they would remain for the rest of the season.

The defining moment for the 1998 Yankees came in Yankee Stadium on Sunday afternoon, May 17, "Beanie Baby Day." The starting pitcher for the Yankees was the eccentric, beer-guzzling, fun-loving lefthander David Wells, who had endeared himself to Yankees fans with outrageous comments, a cavalier lifestyle and a reverence for and knowledge of Yankees tradition.

When he arrived in New York, Wells asked for the uniform number worn by his idol, Babe Ruth. Told that No. 3 was retired and would never be worn again, Wells settled for No. 33—Ruth times two. He had purchased a Yankees cap worn by Ruth for the princely sum of $35,000 and wore it one day during a game until he was told the cap was not uniform with those of his teammates.

On "Beanie Baby Day," the rotund Wells sailed through the Minnesota Twins batting order with ease. Nobody reached base, and when Pat Meares' fly ball nestled into the glove of right fielder O'Neill, Wells had pitched the 13th Perfect Game in modern baseball history and the second ever by a Yankee. The first was accomplished in the fifth game of the 1956 World Series by another pitcher known for his loose lifestyle, Don Larsen, who by the oddest of coincidences had attended the same San Diego high school as Wells some 40 years before Wells passed through its halls.

Wells' Perfect Game was the second of a five-game winning streak for the Yankees that left them with a record of 31-9—and the runaway was on.

Bernie Williams, the 1998 American League batting champion, singles in a run against the Indians in Game 3 of the ALCS. (AP/Wide World)

"What stands out most is how we prepare ourselves for each game," said Darryl Strawberry. "We don't like losing. We don't like losing a game, period. When you have a group of guys with that approach, it's a fun thing to be part of. You rarely see it when the whole team is like that. We're all riding the bus together. If we keep riding it the right way, we know it can take us to a very special place."

The Yankees were on a runaway bus hurtling through the American League, so far in front of the pack that only a disaster could stop them. They faced their first crisis as May turned into June. David Wells' angry left shoulder was barking, and David Cone had been bitten on his right index finger by his mother's Jack Russell terrier and was scratched from his scheduled start against the Tampa Bay Devil Rays on June 3.

In need of a pitcher, the Yankees reached down to their Norfolk farm team for "El Duque."

Orlando Hernandez, "El Duque," was the star pitcher for Cuba's National Team. He was the greatest pitcher in Cuba's history, but he had longed for the chance to try his stuff against the best, especially after watching on television as his half-brother Livan Hernandez won two games for the Florida Marlins in the 1997 World Series and was named Series MVP.

The Yankees' peerless closer, Mariano Rivera, strikes out the Indians' Enrique Wilson for the final out of Game 5 of the ALCS as the Yankees grab a three games-to-two lead and control of the series. (AP/Wide World)

Desperate to gain his freedom, El Duque departed his native Cuba late one December night. Leaving his wife and two small children behind, he boarded a leaky raft and sailed through turbulent, shark-infested waters and miraculously landed safely on the coast of Florida. Three months later, he signed a $6.6 million contract as a free agent with the Yankees.

The intention was to leave Hernandez in the minor leagues for most of the 1998 season, even though his performance in the minors quickly made it clear he was good enough to pitch in the major leagues. But the pitching emergency caused by Wells' sore shoulder and Cone's dog bite forced the Yankees to accelerate El Duque's arrival in New York.

He was to pitch on June 3 and then, no matter what happened, be sent back to Norfolk. But because of his performance against the Devil Rays—one run, five hits, seven strikeouts in seven innings—and his reception by the fans, El Duque would spend the remainder of the season in New York, posting a record of 12-4 in his rookie season.

As the trading deadline approached, rumors circulated that the Mariners were shopping their dominant, All-Star left-hander Randy Johnson to the highest bidder. This period would be rookie GM Brian Cashman's finest moment. He continued to state publicly that the Yankees were a player in the Johnson sweepstakes, while privately urging Boss Steinbrenner not to acquire the lefthander for fear of upsetting team chemistry.

Cashman played his hand like a veteran poker player, trying to discourage the Yankees American League rivals from dealing for Johnson. Cashman knew if Johnson went to a team that eventually came back to beat the Yankees, he would pay dearly for his gaffe with his job. Yet he stubbornly maintained his position and was able to rest easier when Johnson was dealt to a National League team, the Houston Astros.

On September 4, in Chicago, the Yankees beat the White Sox 11-6. It was their 100th win of the season. They had lost only 38. With 24 games remaining, the 1998 Yankees were on course to surpass three

Chili Davis (right) gets a "high five" from Tino Martinez after scoring on rookie Ricky Ledee's double in the second inning of Game 1 of the 1998 World Series.
(AP/Wide World)

Vindication for Chuck Knoblauch's ALCS Game 2 goof came in the form of a game-tying three-run home run in Game 1 of the World Series. (AP/Wide World)

momentous baseball records—the franchise mark of 110 wins by the fabulous 1927 Murderers Row Yankees, often called baseball's greatest team; the American League record of 111 wins by the 1954 Cleveland Indians; and the all-time record of 116 wins by the 1906 Chicago Cubs.

On September 23, the Yankees beat the Indians, 8-4, for their 110th win of the season, matching the win total of the 1927 Yankees. The next day, they broke their team record and tied the 1954 Indians record with their 111th win, a 5-2 victory over the Devil Rays. The next day, they beat the Devil Rays again, 6-1, for win No. 112—the most wins in American League history.

In those frenetic final days of the regular season, the Yankees went through a gamut of emotions, highs and lows, even as they were finishing out a record season. Suffering from stomach pains, fan favorite Darryl Strawberry, a popular and vital member of the team, checked himself into Columbia Presbyterian Hospital for tests. Doctors found a cancerous walnut-sized lump in his colon and scheduled Strawberry for immediate surgery.

The operation was a success with expectations for a full recovery, but Strawberry would miss the chance to be with the Yankees in the postseason. He was there in spirit, however, as his No. 39 was stitched in white on the Yankees caps.

On September 28, David Cone won his 20th game of the season, the second Yankee to win 20 games (Andy Pettitte in 1996) since Ron Guidry in 1985. Cone had won 20 with the New York Mets in 1988, and the nine-year gap between 20-win seasons is the longest in baseball history.

In the final weeks of the regular season, a new star emerged on the Yankees horizon. Shane Spencer, who had spent eight years in the minor leagues and who had never been regarded as a top prospect, came up from Norfolk and set the baseball world on its ear by hitting 10 home runs in 27 games, a pace that exceeded

Cuban defector Orlando Hernandez, "El Duque," pitched and won the critical Game 2 of the World Series. (AP/Wide World)

even that of home-run king Mark McGwire.

In the final game of the season, Bernie Williams rapped out two hits and finished with a batting average of .339, two points better than Boston's Mo Vaughn, to become the ninth batting champion in Yankees' history.

The Yankees would close out the regular season with a flurry, winning their last seven games to finish with a record of 114-48—more wins than any other team in history except the 1906 Chicago Cubs.

"It's been a great season," cautioned owner George Steinbrenner, "but we haven't done anything yet. It won't mean a thing if we don't at least get to the World Series."

The first hurdle of that ultimate goal would be presented by the power-laden Texas Rangers, the American League's most explosive offense, in the division series. But Yankees pitching suffocated the Rangers' bats and the Yankees swept the series in three games, by scores of 2-0, 3-1 and 4-0.

The Rangers, who led the American League with a batting average of .289, scored one run and batted a paltry .141 in three games. The Yankees' bullpen, led by Mariano Rivera who saved two games, did not allow a run in the three games. Rookie Spencer continued his hot hitting with home runs in each of the first two games.

Next up were the Cleveland Indians, who had ended the Yankees 1997 season so abruptly. David Wells

Scott Brosius capped off his, and the Yankees', magical season with a three-run home run in the eighth inning of Game 3 of the World Series. Brosius would be named World Series Most Valuable Player. (AP/Wide World)

pitched the opener of the best-of-seven American League Championship Series and improved his post-season record to 6-1 with $8\frac{1}{3}$ exceptional innings in a 7-2 victory.

But the Yankees lost Game 2, 4-1, in 12 innings when Chuck Knoblauch suffered brain lock on a bunt play. While Knoblauch argued that the bunter, Travis Fryman, should have been ruled out for interference while running to first, the ball, which had hit Fryman on the back, trickled past Knoblauch into short right field as the go-ahead run scored.

Game 3 in Cleveland was an Indians' power show. Two home runs by Manny Ramirez and one each by Jim Thome and Mark Whiten, all against Andy Pettitte, pushed the Indians to a 6-1 victory. For the first time, the Yankees trailed in the postseason, two games to one, their dream season in danger of coming to a disheartening conclusion.

Not since the first week of the season had the Yankees faced a "must win" situation. Now in Game 3 against the Indians, they were banking on a rookie, Orlando Hernandez, to get them back on track. In the Yankees' biggest game of the year, El Duque pitched brilliantly. For seven innings, he baffled the Indians, blunted their awesome power and held them scoreless on three hits.

"I had pressure," Hernandez said through an interpreter, "but I had no fear."

The Yankees evened the series at 2-2 with a 4-0 victory, and it was as if a heavy weight had been lifted from their backs by a rookie who had fled Cuba on a raft just 10 months before.

Game 5 belonged to David Wells, Mariano Rivera and Chili Davis, who finally was contributing after an injury-plagued season. Wells pitched $7\frac{1}{3}$ innings, Rivera finished up and Davis drove in three runs in a

Yankees stream out of the dugout and onto the field to celebrate the team's 24th world championship—their second in three years. Relief pitcher Mariano Rivera falls to his knees and raises his arms to the heavens as jubilant catcher Joe Girardi rushes to him. (AP/Wide World)

Tears of joy flow from owner George Steinbrenner and manager Joe Torre as they accept the 1998 World Series trophy commemorating the team's 24th world championship in their glorious history. (AP/Wide World)

5-3 victory that allowed the Yankees to grab control of the series.

The Yankees returned to Yankee Stadium for Game 6 and, in front of a wildly-cheering crowd of 57,142 fans sensing the kill, clinched their 35th pennant with a 9-5 victory. Scott Brosius belted a three-run homer, Derek Jeter a two-run triple and Bernie Williams had his best game of the postseason with three hits and two RBI.

Now the Yankees were one hurdle away from their ultimate goal.

Standing in their way was not the Atlanta Braves as expected or the Houston Astros with Randy Johnson, but the surprising San Diego Padres, who had first knocked off Houston and then Atlanta to win the second National League pennant in their 30-year history and their first in 14 years.

With Kevin Brown, a big-game pitcher who had baffled both the Astros and the Braves; Greg Vaughn, the almost-Yankee who had belted 50 homers in the regular season; and the redoubtable Tony Gwynn, an eight-time batting champion, the Padres, who also got major contributions from former Yankees Jim Leyritz and Sterling Hitchcock, were a formidable foe.

The 1998 World Series opened in New York on October 17, and the Yankees knew from the outset they were facing a tough rival. The Yankees opened the scoring with two runs in the second, but the Padres came back with two in the third and three more in the fifth off David Wells.

With Kevin Brown leading by three runs entering the seventh, the Padres looked like a good bet to grab the early lead in the series. But when San Diego manager Bruce Bochy lifted Brown with two runners on and one out, Chuck Knoblauch exploded a three-run homer off Donne Wall to tie, 5-5. The Yankees would score seven runs in the inning for a 9-5 victory that took much of the starch out of the Padres. It happened so quickly that the Padres hardly knew what hit them.

Again, Manager Joe Torre turned to El Duque for Game 2, and the Yankees eased his way by scoring three runs in the first, three more in the second and one in the third. Hernandez pitched seven innings for the 9-3 win and a two games-to-nothing lead.

The Padres were hopeful they could mount a comeback in their home ballpark, while the Yankees went to San Diego thinking a sweep would validate their claim as baseball's greatest team.

David Cone and Sterling Hitchcock dueled through five scoreless innings in Game 3. In the sixth, the Padres pushed across three runs, and it looked like the Series was about to take a dramatic turn in their favor.

Once again, late-inning lightning erupted for the Yankees. Scott Brosius started it with a solo homer leading off the seventh. Shane Spencer followed with a double and scored on an error by third baseman Ken Caminiti.

The Padres still held a lead, albeit a slim one, in the seventh when Brosius connected again—a three-run

Unable to compete in the postseason after undergoing surgery for colon cancer, Darryl Strawberry joined the 1998 world champion Yankees as they rode the victory parade through New York's celebrated "Canyon of Heroes." (AP/Wide World)

homer off Trevor Hoffman, San Diego's invincible closer who had saved 53 games during the regular season. Mariano Rivera closed out the 5-3 win with 1 2/3 innings of scoreless relief for his second save of the Series, and the Yankees were one win away from the sweep.

The honor of going for the clincher in Game 4 fell to Andy Pettitte. He hadn't pitched in 11 days, and he had been bombed by the Indians in his last start, but Pettitte was brilliant. He held the Padres scoreless into the eighth, when he was relieved first by Jeff Nelson, then Rivera.

Pitching with only three days' rest, Kevin Brown matched Pettitte zero for zero until Bernie Williams drove in the Yankees' first run with a high chopper to the mound in the sixth. The Yankees took a 3-0 lead in the eighth on Brosius' RBI single. (Brosius hit two homers and drove in six runs during the World Series, batted .471 and was named Most Valuable Player of the Series.)

Again, Mariano Rivera closed it out with 1 1/3 innings of scoreless relief, completing a postseason in which he pitched 13 1/3 innings without allowing a run.

The Yankees had realized their goal—a record of 11-2 in postseason play, a four-game sweep in the World Series and the 24th world championship in team history.

"I never saw the '27 Yankees or the '39 Yankees," said a joyful, sobbing Joe Torre. "But I did see the Oakland A's of the early seventies and Cincinnati's Big Red Machine, and this is the best team I've ever seen."

The greatest baseball team in 40 years? Perhaps.

The greatest baseball team ever?

Let future historians be the judges.

Records & Statistics

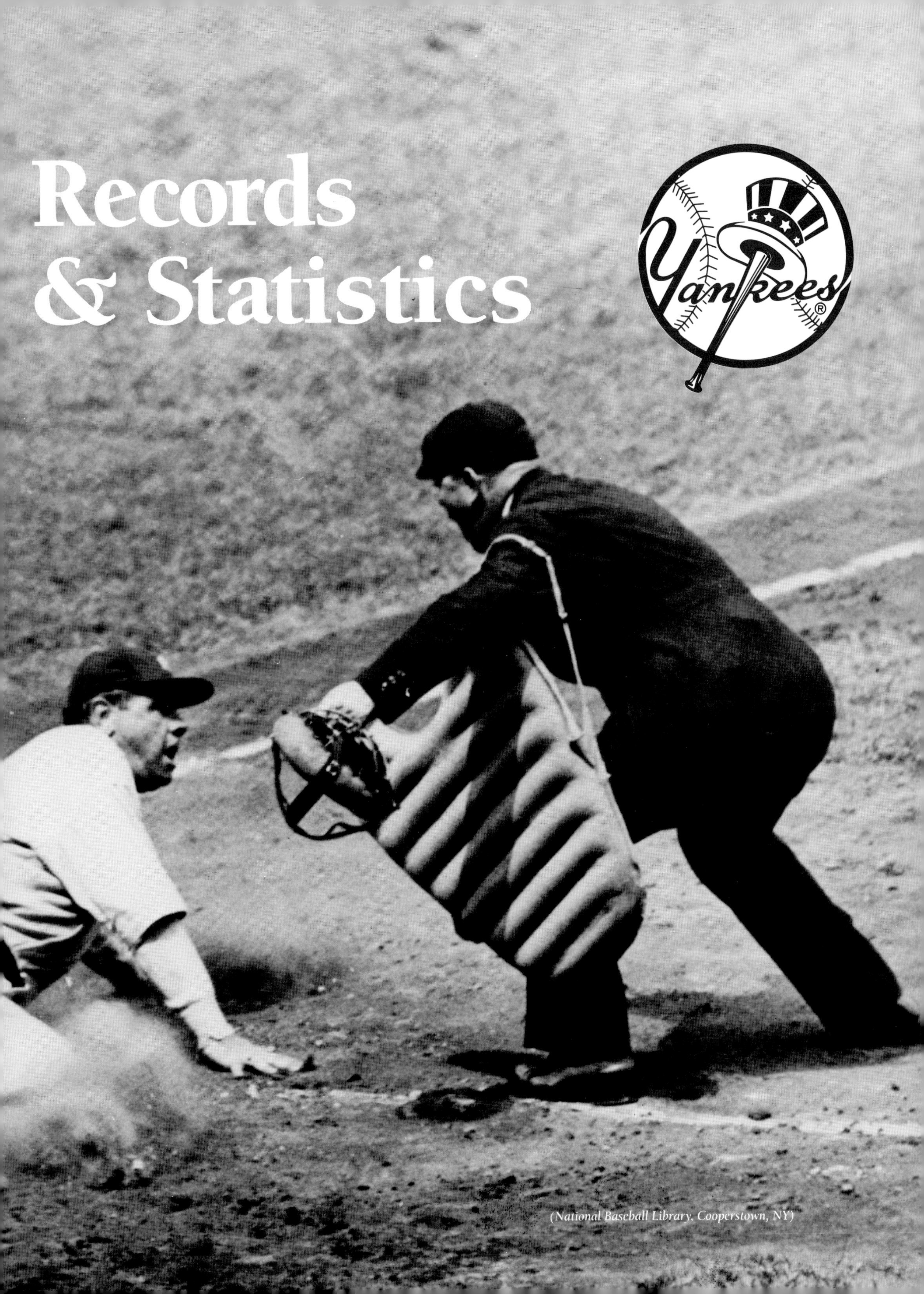

(National Baseball Library, Cooperstown, NY)

YANKEES MEMBERS OF BASEBALL HALL OF FAME

Babe Ruth
1936

Lou Gehrig
1939

Willie Keeler
1939

Clark C. Griffith
1945

Frank Chance
1946

Jack Chesbro
1946

Herb Pennock
1948

Paul Waner
1952

Edward G. Barrow
1953

Bill Dickey
1954

Home Run Baker
1955

Joe DiMaggio
1955

Dazzy Vance
1955

Joe McCarthy
1957

Bill McKechnie
1962

Burleigh Grimes
1964

Miller Huggins
1964

Casey Stengel
1966

Branch Rickey
1967

Red Ruffing
1967

Stan Coveleski
1969

Waite Hoyt
1969

Earle Combs
1970

George M. Weiss
1970

Yogi Berra
1972

Lefty Gomez
1972

Mickey Mantle
1974

Whitey Ford
1974

Bucky Harris
1975

Joe Sewell
1977

Larry MacPhail
1978

Johnny Mize
1981

Enos Slaughter
1985

Catfish Hunter
1987

Gaylord Perry
1991

Tony Lazzeri
1991

Reggie Jackson
1993

Phil Rizzuto
1994

ALL-TIME YANKEE ROSTER

Through 1998, 1,196 players have appeared in at least one game for the Yankees

A

Jim Abbott 1993–94
Harry Ables 1911
Spencer Adams 1926
Doc Adkins 1903
Steve Adkins 1990
Luis Aguayo 1988
Jack Aker 1969–72
Doyle Alexander 1976, 1982–83
Walt Alexander 1915–17
Bernie Allen 1972–73
Johnny Allen 1932–35
Neil Allen 1985, 1987–88
Sandy Alomar 1974–76
Felipe Alou 1971–73
Matty Alou 1973
Dell Alston 1977–78
Ruben Amaro 1966–68
John Anderson 1904–05
Rick Anderson 1979
Ivy Andrews 1931–32, 1937–38
Pete Appleton 1933
Angel Aragon 1914, 1916–17
Rugger Ardizola 1947
Mike Armstrong 1984–86
Brad Arnsberg 1986–87
Luis Arroyo 1960–63
Tucker Ashford 1981
Paul Assenmacher 1993
Joe Ausanio 1994–95
Jimmy Austin 1909–10
Martin Autry 1924
Oscar Azocar 1990

B

Loren Babe 1952–53
Stan Bahnsen 1966, 1968–71
Bill Bailey 1911
Frank Baker 1916–19, 1921–22
Frank Baker 1970–71
Steve Balboni 1981–83, 1989–90
Neal Ball 1907–09
Scott Bankhead 1995
Willie Banks 1997–98
Steve Barber 1967–68
Jesse Barfield 1989–92
Cy Barger 1906–07
Ray Barker 1965–67
Frank Barnes 1930
Honey Barnes 1926
Ed Barney 1915
George Batten 1912
Hank Bauer 1948–59
Paddy Baumann 1915–17
Don Baylor 1983–85
Walter Beall 1924–27
Jim Beattie 1978–79
Rick Beck 1965
Zinn Beck 1918
Fred Beene 1972–74
Joe Beggs 1938
John Bell 1907
Zeke Bella 1957
Benny Bengough 1923–30
Juan Beniquez 1979
Lou Berberet 1954–55
Dave Bergman 1975, 1977
Juan Bernhardt 1976
Walter Bernhardt 1918
Dale Berra 1985–86
Yogi Berra 1946–63
Bill Bevens 1944–47
Monte Beville 1903–04
Harry Billiard 1908
Doug Bird 1980–81
Ewell Blackwell 1952–53
Rick Bladt 1975
Paul Blair 1977–80
Walter Blair 1907–11
Johnny Blanchard 1955, 1959–65
Gil Blanco 1965
Wade Blasingame 1972
Steve Blateric 1972
Gary Blaylock 1959
Curt Blefary 1970–71
Elmer Bliss 1903–04
Ron Blomberg 1969, 1971–76
Mike Blowers 1989–91
Eddie Bockman 1946
Ping Bodie 1918–21
Len Boehmer 1969,1971
Brian Boehringer 1995–96
Wade Boggs 1993–96
Don Bollweg 1953
Bobby Bonds 1975
Ernie Bonham 1940–46
Juan Bonilla 1985,1987
Ricky Bones 1996
Luke Boone 1913–16
Frenchy Bordagaray 1941
Rich Bordi 1985,1987
Joe Borowski 1997–98
Hank Borowy 1942–45
Babe Borton 1913
Daryl Boston 1944
Jim Bouton 1962–68
Clete Boyer 1959–66
Ryan Bradley 1998
Scott Bradley 1984–85
Neal Brady 1915,1917
Ralph Branca 1954
Norm Branch 1941–42
Marshall Brant 1980
Garland Braxton 1925–26
Don Brennan 1933
Jim Brenneman 1965
Ken Brett 1976
Marv Breuer 1939–43
Billy Brewer 1996
Fritzie Brickell 1958–59
Jim Brideweser 1951–53
Marshall Bridges 1962–63
Harry Bright 1963–64
Ed Brinkman 1975
Johnny Broaca 1934–37
Lew Brockett 1907, 1909,1911
Jim Bronstad 1959
Tom Brookens 1989
Scott Brosius 1998
Bob Brower 1989
Boardwalk Brown 1914–15
Bobby Brown 1979–81
Carl Brown 1984
Hal Brown 1962
Jumbo Brown 1932–33, 1935–36
Jim Bruske 1998
Billy Bryan 1966–67
Jess Buckles 1916
Mike Buddie 1998
Jay Buhner 1987–88
Bill Burbach 1969–71
Lew Burdette 1950
Tim Burke 1992
George Burns 1928–29
Alex Burr 1914
Ray Burris 1979
Homer Bush 1997–98
Joe Bush 1922–24
Tom Burkey 1973–74
Ralph Buxton 1949
Joe Buzas 1945
Harry Byrd 1954
Sammy Byrd 1929–34
Tommy Byrne 1943, 1946–51, 1954–57
Marty Bystrom 1984–85

C

Greg Cadaret 1989–92
Charlie Caldwell 1925
Ray Caldwell 1910–18
Johnny Callison 1972–73
Howie Camp 1917
Bert Campaneris 1983
Archie Campbell 1928
John Candelaria 1988–89
Mike Cantwell 1916
Andy Carey 1952–60
Roy Carlyle 1926
Duke Carmel 1965
Dick Carroll 1909
Ownie Carroll 1930
Tommy Carroll 1955–56
Chuck Cary 1989–91
Hugh Casey 1949
Roy Castleton 1907
Bill Castro 1981
Danny Cater 1970–71
Rick Cerrone 1980–84, 1987,1990
Bob Cerv 1951–56, 1960–62
Chris Chambliss 1974–79, 1988
Frank Chance 1913–14
Spud Chandler 1937–47
Les Channell 1910,1914
Darrin Chapin 1991
Ben Chapman 1930–36
Mike Chartak 1940,1942
Hal Chase 1905–13
Jack Chesbro 1903–09
Clay Christiansen 1984
Al Cicotte 1957
Allie Clark 1947
George Clark 1913
Jack Clark 1988
Horace Clarke 1965–74
Walter Clarkson 1904–07
Ken Clay 1977–79
Pat Clements 1987–88
Tex Clevenger 1961–62
Lu Clinton 1966–67
Al Closter 1971–72
Andy Coakley 1911
Jim Coates 1956, 1959–62
Jim Cockman 1905
Rich Coggins 1975–76
Rocky Colavito 1968
King Cole 1914–15
Curt Coleman 1912
Jerry Coleman 1949–57
Rip Coleman 1955–56
Bob Collins 1944
Dave Collins 1982
Joe Collins 1948–57
Orth Collins 1904
Pat Collins 1926–28
Rip Collins 1920–21
Frank Colman 1946–47
Lloyd Colson 1970
Earle Combs 1924–35
David Cone 1995–98
Tom Connelly 1920–21
Joe Connor 1905
Wid Conroy 1903–08
Andy Cook 1993
Doc Cook 1913–16
Dusty Cooke 1930–32
Johnny Cooney 1944
Phil Cooney 1905
Don Cooper 1985
Guy Cooper 1914
Dan Costello 1913
Henry Cotto 1985–87
Ensign Cottrell 1915
Clint Courtney 1951
Ernie Courtney 1903
Stan Coveleski 1928

Billy Cowan	1969
Joe Cowley	1984–85
Bobby Cox	1968–69
Casey Cox	1972–73
Birdie Cree	1908–15
Lou Criger	1920
Herb Crompton	1945
Frankie Crosetti	1943–58
Ivan Cruz	1997
Jose Cruz	1988
Jack Cullen	1962, 1965–66
Roy Cullenbine	1942
Nick Cullop	1916–17
Nick Cullop	1926
John Cumberland	1968–70
Jim Curry	1911
Chad Curtis	1997–98
Fred Curtis	1905

D

Babe Dahlgren	1937–40
Buddy Daley	1961–64
Tom Daley	1914–15
Bert Daniels	1910–13
Bobby Davidson	1989
Chili Davis	1998
George Davis	1912
Kiddo Davis	1926
Lefty Davis	1903
Ron Davis	1978–81
Russ Davis	1994–95
Brian Dayett	1983–84
John Deering	1903
Jim Deidel	1974
Ivan DeJesus	1986
Frank Delahanty	1905–06, 1908
Bobby Del Greco	1957–58
Jim Delsing	1949–50
Joe DeMaestri	1960–61
Ray Demmitt	1909
Rick Dempsey	1973–76
Bucky Dent	1977–82
Claud Derrick	1913
Russ Derry	1944–45
Jim Deshales	1984
Jimmie DeShong	1934–35
Orestes Destrade	1987
Charlie Devens	1932–34
Al DeVormer	1921–22
Bill Dickey	1928–43, 1946
Murry Dickson	1958
Joe DiMaggio	1936–42, 1946–51
Kerry Dineen	1975–76
Al Ditmar	1957–61
Sonny Dixon	1956
Pat Dobson	1973–75
Cozy Dolan	1911–12
Atley Donald	1938–45
Mike Donovan	1908
Wild Bill Donovan	1915–16
Brian Dorsett	1989–90
Richard Dotson	1988–89
Patsy Dougherty	1904–06
John Dowd	1912
Al Downing	1961–69
Brian Doyle	1978–80
Jack Doyle	1905
Slow Joe Doyle	1906–10
Doug Drabek	1986
Bill Drescher	1944–46
Karl Drews	1946–48
Monk Dubiel	1944–45
Joe Dugan	1922–28
Ryne Duren	1958–61
Leo Durocher	1925, 1928–29
Cedric Durst	1927–30

E

Mike Easier	1986–87
Rawly Eastwick	1978
Doc Edwards	1965
Foster Edwards	1930
Robert Eenhoorn	1994–96
Dave Eiland	1988–91, 1995
Kid Elberfeld	1903–09
Gene Elliott	1911
Dock Ellis	1976–77
John Ellis	1969–72
Kevin Elster	1994–95
Red Embree	1948
Clyde Engle	1909–10
John Enright	1917
Todd Erdos	1998
Roger Erickson	1982–83
Juan Espino	1982–83, 1985–86
Alvaro Espinoza	1988–91
Nick Etten	1943–46
Barry Evans	1982

F

Charles Fallon	1905
Steve Farr	1991–93
Doc Farrell	1932–33
Alex Ferguson	1918, 1921,1925
Frank Fernandez	1967–69
Tony Fernandez	1995
Mike Ferraro	1966,1968
Wes Ferrell	1938–39
Tom Ferrick	1950–51
Chick Fewster	1917–22
Cecil Fielder	1996
Mike Figga	1997–98
Ed Figueroa	1976–80
Pete Filson	1987
Happy Finneran	1918
Mike Fischlin	1986
Brian Fisher	1985–86
Gus Fisher	1985–86
Ray Fisher	1910–17
Mike Fitzgerald	1911
Tim Foli	1984
Ray Fontenot	1983–84
Barry Foote	1981–82
Russ Ford	1909–13
Whitey Ford	1950, 1953–67
Eddie Foster	1910
Jack Fournier	1918
Andy Fox	1996–97
Ray Francis	1925
George Frazier	1981–83
Mark Freeman	1959
Ray French	1920
Lonny Frey	1947–48
Bob Friend	1966
John Frill	1910
Bill Fulton	1987
Dave Fultz	1903–05
Liz Funk	1929

G

John Gabler	1959–60
Joe Gallagher	1939
Mike Gallego	1992–94
Oscar Gamble	1976, 1979–84
John Ganzel	1903–04
Mike Garbark	1944–45
Damaso Garcia	1978–79
Billy Gardner	1961–62
Earl Gardner	1908–12
Rob Gardner	1970–72
Ned Garvin	1904
Milt Gaston	1924
Mike Gazelle	1923, 1926–28
Joe Gedeon	1916–17
Lou Gehrig	1923–39
Bob Geren	1988–91
Al Gettell	1945–46
Joe Glard	1927
Jake Gibbs	1962–71
Paul Gibson	1930
Frank Gilhooley	1913–18
Joe Girardi	1996–98
Fred Glade	1908
Fran Gleich	1919–20
Joe Glenn	1932–33, 1935–38
Lefty Gomez	1930–42
Jesse Gonder	1960–61
Fernando Gonzalez	1974
Pedro Gonzalez	1963–65
Wilbur Good	1905
Dwight Gooden	1996
Art Goodwin	1905
Joe Gordon	1938–43, 1946
Tom Gorman	1952–54
Rich Gossage	1978–83, 1989
Dick Gossett	1913–14
Larry Gowell	1972
Johnny Grabowski	1927–29
Wayne Granger	1973
Ted Gray	1955
Eli Grba	1959–60
Willie Greene	1903
Ken Griffey	1982–86
Mike Griffin	1979–81
Clark Griffith	1903–07
Bob Grim	1954–58
Burleigh Grimes	1934
Oscar Grimes	1943–46
Lee Grissom	1940
Cecilio Guante	1987–88
Lee Guetterman	1988–92
Ron Guidry	1975–78
Brad Gulden	1979–80
Don Gullett	1977–78
Bill Gullickson	1987
Randy Gumpert	1946–48
Larry Gura	1974–75

H

John Habyan	1990–93
Bump Hadley	1936–40
Kent Hadley	1960
Ed Hahn	1905–06
Noodles Hahn	1906
Hinkey Haines	1923
George Hales	1919
Bob Hale	1961
Jimmie Hall	1969
Mel Hall	1989–92
Roger Hambright	1971
Steve Hamilton	1963–70
Mike Handiboe	1911
Jim Hanley	1913
Truck Hannah	1918–20
Ron Hansen	1970–71
Joe Hanson	1913
Jim Hardin	1971
Bubbles Hargrave	1930
Harry Harper	1921
Toby Harrah	1984
Greg Harris	1994
Joe Harris	1914
Jim Hart	1973–74
Roy Hartzell	1911–16
Buddy Hassett	1942
Ron Hassey	1985–86
Andy Hawkins	1989–91
Chicken Hawks	1921
Charlie Hayes	1992,1996
Fran Healy	1976–78
Mike Heath	1978
Neal Heaton	1993
Don Heffner	1934–37
Mike Hegan	1964, 1966–67, 1973–74
Fred Heimach	1928–29
Woodie Held	1954
Charlie Hemphill	1908–11
Rollie Hernsley	1942–44
Bill Henderson	1930
Rickey Henderson	1985–89
Harvey Hendrick	1923–24
Elroy Hendricks	1976–77
Tim Hendryx	1915–17
Tommy Henrich	1937–42, 1946–50
Bill Henry	1966
Leo Hernandez	1986
Orlando Hernandez	1998
Xavier Hernandez	1994
Ed Hermann	1975
Hugh High	1915–18
Oral Hildebrand	1939–40
Jesse Hill	1935
Shawn Hillegas	1992
Frank Hiller	1946, 1948–49
Mack Hillis	1924
Rich Hinton	1972
Sterling Hitchcock	1992–95
Myril Hoag	1931–32, 1934–38
Butch Hobson	1982
Red Hoff	1911–13
Danny Hoffman	1906–07
Solly Hofman	1916
Fred Hofmann	1919–25
Bill Hogg	1905–08
Bobby Hogue	1951–52

Ken Holcombe	1945
Bill Holden	1913–14
Al Holland	1986–87
Ken Holloway	1930
Darren Holmes	1998
Fred Holmes	1903
Roger Holt	1980
Ken Holtzman	1976–78
Rick Honeycutt	1995
Don Hood	1979
Wally Hood	1949
Johnny Hopp	1950–52
Shags Horan	1924
Ralph Houk	1947–54
Elston Howard	1955–67
Matt Howard	1996
Steve Howe	1991–96
Harry Howell	1903
Jay Howell	1982–84
Dick Howser	1967–68
Waite Hoyt	1921–30
Rex Hudler	1984–85
Charles Hudson	1987–88
Keith Hughes	1987
Long Tom Hughes	1904
Tom Hughes	1906–07, 1909–10
John Hummel	1918
Mike Humphreys	1991–93
Ken Hunt	1959–60
Billy Hunter	1955–56
Catfish Hunter	1975–79
Mark Hutton	1993–94, 1996
Ham Hyatt	1918

I

Pete Incaviglia	1997
Hideki Irabu	1997–98

J

Fred Jacklitsch	1905
Grant Jackson	1976
Reggie Jackson	1977–81
Dion James	1992–93, 1995–96
Johnny James	1958, 1960–61
Stan Javier	1984
Domingo Jean	1993
Stanley Jefferson	1989
Jackie Jensen	1950–52
Mike Jerzembeck	1998
Derek Jeter	1995–98
Elvio Jimenez	1964
Tommy John	1979–82, 1986–89
Alex Johnson	1974–75
Billy Johnson	1943, 1946–51
Cliff Johnson	1977–79
Darrell Johnson	1957–58
Deron Johnson	1960–61
Don Johnson	1947,1950
Ernie Johnson	1923–25
Hank Johnson	1925–26, 1928–32
Jeff Johnson	1991–93
Johnny Johnson	1944
Ken Johnson	1969
Otis Johnson	1911
Roy Johnson	1936–37
Jay Johnstone	1978–79
Darryl Jones	1979
Gary Jones	1970–71
Jimmy Jones	1989–90
Ruppert Jones	1980
Sad Sam Jones	1922–26
Tim Jordan	1903
Art Jorgens	1929–39
Mike Jurewicz	1965

K

Jim Kaat	1979–80
Scott Kamieniecki	1991–96
Bob Kammeyer	1978–79
Frank Kane	1919
Bill Karlon	1930
Herb Karpel	1946
Benny Kauff	1912
Curt Kaufman	1982–83
Eddie Kearse	1942
Ray Keating	1912–16, 1918
Bob Keefe	1907
Willie Keeler	1903–09
Mike Kekich	1969–73
Charlie Keller	1939–43, 1945–49, 1952
Pat Kelly	1991–96
Roberto Kelly	1987–92
Steve Kemp	1983–84
John Kennedy	1967
Jerry Kenney	1967, 1969–72
Matt Keough	1983
Jimmy Key	1993–96
Steve Kiefer	1989
Dave Kingman	1977
Harry Kingman	1914
Fred Kipp	1960
Frank Kitson	1907
Ron Kittle	1986–87
Ted Kleinhans	1936
Red Kleinow	1904–10
Ed Klepfer	1911,1913
Ron Klimkowski	1969–70, 1972
Steve Kline	1970–74
Mickey Klutts	1976–78
Bill Knickerbocker	1938–40
John Knight	1909–11, 1913
Chuck Knoblauch	1998
Mark Koenig	1925–30
Jim Konstanty	1954–56
Andy Kosco	1968
Steve Kraly	1953
Jack Kramer	1951
Ernie Krueger	1915
Dick Kryhoski	1949
Tony Kubek	1957–65
Johnny Kucks	1955–59
Bill Kunkel	1963
Bob Kuzava	1951–54

L

Joe Lake	1908–09
Bill Lamar	1917–19
Hal Lanier	1972–73
Dave LaPoint	1989–90
Frank LaPorte	1905–10
Dave LaRoche	1981–83
Don Larsen	1955–59
Lyn Lary	1929–34
Marcus Lawton	1989
Gene Layden	1915
Tony Lazzeri	1926–37
Tim Leary	1990–92
Ricky Ledee	1998
Joe Lefebvre	1980
Al Leiter	1990
Frank Lela	1954–55
Jack Lelivelt	1912–13
Eddie Leon	1975
Louis LeRoy	1905–06
Ed Levy	1942–44
Duffy Lewis	1918–20
Jim Lewis	1982
Terry Ley	1972
Jim Leyritz	1990–94
Paul Lindblad	1978
Johnny Lindell	1941–50
Phil Linz	1962–65
Bryan Little	1986
Jack Little	1912
Clem Llewellyn	1922
Graeme Lloyd	1996–98
Gene Locklear	1976–77
Sherm Lollar	1947–48
Tim Lollar	1980
Phil Lombardi	1985–87
Dale Long	1960, 1962–63
Herman Long	1903
Ed Lopat	1948–55
Art Lopez	1965
Hector Lopez	1959–66
Baldy Louden	1907
Slim Love	1916–18
Torey Lovullo	1991
Mike Lowell	1998
Johnny Lucadello	1947
Joe Lucey	1920
Ray Luebbe	1925
Matt Luke	1996
Jerry Lumpe	1956–59
Scoff Lusader	1991
Sparky Lyle	1972–78
Al Lyons	1944, 1946–47
Jim Lyttle	1969–71

M

Duke Maas	1958–61
Kevin Maas	1990–93
Bob MacDonald	1995
Danny MacFayden	1932–34
Ray Mack	1947
Bunny Madden	1910
Elliott Maddox	1974–76
Dave Madison	1950
Lee Magee	1916–17
Sal Maglie	1957–58
Stubby Magner	1911
Jim Magnuson	1973
Fritz Maisel	1913–17
Hank Majeski	1946
Frank Makosky	1937
Pat Malone	1935–37
Pat Maloney	1912
Al Mamaux	1924
Rube Manning	1907–10
Mickey Mantle	1951–68
Josias Manzanillo	1995
Cliff Mapes	1948–51
Roger Maris	1960–66
Cliff Markle	1915–16, 1924
Jim Marquis	1925
Armando Marsans	1917–18
Cuddles Marshall	1946, 1948–49
Billy Martin	1950–53, 1955–57
Hersh Martin	1944–45
Jack Martin	1912
Tino Martinez	1996–98
Tippy Martinez	1974–76
Jim Mason	1974–76
Vic Mata	1984–85
Don Mattingly	1982–95
Carlos May	1976–77
Rudy May	1974–76, 1980–83
John Mayberry	1982
Carl Mays	1919–23
Lee Mazilli	1982
Larry McCall	1977–78
Joe McCarthy	1905
Pat McCauley	1903
Larry McClure	1910
George McConnell	1909, 1912–13
Mike McCormick	1970
Lance McCullers	1989–90
Lindy McDaniel	1968–73
Mickey McDermott	1956
Danny McDevitt	1961
Dave McDonald	1969
Jim McDonald	1952–54
Gil McDougald	1951–60
Jack McDowell	1995
Sam McDowell	1973
Lou McEvoy	1930–31
Herm McFarland	1903
Andy McGaffigan	1981
Lynn McGlothen	1982
Bob McGraw	1917–20
Deacon McGuire	1904–07
Marty McHale	1913–15
Irish McIlveen	1908–09
Tim McIntosh	1996
Bill McKechnie	1913
Rich McKinney	1972
Frank McManus	1904
Norm McMillan	1922
Tommy McMillan	1912
Mike McNally	1921–24
Herb McQuaid	1926
George McQuinn	1947–48
Bobby Meacham	1983–88
Charlie Meara	1914
Jim Mecir	1996
George Medich	1972–75
Bob Melvin	1994
Ramiro Mendoza	1996–98
Fred Merkle	1925–26
Andy Messersmith	1978

Tom Metcalf	1963
Bud Metheny	1943–46
Hensley Meulens	1989–93
Bob Meusel	1920–29
Bob Meyer	1964
Gene Michael	1968–74
Ezra Midkiff	1912–13
Pete Mikkelsen	1964–65
Larry Milbourne	1981–83
Sam Millitello	1992–93
Bill Miller	1952–54
Elmer Miller	1915–18, 1921–22
John Miller	1966
Alan Mills	1990–91
Buster Mills	1940
Mike Milosevich	1944–45
Paul Mirabella	1979
Willie Miranda	1953–54
Bobby Mitchell	1970
Fred Mitchell	1910
Johnny Mitchell	1921–22
Johnny Mize	1949–53
Kevin Mmahat	1989
George Mogridge	1915–23
Dale Mohorcic	1988–89
Fenton Mole	1959
Bill Monbouquette	1967–68
Ed Monroe	1917–18
Zack Monroe	1958–59
John Montefusco	1983–86
Rich Monteleone	1990–93
Archie Moore	1964–65
Earl Moore	1907
Wilcy Moore	1927–29, 1932–33
Ray Morehart	1927
Omar Moreno	1983–85
Mike Morgan	1982
Tom Morgan	1951–52, 1954–56
George Moriarty	1906–08
Jeff Moronko	1987
Hal Morris	1988–89
Ross Moschitto	1965,1967
Gerry Moses	1973
Terry Mulholland	1994
Charlie Mullen	1914–16
Jerry Mumphrey	1981–83
Bob Muncrief	1951
Bobby Munoz	1993
Thurman Munson	1969–79
Bobby Murcer	1965–66, 1969–74, 1979–83
Johnny Murphy	1932, 1934–43, 1946
Rob Murphy	1994
Dale Murray	1983–85
George Murray	1922
Larry Murray	1974–76

N

Jerry Narron	1979
Bots Nekola	1929
Gene Nelson	1981
Jeff Nelson	1996–98
Luke Nelson	1919
Craig Nettles	1973–83
Tex Neuer	1907
Ernie Nevel	1950–51
Floyd Newkirk	1934
Bobo Newsom	1947
Doc Newton	1905–09
Gus Niarhos	1946–50
Joe Niekro	1985–87
Phil Niekro	1984–85
Jerry Nielsen	1992
Scott Nielsen	1986, 1988–89
Harry Niles	1908
Otis Nixon	1983
Man Nokes	1990–94
Irv Noren	1952–56
Don Nottebart	1969
Les Nunamaker	1914–17

O

Johnny Oates	1980–81
Mike O'Berry	1984
Andy O'Connor	1908
Jack O'Connor	1903
Paddy O'Connor	1918
Heinie Odom	1925
Lefty O'Doul	1919–20, 1922
Rowland Office	1983
Bob Ojeda	1994
Rube Oldring	1905,1916
Bob Oliver	1975
Nate Oliver	1969
Paul O'Neill	1993–98
Steve O'Neill	1925
Queenie O'Rourke	1908
Al Orth	1904–09
Champ Osteen	1904
Joe Ostrowski	1950–52
Bill Otis	1912
Stubby Overmire	1951
Spike Owen	1993

P

John Pacella	1982
Del Paddock	1912
Dave Pagan	1973–76
Joe Page	1944–50
Mike Pagliarulo	1984–89
Donn Pall	1994
Clay Parker	1989–90
Ben Paschal	1924–29
Dan Pasqua	1985–87
Gil Patterson	1977
Jeff Patterson	1995
Mike Patterson	1981–82
Dave Pavlas	1995–96
Monte Pearson	1936–40
Roger Peckinpaugh	1913–21
Steve Peek	1941
Hipolito Pena	1988
Herb Pennock	1923–33
Joe Pepitone	1962–69
Marty Perez	1977
Melido Perez	1992–95
Pascual Perez	1990–91
Cecil Perkins	1967
Cy Perkins	1931
Gaylord Perry	1980
Fritz Peterson	1966–74
Andy Pettitte	1995–98
Ken Phelps	1988–89
Eddie Phillips	1932
Jack Phillips	1947–49
Cy Pieh	1913–15
Bill Piercy	1917,1921
Duane Pillette	1949–50
Lou Piniella	1974–84
George Pipgras	1923–24, 1927–33
Wally Pipp	1915–25
Jim Pisoni	1959–60
Eric Plunk	1989–91
Dale Polley	1996
Luis Polonia	1989–90, 1994
Bob Porterfield	1948–51
Jorge Posada	1995–98
Jack Powell	1904–05
Jake Powell	1936–40
Mike Powers	1905
Del Pratt	1918–20
Gerry Priddy	1941–42
Johnnie Priest	1911–12
Alfonso Pulido	1986
Ambrose Puttman	1903–05

Q

Mel Queen	1942,1944 1946–47
Ed Quick	1903
Jack Quinn	1909–12, 1919–21
Jamie Quirk	1989

R

Tim Raines	1996–98
Dave Rajsich	1978
Bobby Ramos	1982
Domingo Ramos	1978
John Ramos	1991
Pedro Ramos	1964–66
Lenny Randle	1979
Willie Randolph	1976–88
Vic Raschi	1946–53
Dennis Rasmussen	1984–87
Shane Rawley	1982–84
Jeff Reardon	1994
Jack Reed	1961–63
Jimmy Reese	1930–31
Hal Reniff	1961–67
Bill Renna	1953
Tony Rensa	1933
Roger Repoz	1964–66
Rick Reuschel	1981–82
Dave Revering	1981–82
Allie Reynolds	1947–54
Bill Reynolds	1913–14
Rick Rhoden	1987–88
Gordon Rhodes	1929–32
Harry Rice	1930
Bobby Richardson	1955–66
Nolen Richardson	1935
Branch Rickey	1907
Dave Righetti	1979, 1981–90
Jose Rijo	1984
Danny Rios	1997
Mariano Rivera	1995–98
Ruben Rivera	1995–96
Mickey Rivers	1976–79
Phil Rizzuto	1941–42, 1946–56
Roxy Roach	1910–11
Dale Roberts	1967
Andre Robertson	1981–85
Gene Robertson	1928–29
Aaron Robinson	1943, 1945–47
Bill Robinson	1967–69
Bruce Robinson	1979–80
Eddie Robinson	1954–56
Hank Robinson	1918
Jeff Robinson	1990
Aurelio Rodriguez	1980–81
Carlos Rodriguez	1991
Edwin Rodriguez	1982
Ellie Rodriguez	1968
Oscar Roettger	1923–24
Jay Rogers	1914
Kenny Rogers	1996
Tom Rogers	1921
Jim Roland	1972
Red Rolfe	1931, 1934–42
Buddy Rosar	1939–42
Larry Rosenthal	1944
Steve Roser	1944–46
Braggo Roth	1921
Jerry Royster	1987
Muddy Ruel	1917–20
Dutch Ruether	1926–27
Red Ruffing	1930–42, 1945–46
Allen Russell	1915–19
Marius Russo	1939–43, 1946
Babe Ruth	1920–34
Blondy Ryan	1935
Rosy Ryan	1928

S

Johnny Sain	1951–56
Lenn Sakata	1987
Mark Salas	1987
Jack Saltzgaver	1932, 1934–37
Billy Sample	1985
Celerino Sanchez	1972–73
Deion Sanders	1989–90
Roy Sanders	1918
Scott Sanderson	1991–92
Charlie Sands	1967
Fred Sanford	1949–51
Rafael Santana	1988
Don Savage	1944–45
Rick Sawyer	1974–75
Steve Sax	1989–91
Ray Scarborough	1952–53
Germany Schaefer	1916
Harry Schaeffer	1952
Roy Schalk	1932
Art Schallock	1951–55
Wally Schang	1921–25
Bob Schmidt	1909
Johnny Schmitz	1952–53
Pete Schneider	1919
Dick Schofield	1966
Paul Schreiber	1945
Art Schult	1953
Al Schulz	1912–14

Name	Years
Don Schulze	1989
Bill Schwartz	1914
Plus Schwert	1914–15
Everett Scott	1922–25
George Scott	1979
Rodney Scott	1982
Rod Scurry	1985–86
Ken Sears	1943
Bob Seeds	1936
Kal Segrist	1952
George Selkirk	1934–42
Ted Sepkowski	1947
Hank Severeid	1926
Joe Sewell	1931–33
Howard Shanks	1925
Billy Shantz	1960
Bobby Shantz	1957–60
Bob Shawkey	1915–27
Spec Shea	1947–49, 1951
Al Shealy	1928
George Shears	1912
Tom Sheehan	1921
Rollie Sheldon	1961–62, 1964–65
Skeeter Shelton	1915
Roy Sherid	1929–31
Pat Sheridan	1991
Dennis Sherrill	1978,1980
Ben Shields	1924–25
Steve Shields	1988
Bob Shirley	1983–87
Urban Shocker	1916–17, 1925–28
Tom Shopay	1967,1969
Ernie Shore	1919–20
Bill Short	1960
Norm Siebern	1956, 1958–59
Charlie Silvera	1948–56
Dave Silvestri	1991–95
Ken Silvestri	1941, 1946–47
Hack Simmons	1912
Dick Simpson	1969
Harry Simpson	1957–58
Duke Sims	1973–74
Bill Skiff	1926
Camp Skinner	1922
Joel Skinner	1986–88
Lou Skizas	1956
Bill Skowron	1954–62
Roger Slagle	1979
Don Slaught	1988–89
Enos Slaughter	1954–59
Roy Smalley	1982–84
Walt Smallwood	1917,1919
Charley Smith	1967–68
Elmer Smith	1922–23
Joe Smith	1913
Keith Smith	1984–85
Klondike Smith	1912
Lee Smith	1993
Harry Smythe	1934
J.T. Snow	1992
Eric Soderholm	1980
Luis Sojo	1998
Tony Solaita	1968
Steve Souchock	1946,1948
Jim Spencer	1978–81
Shane Spencer	1998
Charlie Spikes	1972
Russ Springer	1992
Bill Stafford	1960–65
Jake Stahl	1908
Roy Staiger	1979
Tuck Stainback	1942–45
Gerry Staley	1955–56
Charley Stanceu	1941
Andy Stankiewicz	1992–93
Fred Stanley	1973–80
Mike Stanley	1992–95
Mike Stanton	1997–98
Dick Starr	1947–48
Dave Stegman	1982
Dutch Sterrett	1912–13
Bud Stewart	1948
Lee Stine	1938
Snuffy Stirnweiss	1943–50
Tim Stoddard	1986–88
Mel Stottlemyre	1964–74
Hal Stowe	1960
Darryl Strawberry	1995–98
Gabby Street	1912
Marlin Stuart	1954
Bill Stumpf	1912–13
Tom Sturdivant	1955–59
Johnny Sturm	1941
Bill Sudakis	1974
Steve Sundra	1936, 1938–40
Dale Sveum	1998
Jeff Sweeney	1908–15
Ron Swoboda	1971–73

T

Name	Years
Fred Talbot	1966–69
Vito Tamulis	1934–35
Frank Tanana	1993
Jesse Tannehill	1903
Danny Tartabull	1992–95
Wade Taylor	1991
Zack Taylor	1934
Frank Tepedino	1967, 1969–72
Walt Terrell	1989
Ralph Terry	1956–57, 1959–64
Dan Tessmer	1998
Dick Tettelbach	1955
Bob Tewksbury	1986–87
Ira Thomas	1906–07
Lee Thomas	1961
Myles Thomas	1926–29
Stan Thomas	1977
Gary Thomasson	1978
Homer Thompson	1912
Tommy Thompson	1912
Jack Thoney	1904
Hank Thormahlen	1917–20
Marv Throneberry	1955, 1958–59
Luis Tiant	1979–80
Dick Tidrow	1974–79
Bobby Tiefenauer	1965
Eddie Tierneyer	1909
Ray Tift	1907
Bob Tillman	1967
Thad Tillotson	1967–68
Dan Tipple	1915
Wayne Tolleson	1986–90
Earl Torgeson	1961
Rusty Torres	1971–72
Mike Torrez	1977
Cesar Tovar	1976
Tom Tresh	1961–69
Gus Triandos	1953–54
Steve Trout	1987
Virgil Trucks	1958
Frank Truesdale	1914
Bob Turley	1955–62
Jim Turner	1942–45

U

Name	Years
George Uhle	1933–34
Tom Underwood	1980–81
Bob Unglaub	1904
Cecil Upshaw	1974

V

Name	Years
Elmer Valo	1960
Russ Van Atta	1933–35
Dazzy Vance	1915,1918
Joe Vance	1937–38
Bobby Vaughn	1909
Hippo Vaughn	1908, 1910–12
Bobby Veach	1925
Randy Velarde	1987–95
Otto Velez	1973–76
Joe Verbanic	1967–68, 1970
Frank Verdi	1953
Sammy Vick	1917–20

W

Name	Years
Jake Wade	1946
Dick Wakefied	1950
Jim Walewander	1990
Curt Walker	1919
Dixie Walker	1931, 1933–36
Mike Wallace	1974–75
Jimmy Walsh	1914
Joe Walsh	1910–11
Roxy Walters	1915–18
Danny Walton	1971
Paul Waner	1944–45
Jack Wanner	1909
Pee Wee Wanninger	1925
Aaron Ward	1917–26
Gary Ward	1987–89
Joe Ward	1909
Pete Ward	1970
Jack Warhop	1908–15
George Washburn	1941
Claudell Washington	1986–88, 1990
Gary Waslewski	1970–71
Bob Watson	1980–82
Roy Weatherly	1943,1946
David Weathers	1996
Jim Weaver	1931
Dave Wehmneister	1981
Lefty Weinert	1931
David Wells	1997–98
Ed Wells	1929–32
Butch Wensloff	1942,1947
Julie Wera	1927,1929
Bill Werber	1930,1933
Dennis Werth	1979–81
John Wetteland	1995–96
Stefan Wever	1982
Steve Whitaker	1966–68
Roy White	1965–79
Wally Whitehurst	1996
George Whiteman	1913
Terry Whitfield	1974–76
Ed Whitson	1985–86
Kemp Wicker	1936–38
Al Wickland	1919
Bob Wickman	1992–97
Bob Wiesler	1951, 1954–55
Bill Wight	1946–47
Ted Wilborn	1980
Ed Wilkinson	1911
Bernie Williams	1991–98
Bob Williams	1911–13
Gerald Williams	1992–96
Harry Williams	1913–14
Jimmy Williams	1903–07
Stan Williams	1963–64
Walt Williams	1974–75
Archie Wilson	1951–52
Pete Wilson	1908–09
Ted Wilson	1956
Snake Wiltse	1903
Gordie Windhorn	1959
Dave Winfield	1981–90
Mickey Witek	1949
Mike Witt	1990–93
Whitey Witt	1922–25
Bill Wolfe	1903–04
Harry Wolter	1910–13
Harry Wolverton	1912
Dooley Womack	1966–68
Gene Woodling	1949–54
Ron Woods	1969–71
Dick Woodson	1974
Hank Workman	1950
Ken Wright	1974
Yats Wuestling	1930
John Wyatt	1968
Butch Wynegar	1982–86
Jimmy Wynn	1977

Y

Name	Years
Joe Yeager	1905–06
Jim York	1976
Curt Young	1992
Ralph Young	1913

Z

Name	Years
Tom Zachary	1928–30
Jack Zalusky	1903
George Zeber	1977–78
Rollie Zeider	1913
Guy Zinn	1911–12
Bill Zuber	1943–46
Paul Zuvella	1986–87

CHAMPIONSHIP YANKEE CLUBS

35 American League Pennant Winners

24 World Championship Teams

Casey Stengel (New York Yankees Archives)

Year	Won	Lost	Pct.	GA	Manager	World Series Opp	Record W	L
1921	98	55	.641	4.5	Miller Huggins	Giants	3	5
1922	94	60	.610	1.0	Miller Huggins	Giants	**0	4
*1923	98	54	.645	16.0	Miller Huggins	Giants	4	2
1926	91	63	.591	3.0	Miller Huggins	Cardinals	3	5
*1927	110	44	.714	19.0	Miller Huggins	Pirates	4	0
*1928	101	53	.656	2.5	Miller Huggins	Cardinals	4	0
*1932	107	47	.695	13.0	Joe McCarthy	Cubs	4	0
*1936	102	51	.667	19.5	Joe McCarthy	Giants	4	2
*1937	102	52	.662	13.0	Joe McCarthy	Giants	4	1
*1938	99	53	.651	9.5	Joe McCarthy	Cubs	4	0
*1939	106	45	.702	17.0	Joe McCarthy	Reds	4	0
*1941	101	53	.656	17.0	Joe McCarthy	Dodgers	4	1
1942	103	51	.689	9.0	Joe McCarthy	Cardinals	1	4
*1943	98	56	.636	13.5	Joe McCarthy	Cardinals	4	1
*1947	97	57	.630	12.0	Bucky Harris	Dodgers	4	3
*1949	97	57	.630	1.0	Casey Stengel	Dodgers	4	1
*1950	98	56	.636	3.0	Casey Stengel	Phillies	4	0
*1951	98	56	.636	5.0	Casey Stengel	Giants	4	2
*1952	95	59	.617	2.0	Casey Stengel	Dodgers	4	3
*1953	99	52	.656	8.5	Casey Stengel	Dodgers	4	2
1955	96	58	.623	3.0	Casey Stengel	Dodgers	3	4
*1956	97	57	.630	9.0	Casey Stengel	Dodgers	4	3
1957	98	56	.636	8.0	Casey Stengel	Braves	3	4
*1958	92	62	.597	10.0	Casey Stengel	Braves	4	3
1960	97	57	.630	8.0	Casey Stengel	Pirates	3	4
*1961	109	53	.673	8.0	Ralph Houk	Reds	4	3
*1962	96	66	.593	5.0	Ralph Houk	Giants	4	3
1963	104	57	.646	10.5	Ralph Houk	Dodgers	0	4
1964	99	63	.611	1.0	Yogi Berra	Cardinals	3	4
1976	97	62	.610	10.5	Billy Martin	Reds	0	4
*1977	100	62	.617	2.5	Billy Martin	Dodgers	4	2
*1978	100	63	.613	1.0	Martin-Lemon	Dodgers	4	2
†1981	34	22	.607	2.0	Gene Michael			
	25	26	.490	-5.0	Michael-Lemon	Dodgers	2	4
*1996	92	70	.568	4.0	Joe Torre	Braves	4	2
*1998	114	48	.704	22.0	Joe Torre	Padres	4	0
					(Yankees' World Series Totals)		117	79

*World Champions

†1st-Half Winners ** Tie game in 1922

Micky Mantle, Bobby Richardson, and Whitey Ford (New York Yankees Archives)

NEW YORK YANKEES—YEAR BY-YEAR

Year	Position	GA/GB	Won	Lost	Pct.	Manager	Attendance
1903	Fourth	17.0	72	62	.537	Clark Griffith	211,808
1904	Second	1.5	92	59	.609	Clark Griffith	438,919
1905	Sixth	21.5	71	78	.477	Clark Griffith	309,100
1906	Second	3.0	90	61	.596	Clark Griffith	434,700
1907	Fifth	21.0	70	78	.473	Clark Griffith	350,020
1908	Eighth	39.5	51	103	.331	Griffith-N. Elberfeld	305,500
1909	Fifth	23.5	74	77	.490	George T. Stallings	501,000
1910	Second	14.5	68	63	.583	Stallings-Hal Chase	355,857
1911	Sixth	25.5	76	76	.500	Hal Chase	302,444
1912	Eighth	55.0	50	102	.329	Harry Wolverton	242,194
1913	Seventh	38.0	57	94	.377	Frank Chance	302,444
1914a	Sixth	30.0	70	84	.455	Chance-R. Peckinpaugh	359,477
1915	Fifth	32.5	69	83	.454	William E. Donovan	256,035
1916	Fourth	11.0	80	74	.519	William E. Donovan	469,211
1917	Sixth	28.5	71	82	.464	William E. Donovan	330,294
1918	Fourth	13.5	60	63	.488	Miller J. Huggins	282,047
1919	Third	7.5	80	59	.576	Miller J. Hugginsa	619,164
1920	Third	3.0	95	59	.617	Miller J. Huggins	1,289,422
1921	First	4.5	98	55	.641	Miller J. Huggins	1,230,096
1922	First	1.0	94	60	.610	Miller J. Huggins	1,026,134
1923*	First	16.0	98	54	.645	Miller J. Huggins	1,007,060
1924	Second	2.0	89	63	.586	Miller J. Huggins	1,053,533
1925	Seventh	28.5	69	85	.448	Miller J. Huggins	697,267
1926	First	3.0	91	63	.591	Miller J. Huggins	1,027,095
1927*	First	19.0	110	44	.714	Miller J. Huggins	1,164,015
1928*	First	2.5	101	53	.656	Miller J. Huggins	1,072,132
1929	Second	18.0	88	66	.571	Huggins-Fletcher	960,148
1930	Third	16.0	86	68	.558	Bob Shawkey	1,109, 230
1931	Second	13.5	94	59	.614	Joe McCarthy	912,437
1932*	First	13.0	107	47	.695	Joe McCarthy	962,320
1933	Second	7.0	91	59	.607	Joe McCarthy	728,014
1934	Second	7.0	94	60	.610	Joe McCarthy	854,082
1935	Second	3.0	89	60	.597	Joe McCarthy	657,508
1936*	First	19.5	102	51	.667	Joe McCarthy	976,913
1937*	First	13.0	102	52	.662	Joe McCarthy	998,148
1938*	First	9.5	99	53	.651	Joe McCarthy	970,916
1939*	First	17.0	106	45	.702	Joe McCarthy	859,785
1940	Third	2.0	88	66	.571	Joe McCarthy	988,975
1941*	First	17.0	101	53	.656	Joe McCarthy	964,731
1942	First	9.0	103	51	.669	Joe McCarthy	988,251
1943*	First	13.5	98	56	.636	Joe McCarthy	645,006
1944	Third	6.0	83	71	.539	Joe McCarthy	822,864
1945	Fourth	6.5	81	71	.531	Joe McCarthy	881,846
1946	Third	17.0	87	67	.565	McCarthy-W. Dicky-Neun	2,265,532
1947*	First	12.0	97	57	.630	Bucky Harris	2,178,937
1948	Third	2.5	94	60	.610	Bucky Harris	2,373,901
1949*	First	1.0	97	57	.630	Casey Stengel	2,281,676
1950*	First	3.0	98	56	.636	Casey Stengel	2,081,380
1951*	First	5.0	98	56	.636	Casey Stengel	1,950,017
1952*	First	2.0	95	59	.617	Casey Stengel	1,629,665
1953*	First	8.5	99	52	.656	Casey Stengel	1,537,811
1954	Second	8.0	103	51	.669	Casey Stengel	1,475,171
1955	First	3.0	96	58	.623	Casey Stengel	1,490,138
1956*	First	9.0	97	57	.680	Casey Stengel	1,491,784
1957	First	8.0	98	56	.636	Casey Stengel	1,497,134
1958*	First	10.0	92	62	.597	Casey Stengel	1,428,428
1959	Third	15.0	79	75	.513	Casey Stengel	1,552,030
1960	First	8.0	97	57	.630	Casey Stengel	1,627,349
1961*	First	8.0	109	53	.673	Ralph Houk	1,747,736
1962*	First	5.0	96	66	.593	Ralph Houk	1,493,574
1963	First	10.5	104	57	.646	Ralph Houk	1,308,920
1964	First	1.0	99	63	.611	Yogi Berra	1,305,838
1965	Sixth	25.0	77	85	.475	Johnny Keane	1,213,552
1966	Tenth	26.5	70	89	.440	Keane-Houk	1,124,648
1967	Ninth	20.0	72	90	.444	Ralph Houk	1,141,714
1968	Fifth	20.0	83	79	.512	Ralph Houk	1,125,124
1969	Fifth	28.5	80	81	.497	Ralph Houk	1,067,996
1970	Second	15.0	93	69	.574	Ralph Houk	1,136,879
1971	Fourth	21.0	82	80	.506	Ralph Houk	1,070,771
1972	Fourth	6.5	79	76	.510	Ralph Houk	966,328
1973	Fourth	17.0	80	82	.494	Ralph Houk	1,262,077
1973	Second	2.0	89	73	.549	Bill Virdon	1,273,075
1975	Third	12.0	83	77	.519	Virdon-Martin	1,288,048
1976	First	10.5	97	62	.610	Billy Martin	2,012,434
1977*	First	2.5	100	62	.617	Billy Martin	2,103,092
1978*	First	1.0	100	63	.613	Martin-Lemon	2,335,871
1979	Fourth	13.5	89	71	.556	Lemon-Martin	2,537,765
1980b	First	3.0	103	59	.630	Dick Howser	2,627,417
1981	First	2.0	34	22	.607	Gene Michael	
	Sixth	5.0	25	26	.490	Michael-Lemon	1,614,533
1982	Fifth	16.0	79	83	.488	Lemon-Michael-King	2,041,219
1983	Third	7.0	91	71	.562	Billy Martin	2,257,976
1984	Third	17.0	87	75	.537	Yogi Berra	1,821,815
1985	Second	2.0	97	64	.602	Berra-Martin	2,214,587
1986	Second	5.5	90	72	.556	Lou Piniella	2,268,116
1987	Fourth	9.0	89	73	.549	Lou Piniella	2,427,672
1988	Fifth	3.5	85	76	.528	Martin-Piniella	2,633,701
1989	Fifth	14.5	74	87	.460	Green-Dent	2,170,485
1990	Seventh	21.0	67	95	.414	Dent-Merrill	2,006,436
1991	Fifth	21.0	71	91	.438	Stump Merrill	1,863,731
1992c	Fourth	20.0	76	86	.469	Buck Showalter	1,748,737
1993	Second	7.0	88	74	.543	Buck Showalter	2,416,942
1994d	First	6.5	70	43	.619	Buck Showalter	1,675,557
1995e	Second	7.0	79	65	.549	Buck Showalter	1,705,257
1996*	First	4.0	92	90	.568	Joe Torre	2,250,839
1997	Second	2.0	96	66	.593	Joe Torre	2,580,325
1998*	First	22.0	114	48	.704	Joe Torre	2,949,734
	Totals		8,394	6,426	.566		

a Tied with Chicago
b Lost to KC in ALCS
c Tied with Cleveland
d No postseason
e Won wild card playoff berth by 1 game over Seattle and California; lost to Seattle in AL Division Series
*World Champions

World Championships-24
American League Championships-35
Finished First-6; Second-17; Third-11; Fourth-10; Fifth-9; Sixth-6; Seventh-3; Eighth-2; Ninth-1; Tenth-1.
Highest Percentage .714 in 1927
Lowest .329 in 1912.

The 1936 World Champion New York Yankees. Team owner Jacob Ruppert is center foreground. (New York Yankees Archives)

JOE DIMAGGIO'S 56-GAME HITTING STREAK

DATE 1941	SITE	OPPONENT	STARTING PITCHER	JOE D AT-BAT	GAME SCORE
May 15	Yankee Stadium	Chicago	Edgar Smith	1-for-4	1-13
16	Yankee Stadium	Chicago	Thornton Lee	2-for-4	6-5
17	Yankee Stadium	Chicago	John Rigney	1-for-3	2-3
18	Yankee Stadium	St. Louis	Bob Harris	3-for-3	12-2
19	Yankee Stadium	St. Louis	Dennis Galehouse	1-for-3	1-5
20	Yankee Stadium	St. Louis	Eldon Auker	1-for-5	10-9
21	Yankee Stadium	Detroit	Schoolboy Rowe	2-for-5	5-4
22	Yankee Stadium	Detroit	Bobo Newsom	1-for-5	6-5
23	Yankee Stadium	Boston	Dick Newsome	1-for-5	9-9
24	Yankee Stadium	Boston	Earl Johnson	1-for-4	7-6
25	Yankee Stadium	Boston	Lefty Grove	1-for-5	3-10
27	Griffith Stadium	Washington	Ken Chase	4-for-5	10-8
28	Griffith Stadium	Washington	Sid Hudson	1-for-4	6-5
29	Griffith Stadium	Washington	Steve Sundra	1-for-3	2-2
30*	Fenway Park	Boston	Earl Johnson	1-for-2	4-3
30	Fenway Park	Boston	Mickey Harris	1-for-3	0-13
June 1*	Municipal Stadium	Cleveland	Al Milnar	1-for-4	2-0
1	Municipal Stadium	Cleveland	Mel Harder	1-for-4	5-3
2	Municipal Stadium	Cleveland	Bob Feller	2-for-4	5-7
3	Briggs Stadium	Detroit	Dizzy Trout	1-for-4	2-4
5	Briggs Stadium	Detroit	Hal Newhouser	1-for-5	4-5
7	Sportsman's Park	St. Louis	Bob Muncrief	3-for-5	11-7
8*	Sportsman's Park	St. Louis	Eldon Auker	2-for-4	9-3
8	Sportsman's Park	St. Louis	Bob Harris 2-for-4	8-3	
10	Comiskey Park	Chicago	John Rigney	1-for-5	8-3
12	Comiskey Park	Chicago	Thornton Lee	2-for-4	3-2
14	Yankee Stadium	Cleveland	Bob Feller	1-for-2	4-1
15	Yankee Stadium	Cleveland	Jim Bagby	1-for-3	3-2
18	Yankee Stadium	Cleveland	Al Milner	1-for-5	6-4
17	Yankee Stadium	Cleveland	John Rigney	1-for-4	7-8
18	Yankee Stadium	Cleveland	Thornton Lee	1-for-3	2-3
19	Yankee Stadium	Cleveland	Edgar Smith	3-for-3	7-2
20	Yankee Stadium	Detroit	Bobo Newsom	4-for-5	14-4
21	Yankee Stadium	Detroit	Dizzy Trout	1-for-4	2-7
22	Yankee Stadium	Detroit	Hal Newhouser	2-for-5	5-4
24	Yankee Stadium	St. Louis	Bob Muncrief	1-for-4	9-1
25	Yankee Stadium	St. Louis	Dennis Galehouse	1-for-4	7-5
26	Yankee Stadium	St. Louis	Eldon Auker	1-for-4	4-1
27	Shibe Park	Philadelphia	Chubby Dean	2-for-3	6-7
28	Shibe Park	Philadelphia	Johnny Babich	2-for-5	7-4
29*	Griffith Stadium	Washington	Dutch Leonard	1-for-4	9-4
29	Griffith Stadium	Washington	Sid Hudson	1-for-5	7-5
July 1*	Yankee Stadium	Boston	Mickey Harris	2-for-4	7-2
1	Yankee Stadium	Boston	Jack Wilson	1-for-3	9-2
2	Yankee Stadium	Boston	Dick Newsome	1-for-5	8-4
5	Yankee Stadium	Philadelphia	Phil Marchildon	1-for-4	10-5
6*	Yankee Stadium	Philadelphia	Johnny Babich	4-for-5	
6	Yankee Stadium	Philadelphia	Jack Knott	2-for-4	3-1
10	Sportsman's Park	St. Louis	John Niggeling	1-for-2	1-0
11	Sportsman's Park	St. Louis	Bob Harris	4-for-5	6-2
12	Sportsman's Park	St. Louis	Eldon Auker	2-for-5	7-5
13*	Comiskey Park	Chicago	Ted Lyons	3-for-4	8-1
13	Comiskey Park	Chicago	Thornton Lee	1-for-4	1-0
14	Comiskey Park	Chicago	John Rigney	1-for-3	1-7
15	Comiskey Park	Chicago	Edgar Smith	2-for-4	5-4
16	Municipal Stadium	Cleveland	Al Milnar	3-for-4	10-3

(Cranston & Elkins)

(National Baseball Library, Cooperstown, NY)

YANKEE AMERICAN LEAGUE BATTING CHAMPIONS

Year	Yankee	AVG.	G	AB	R	H	2B	3B	HR	RBI
1924	Babe Ruth	.378*	153	529	143*	200	39	7	46*	121
1934	Lou Gehrig	.363*	154	579	128	210	40	6	49*	165*
1939	Joe DiMaggio	.381	120	462	108	176	32	6	30	126
1940	Joe DiMaggio	.352*	132	508	93	179	28	9	31	133
1945	Snuffy Stimweiss	.309*	152	632	107*	195*	32	22*	10	64
1956	Mickey Mantle	.353*	150	533	132*	188	22	5	52*	130*
1984	Don Mattingly	.343*	153	603	91	207*	44*	2	23	110
1994	Paul O'Neill	.359*	103	368	68	132	25	1	21	83
1998	Bernie Williams	.339*	128	499	101	169	30	5	26	97

*League Leaders

LEFT: ***Bob Fishel, Yankees public relations director from 1954-74.***

BELOW: ***Long-time voice of the Yankees, Mel Allen.*** *(New York Yankees Archives)*

ABOVE: *Rookie infielder Leo Durocher with Babe Ruth, 1929. (New York Yankees Archives.)*

BELOW: *Babe Ruth homers in the 1932 World Series vs. the Chicago Cubs; #4 is Lou Gehrig, #21 is Joe Sewell (New York Yankees Archives)*

ALL-TIME YANKEE TEAM RECORDS

Most players	50 in 1989
Fewest players	25 in 1923, 1927
Most games	164 in 1964, 1968
Most at bats	5705 in 1964
Most runs	1067 in 1931
Fewest runs	549 in 1908
Most opponents runs	898 in 1930
Most hits	1683 in 1930
Fewest hits	1137 in 1968
Most singles	1237 in 1988
Most doubles	315 in 1936
Most triples	110 in 1930
Most homers	240 in 1961
Most home runs by pinch-hitters, season	10 in 1961
Most home runs with bases filled	10 in 1987
Most total bases	2703 in 1936
Most sacrifices (SH and SF)	218 in 1922, 1926
Most sacrifice hits	178 in 1906
Most sacrifice flies	72 in 1974, 1996
Most stolen bases	289 in 1910
Most times caught stealing	82 in 1920
Most bases on balls	766 in 1932
Most strikeouts	1043 in 1967
Fewest strikeouts	420 in 1924
Most times hit by pitch	53 in 1990
Fewest times hit by pitch	14 in 1969
Most runs batted in	995 in 1936
Highest batting average	.309 in 1930
Lowest batting average	.214 in 1968
Highest slugging average	.489 in 1927
Lowest slugging average	.287 in 1914
Most times grounded into double play	152 in 1982
Fewest times grounded into double play	91 in 1963
Most times left on base	1258 in 1996
Fewest times left on base	1010 in 1920
Most .300 hitters	9 in 1930
Most putouts	4520 in 1964
Fewest putouts	3993 in 1935
Most assists	2086 in 1904
Fewest assists	1493 in 1948
Most chances accepted	6383 in 1980
Fewest chances accepted	5551 in 1935
Most errors	386 in 1912
Fewest errors	91 in 1996
Most errorless games	91 in 1964
Most consecutive errorless games	10 in 1977, 1993, 1995
Most double plays	214 in 1956
Fewest double plays	81 in 1912
Most consecutive games, one or more double plays turned	19 (27 double plays), 1992
Most passed balls	32 in 1913
Fewest passed balls	0 in 1931
Highest fielding average	.985 in 1996
Lowest fielding average	.939 in 1912
Most games won	114 in 1998
Most home games won	65 in 1961
Most road games won	54 in 1939
Most games lost	103 in 1908
Highest percentage games won	.714 in 1927
Lowest percentage games won	.329 in 1912
Most shutouts won, season	24 in 1951
Most shutouts lost, season	27 in 1914
Most 1-0 games won	6 in 1908, 1968
Most 1-0 games lost	9 in 1914
Most consecutive games won, season	19 in 1947
Most consecutive games lost, season	13 in 1913
Most consecutive extra-inning games	4 in 1992
Most times league champions	35
Most runs, game	New York 25, Philadelphia 2, May 24, 1936
by opponent, on road	Cleveland 24, New York 6, July 29, 1928
by opponent, at home	Detroit 19, New York 1, June 17, 1925 Toronto 19, New York 3, September 10, 1977
Most runs, shutout game	New York 21, Philadelphia 0, August 13, 1939, Game 2, 8 innings
by opponent	Chicago 15, New York 0, July 15, 1907 Chicago 15, New York 0, May 5, 1950
Most runs, doubleheader shutout	24, New York vs. Philadelphia, September 4, 1944
Longest 1-0 game won	15 innings, New York 1, Philadelphia 0, July 4, 1925, Game 1
Longest 1-0 game lost	14 innings, Boston 1, New York 0, September 24, 1969
Most runs, inning	14, N.Y. vs. Washington, July 6, 1920, fifth inning
Most hits, game	30, New York vs. Boston, September 28, 1923
Most doubles, game	10, New York at Toronto, April 12, 1988
Most home runs, game	8, New York vs. Philadelphia, June 28, 1939, Game 1
Most consecutive games, one or more home runs	25 (40 homers), 1941
Most home runs in consecutive games in which home runs were made	40 25 games), 1941
Most total bases, game	53, New York vs. Philadelphia, June 28, 1939, Game 1
Most grand slams, game	2, New York vs. Philadelphia, May 24, 1936 New York at Toronto, June 29, 1987

1962 was a good year for the Yankees. Showing off their hardware left to right: Ralph Terry, World Series MVP; Mickey Mantle, American League MVP; Tom Tresh, American League Rookie of the Year (New York Yankees Archive)

YANKEES AMERICAN LEAGUE MOST VALUABLE PLAYERS

YEAR	PLAYER	AGE	POS	G	AB	R	H	2B	3B	HR	RBI	BA	E
1923	Babe Ruth	28	OF-1B	152	522	151*	205	45	13	41*	130**	.393	11
1927	Lou Gehrig	24	1B	155*	584	149	218	52*	18	47	175*	.373	15
1936	Lou Gehrig	33	1B	155**	579	167	205	37	7	49*	152	.354	9
1939	Joe DiMaggio	25	OF	120	462	108	176	32	6	30	126	.381*	5
1941	Joe DiMaggio	27	OF	139	541	122	193	43	11	30	125*	.357	9
1942	Joe Gordon	27	2B	147	538	88	173	29	4	18	103	.322	28*

YEAR	PLAYER	AGE	POS	G	IP	W	L	PCT.	H	R	ER	SO	BB	ERA
1943	Spud Chandler	36	RHP	30	253	20*	4	.833*	197	62	46	134	54	1.64*

YEAR	PLAYER	AGE	POS	G	AB	R	H	2B	3B	HR	RBI	BA	E
1947	Joe DiMaggio	33	OF	141	534	97	168	31	10	20	97	.315	1
1950	Phil Rizzuto	32	SS	155	617	125	200	36	7	7	66	.324	14
1951	Yogi Berra	26	C	141	547	92	161	19	4	27	88	.294	13**
1954	Yogi Berra	29	C-3B	151	584	88	179	28	6	22	125	.307	8
1955	Yogi Berra	30	C	147	541	84	147	20	3	27	108	.272	13*
1956	Mickey Mantle	24	OF	150	533	132*	188	22	5	52*	130*	.353*	4
1957	Mickey Mantle	26	OF	144	474	121*	173	28	6	34	94	.365	7
1960	Roger Maris	26	OF	136	499	98	141	18	7	39	112*	.283	4
1961	Roger Maris	27	OF	161	590	132**	159	16	4	61*	142*	.269	9
1962	Mickey Mantle	31	OF	123	377	96	121	15	1	30	89	.321	5
1963	Elston Howard	34	C	135	487	75	140	21	6	28	85	.287	5
1976	Thurman Munson	29	C-OF-DH	152	616	79	186	27	1	17	105	.302	14
1985	Don Mattingly	24	1B	159	652	107	211	48	3	35	145*	.324	7

* League Leader ** Tied for League Lead

NEW YORK YANKEES 20-GAME WINNERS

Year	Pitcher	W	L
1903	Jack Chesbro	21	15
1904	Jack Chesbro	41	12
	Jack Powell	23	19
1906	Albert Orth	27	17
	Jack Chesbro	24	16
1910	Russell Ford	26	6
1911	Russell Ford	22	11
1916	Bob Shawkey	24	14
1919	Bob Shawkey	20	11
1920	Carl Mays	26	11
	Bob Shawkey	20	13
1921	Carl Mays	27	9
1922	Joe Bush	26	7
	Bob Shawkey	20	12
1923	Sad Sam Jones	21	8
1924	Herb Pennock	21	9
1926	Herb Pennock	23	11
1927	Waite Hoyt	22	7
1928	George Pipgras	24	13
	Waite Hoyt	23	7
1931	Lefty Gomez	21	9
1932	Lefty Gomez	24	7
1934	Lefty Gomez	26	5
1936	Red Ruffing	20	12
1937	Lefty Gomez	21	11
	Red Ruffing	20	7
1938	Red Ruffing	21	7
1939	Red Ruffing	21	7
1942	Ernie Bonham	21	5
1943	Spud Chandler	20	4
1946	Spud Chandler	20	8
1949	Vic Raschi	21	10
1950	Vic Raschi	21	8
1951	Eddie Lopat	21	9
	Vic Raschi	21	10
1952	Allie Reynolds	20	8
1954	Bob Grim	20	6
1958	Bob Turley	21	7
1961	Whitey Ford	25	4
1962	Ralph Terry	23	12
1963	Whitey Ford	24	7
	Jim Bouton	21	7
1965	Mel Stottlemyre	20	9
1968	Mel Stottlemyre	21	12
1969	Mel Stottlemyre	20	14
1970	Fritz Peterson	20	11
1975	Catfish Hunter	23	14
1978	Ron Guidry	25	3
	Ed Figueroa	20	9
1979	Tommy John	21	9
1980	Tommy John	22	9
1983	Ron Guidry	21	9
1985	Ron Guidry	22	6
1996	Andy Pettitte	21	8
1998	David Cone	20	7

YANKEE ALL-TIME PACE SETTERS

BATTING CHAMPIONS

Babe Ruth	1924
Lou Gehrig	1934
Joe DiMaggio	1939, 1940
Snuffy Stirnweiss	1945
Mickey Mantle	1956
Don Mattingly	1984
Paul O'Neill	1994
Bernie Williams	1998

A.L. ROOKIE OF THE YEAR AWARDS

Gil McDougald, 3b	1951
Bob Grim, p	1954
Tony Kubek, inf-of	1957
Tom Tresh, ss-of	1962
Stan Bahnsen, p	1968
Thurman Munson, c	1970
Dave Righetti, p	1981
Derek Jeter, ss	1996

RBI LEADERS

Wally Pipp	1916
Babe Ruth	1920, 1921, 1923, 1926, 1928
Bob Meusel	1925
Lou Gehrig	1927, 1928, 1930, 1931, 1934
Joe DiMaggio	1941, 1948
Nick Etten	1945
Mickey Mantle	1956
Roger Maris	1960, 1961
Don Mattingly	1985

HOME RUN CHAMPIONS

Wally Pipp	1916, 1917
Babe Ruth	1920, 1921, 1923, 1924, 1926, 1927, 1928, 1929, 1930, 1931
Bob Meusel	1925
Lou Gehrig	1931, 1934, 1936
Joe DiMaggio	1937, 1948
Nick Etten	1944
Mickey Mantle	1955, 1956, 1958, 1960
Roger Maris	1961
Graig Nettles	1976
Reggie Jackson	1980

MOST VALUABLE PLAYER

Babe Ruth	1923
Lou Gehrig	1927, 1936
Joe DiMaggio	1939, 1941, 1947
Joe Gordon	1942
Spud Chandler	1943
Phil Rizzuto	1950
Yogi Berra	1951, 1954, 1955
Mickey Mantle	1956, 1957, 1962
Roger Maris	1960, 1961
Elston Howard	1963
Thurman Munson	1976
Don Mattingly	1985

CY YOUNG AWARD

Bob Turley	1958
Whitey Ford	1961
Sparky Lyle	1977
Ron Guidry	1978

NEW YORK YANKEES SINGLE-GAME RECORDS

BATTING

AT-BATS			
11	Bobby Richardson	06/24/62	(22 innings)
HITS			
6	Myril Hoag	06/06/34	
DOUBLES			
4	Johnny Lindell	08/17/44	
4	Jim Mason	07/08/74	
TRIPLES			
3	Hal Chase	08/30/06	
3	Earle Combs	09/22/27	
3	Joe DiMaggio	08/28/38	
HOME RUNS			
4	Lou Gehrig	06/03/32	
SACRIFICE FLIES			
3	Bob Meusel	09/15/26	
3	Don Mattingly	05/03/88	
TOTAL BASES			
16	Lou Gehrig	06/03/32	
RBI			
11	Tony Lazzeri	05/24/36	
GRAND SLAMS			
2	Tony Lazzeri	05/24/36	
RUNS			
5	Twelve times, last by Don Mattingly	04/30/88	
CAUGHT STEALING			
3	Fritz Maisel	04/26/16	
3	Lee Magee	06/29/16	
WALKS			
5	Harry Hemphill	08/04/11	
5	Roger Peckinpaugh	06/02/19	
5	Whitey Witt	07/02/24	
5	Lou Gehrig	08/27/35	
5	Ben Chapman	05/24/36	
5	Hersh Martin	09/01/45	
STRIKEOUTS			
5	Johnny Broaca	06/25/34	
5	Bernie Williams	08/21/91	
GROUNDED INTO DOUBLE PLAYS			
3	Eddie Robinson	05/30/55	
3	Jim Leyritz	07/14/90	
3	Matt Nokes	05/03/92	

PITCHING

WALKS		
15	Boardwalk Brown	07/12/14
STRIKEOUTS		
18	Ron Guidry	06/17/78
BALKS		
4	Vic Raschi	05/30/50
CONSECUTIVE STRIKEOUTS		
8	Ron Davis	05/04/81

YANKEE RAWLINGS GOLD GLOVE WINNERS

1957	Bobby Shantz	Pitcher
1958	Bobby Shantz	Pitcher
	Norm Siebern	Outfield
1959	Bobby Shantz	Pitcher
1960	Bobby Shantz	Pitcher
	Roger Maris	Outfield
1961	Bobby Richardson	Second Base
1962	Bobby Richardson	Second Base
	Mickey Mantle	Outfield
1963	Elston Howard	Catcher
	Bobby Richardson	Second Base
1964	Elston Howard	Catcher
	Bobby Richardson	Second Base
1965	Joe Pepitone	First Base
	Bobby Richardson	Second Base
	Tom Tresh	Outfield
1966	Joe Pepitone	First Base
1969	Joe Pepitone	First Base
1972	Bobby Murcer	Outfield
1973	Thurman Munson	Catcher
1974	Thurman Munson	Catcher
1975	Thurman Munson	Catcher
1977	Graig Nettles	Third Base
1978	Chris Chambliss	First Base
	Graig Nettles	Third Base
1982	Ron Guidry	Pitcher
	Dave Winfield	Outfield
1984	Ron Guidry	Pitcher
	Dave Winfield	Outfield
1985	Ron Guidry	Pitcher
	Don Mattingly	First Base
	Dave Winfield	Outfield
1986	Ron Guidry	Pitcher
	Don Mattingly	First Base
1987	Don Mattingly	First Base
	Dave Winfield	Outfield
1988	Don Mattingly	First Base
1989	Don Mattingly	First Base
1991	Don Mattingly	First Base
1992	Don Mattingly	First Base
1993	Don Mattingly	First Base
1994	Don Mattingly	First Base
	Wade Boggs	Third Base
1995	Wade Boggs	Third Base

(New York Yankees Archives)

(UPI/Bettmann)

ROGER MARIS HOME RUNS—1961

Number Homer	Number Game	Date	Opposing Team	Pitcher	Inning	On Base	Final Score
1	11	4/26	at Detroit	Foytack	5	0	13-11
2	17	5/3	at Minnesota	Ramos	7	2	7-3
3	20	5/6 night	at Los Angeles	Grba	5	0	3-5
4	29	5/17	Washington	Burnside	8	1	7-8
5	30	5/19 night	at Cleveland	Perry	1	1	7-9
6	31	5/20	at Cleveland	Bell	3	0	3-4
7	32	5/21	Baltimore	Estrada [1]	1	1	4-2
8	35	5/24	Boston	Conley	4	1	3-2
9	38	5/28	Chicago	McLish [2]	2	0	5-3
10	40	5/30	at Boston	Conley	3	0	12-3
11	40	5/30	at Boston	Fornieles	8	2	12-3
12	41	5/31 night	at Boston	Muffett	3	0	7-6
13	43	6/2 night	at Chicago	McLish	3	1	6-2
14	44	6/3	at Chicago	Shaw	8	2	5-6
15	45	6/4	at Chicago	Kemmerer	3	0	10-1
16	46	6/6 night	Minnesota	Palmquist	6	2	7-2
17	49	6/7	Minnesota	Ramos	3	2	5-1
18	52	6/9 night	Kansas Clty	Herbert	7	1	8-6
19	55	6/11	Los Angeles	Grba [2]	3	0	5-1
20	55	6/11	Los Angeles	James [2]	7	0	5-1
21	57	6/13 night	at Cleveland	Perry	6	0	2-7
22	58	6/14 night	at Cleveland	Bell	4	1	11-5
23	61	6/17 night	at Detroit	Mossi	4	0	10-12
24	62	6/18	at Detroit	Casale	8	1	9-0
25	63	6/19 night	at Kansas Clty	Archer	9	0	3-4
26	64	6/20 night	at Kansas Clty	Nuxhall	5	0	6-2
27	66	6/22 night	at Kansas Clty	Bass	1	2	8-3
28	74	7/1	Washington	Sisler	9	1	7-6
29	75	7/2	Washington	Burnside	3	2	13-4
30	75	7/2	Washington	Klippstein	7	0	13-4
31	77	7/4	Detroit	Larry [2]	8	1	3-4
32	78	7/5	Cleveland	Funk	7	0	6-0
33	82	7/9	Boston	Monbouquette [1]	7	0	3-0
34	84	7/13 night	at Chicago	Wynn	1	1	6-2
35	86	7/15	at Chicago	Herbert	3	0	9-8
36	92	7/21 night	at Boston	Monbouquette	1	1	11-8
37	95	7/25 twi	Chicago	Baumann [1]	4	1	5-1
38	95	7/25 twi	Chicago	Larsen [1]	9	0	5-1
39	96	7/25 twi	Chicago	Kemmerer [2]	4	0	12-0
40	96	7/25 twi	Chicago	Hacker [2]	6	2	12-0
41	106	8/4n	Minnesota	Pascual	1	2	8-5
42	114	8/11 night	at Washington	Burnside	5	0	12-5
43	115	8/12	at Washington	Donovan	4	0	1-5
44	116	8/13	at Washington	Daniels [1]	4	0	2-12
45	117	8/13	at Washington	Kutyna [2]	1	1	9-4
46	118	8/15 night	Chicago	Pizarro	4	0	1-2
47	119	8/16	Chicago	Pierce	1	1	5-4
48	119	8/16	Chicago	Pierce	4	1	5-4
49	123	8/20	at Cleveland	Perry [1]	3	1	6-0
50	125	8/22 night	at Los Angeles	McBride	6	1	3-4
51	129	8/26	at Kansas Clty	Walker	6	0	5-1
52	135	9/2	Detroit	Lary	6	0	7-2
53	135	9/2	Detroit	Aguirre	9	1	7-2
54	140	9/6	Washington	Cheney	4	0	8-0
55	141	9/7 night	Cleveland	Stigman	3	0	7-3
56	143	9/9	Cleveland	Grant	7	0	8-7
57	151	9/16	at Detroit	Lary	3	1	4-10
58	152	9/17	at Detroit	Fox	12	1	6-4
59	155	9/20 night	at Baltimore	Pappas	3	0	4-2
60	159	9/26 night	Baltimore	Fisher	3	0	3-2
61	163	10/1	Boston	Stallard	4	0	1-0

Maris Homers with Men on Base

1 on	21
2 on	9
3 on	0
0 on	31
Home	30
Road	31
Off Lefties	12
Off Righties	49

Home Runs by Parks

Baltimore	1
Boston	4
Chicago	5
Cleveland	5
Detroit	5
Kansas City	4
Los Angeles	2
MInnesota	1
New York	30
Washington	4

Yes, Babe Ruth pitched for New York!
This rare photos shows him in one of only two mound appearances as a Yankees.
A complete game, 6-5 victory over the Boston Red Sox, October 1, 1933 [est]. (New York Yankees Archives)

(New York Yankees Archives)